The Challenge
of Effective Speaking

Rudolph F. Verderber

University of Cincinnati

Wadsworth Publishing Company, Inc., Belmont, California

L. C. Cat. Card No.: 70–93896
Printed in the
United States of America
1 2 3 4 5 6 7 8 9 10—74 73 72 71 70

Preface

You are embarking upon a study that is nearly as old as mankind itself. Speech, the second oldest of the liberal arts, is exceeded in heritage only by the study of music. What you will study in this textbook will be in the tradition of Plato's *Phaedrus* (c. 380 B.C.), Aristotle's *Rhetoric* (c. 330 B.C.), Cicero's *De Oratore* (55 B.C.), Quintilian's *Institutio Oratoria* (A.D. c. 95), St. Augustine's *De Doctrina Christiana* (c. 426), Campbell's *Philosophy of Rhetoric* (1776), Whately's *Elements of Rhetoric* (1826), and Winan's *Public Speaking* (1915). The art of rhetoric (public speaking for a purpose) was forged by the Greeks, refined by the Romans, and mastered as an instrument of democracy by the British and Americans.

Whether your name will be remembered in the history of speechmaking is of course unknown. Nevertheless, whether you give a formal speech or express your opinion in class, at a group meeting, or at a party, what you say and how you say it will affect you, your associates, and perhaps society itself. Because so many ideas are communicated orally, you will be called upon to accept the challenge of public speaking often. Perhaps you are a little uneasy about standing before an audience and speaking. Perhaps you wonder whether the principles of speaking can be learned. Actually, purposeful speaking is neither as nerve-shattering nor as difficult as you may think. If you are willing to make a commitment to yourself, you can learn to give purposeful, interesting speeches during this term.

I believe the procedure discussed in this textbook will provide you with a practical approach to speaking that is applicable to any speech situation. Since one of the first steps in becoming a good speaker is to be a good listener, Part One is concerned with efficient listening. Part Two contains five short chapters covering fundamental speech principles. Since each principle of preparation and delivery is explained in the order of speech preparation, you should read them in that order. The exercises incorporated within the context will give you a chance to apply the principles as you learn them. Part Three covers the kind of speeches you will be giving first in class and perhaps most often outside of class, informative speeches. The first chapter of Part Three is concerned with the common features of all information exchange. The principles in each succeeding chapter are illustrated by a representative student speech, an outline of the speech, and a detailed analysis and criticism of that speech. The speeches and the outlines, appearing essentially as produced by the students, show you how typical students have met the assignments. Because the material is arranged topically in this section, you can study the units in any order that meets your needs or class goals.

Part Four is concerned with persuasive speeches. The first chapter of this unit analyzes how persuasive and informative speaking differ. The three succeeding chapters consider three of the most common kinds of persuasive speech assignments. Again, each chapter is illustrated with a student speech, an outline, and an analysis and criticism of the speech. Part Five is concerned with group discussion. Since much of your speaking outside the classroom will be done in the small-group format, the goals and requirements of discussion are analyzed for you. To establish the application of the principles covered in this textbook, an appendix contains four contemporary speeches for your analysis and criticism.

A special word of thanks is due all the students who showed me the need for a book of this kind, who contributed speeches and outlines appearing in the text, and who supplied the ideas for much of the illustrative material. Likewise, I owe a debt of gratitude to the following for their valuable suggestions: Duane L. Aschenbrenner of the University of Nebraska at Omaha; Virginia Kersting of Pasadena City College; Gordon B. Mills of American River College; and Donald K. Orban of Indiana University; and to all my colleagues at the University of Cincinnati (and especially Dr. Warren Lashley) who read and reread portions of the text in draft stages; to Dr. Loren Reid, University of Missouri, who has had such an influence on my writing; and to my wife, Mary Jo, for her patience and understanding.

R.F.V.

Contents

Part One   Introduction

1 Listening to Speeches   3

Why You Should Listen, 3   How You Can
Improve Your Listening, 4   Get Ready to
Listen, 4   Withhold Evaluation, 5   Listen
Actively, 5   Criteria for Evaluating
Speeches, 6

Part Two   Fundamental Principles

2 Selecting Topics and Determining Purposes   11

Selecting a Speech Topic, 11   Speaker
Interest, 12   Audience Consideration, 14
The Occasion, 17   Determining Speech
Purposes, 18

3 Establishing a Body of Speech Materials   21

Locating Material, 21   Speaker's Prior
Knowledge, 21   Observation, 22   Source
Material, 22   What to Look for, 24
How to Record Material, 28

**4 Arranging, Developing, and
    Adapting Speech Materials   30**

Preparing the Body of the Speech, 30
Selecting and Stating Main Points, 30
Selecting and Adapting Developmental
Materials, 35   Preparing the Introduction,
37   Preparing the Conclusion, 40
Evaluating the Speech Structure—The
Complete Outline, 41

5 Developing Speech Style   45

Characteristics of Oral Style, 45
Clarity, 47   Vividness, 50   Emphasis, 51

6 Practicing the Delivery of the Speech   53

Modes of Delivery, 53   Standards of
Delivery, 54   Desire to Communicate, 55
Audience Contact, 56   Spontaneity, 57
Voice, 58   Articulation, 61   Bodily Action, 62
A Program of Speech Practice, 63

Part Three   Informative Speaking

7 Requirements of Informative Speaking   69

The Goal of Informative Speaking, 69
Informative Speech Development, 71
Kinds of Informative Speeches, 73

8 Speeches Illustrating Organization   74

Inherent Organization, 74   Perceptible
Organization, 75   Placement, 75
Proportion, 76   Transition, 76   Outline, 78
Speech and Analysis, 79

9 Speeches Illustrating Audience Adaptation   82

Knowing the Frame of Reference of Your
Audience, 82   Characteristics of Audience
Adaptation, 82   Outline, 87   Speech and
Analysis, 89

10 Speeches of Definition   92

How Words Are Defined, 92   Developing a
Speech of Definition, 94   Outline, 96
Speech and Analysis, 97

11 Speeches Utilizing Visual Aids   100

Kinds of Visual Aids, 100   Using Visual
Aids, 103   Outline, 105   Speech
and Analysis, 106

12 Descriptive Speeches   111

Topics for Descriptive Speeches, 111
Essentials of Description, 112   Organization
of Description, 114   Language, 115
Outline, 116   Speech and Analysis, 117

13 Expository Speeches   119

The Types of Expository Topics, 119
Political, Economic, and Social Issues, 120
Historical Events and Forces, 121   Theory,
Principle, or Law, 122   Critical Appraisal,
124   Originality, Imagination, and
Creativity, 125   Outline, 126   Speech and
Analysis, 128

14 Research Reports   132

Research, 132   Limiting the Topic, 133
Idea Development, 134   Outline, 136
Speech and Analysis, 138

Part Four   Persuasive Speaking

15 Requirements of Persuasive Speaking   147

Statement of Purpose Sentence, 147
Function of Main Points, 148   Function
of Idea Development, 149   Speech
Organization, 152

16 Speeches of Reasons   156

Selecting Reasons, 156   Testing the Logic
of Your Development, 157   Testing
Structure, 157   Testing Argument, 158
Outline, 164   Speech and Analysis, 167

17 Speeches of Refutation   171

What Can Be Refuted, 171   How to Refute,
174   Outline, 176   Speeches and
Analyses, 177

18 Speeches of Motivation   183

Audience Attitude, 184   Kinds of Motivation, 186   Outline, 191   Speech and Analysis, 193   Outline, 197   Speech and Analysis, 198

Part Five   Small-Group Communication

19 Group Discussion   205

The Forms of Discussion, 205   Preparation for Discussion, 207   Topics, 207   Main Points, 210   Idea Development, 212   The Discussion Outline, 213   Participation in Discussion, 214   Discussion and Analysis, 221

Appendix   Four Contemporary Speeches

"Interpol: History and Mission" by James Hendrick, 227

"A Changing World: Communicate, Learn, and Understand" by H. I. Romnes, 233

"The Corporate Deaf Ear: Consumerism" by E. B. Weiss, 239

"Military Conscription: Abolish the Draft" by W. Allen Wallis, 243

Index   249

Introduction

Part One

Listening
to Speeches

1

Your study of the next five chapters in this textbook will enable you to prepare speeches systematically. Yet in contrast to the five to ten speeches you will be giving, you can expect to hear somewhere between one hundred and two hundred speeches this term! You can make the best use of those speeches and your professor's analysis of them if you understand why you should listen, how you can improve your listening, and what criteria you should apply in evaluating those speeches.

Why You Should Listen

You are taking this course to become a more effective speaker. You will improve faster and enjoy the process more if you also learn to be a better listener. Good listening enables you to test the way theory is applied in speeches. Of these one hundred to two hundred speeches you will hear, a few will be excellent—even some of the average ones will demonstrate characteristics of effective speaking. By listening carefully and critically, you can determine *why* certain speeches were effective. You will be able to identify effective application of theory, and you will be able to judge why those applications were good. Also, careful analysis of classroom speeches will provide you with a wide selection of methods and techniques that you can consider for your speeches. You will hear twenty to thirty times the number of speeches you will give. By identifying the accomplishments and mistakes of others, you may be able to utilize workable methods and avoid the mistakes of others in your speeches.

In addition to the effect of listening on your own speechmaking, there is another good reason for listening carefully. Regardless of how good or how bad your classmates' speeches are, you can learn about more subjects in this course than in any other course you are taking. Much of what your classmates say will be new information or will give new insights. In this respect, speech is truly a liberal arts course.

How You Can Improve Your Listening

Perhaps you believe you are already a good listener. Most college students are not. Estimates of listening efficiency among college students vary from a high of about 70 percent—really very good—to a low of 10 percent. The average college student listens at between 30 percent and 50 percent efficiency. These estimates refer to listening, not hearing. What's the difference? Hearing is your ability to record the sound vibrations that are transmitted. Listening means making sense out of what you hear. You may be startled when you realize that one half to two thirds of all you hear may not register in your mind. These percentages are especially important when you realize that roughly half your daily communication time is spent listening. Of the other 55 percent, you spend 9 percent writing, 16 percent reading, and 30 percent speaking! [1] Since listening and speaking are by far the two most important communication tools, you should try to improve them as much as you try to improve your reading and writing. Assuming for a moment that your listening efficiency is about average, what can you do about it? An average listener can almost double his listening efficiency in a few months if he wants to. In fact, by following a few simple steps, you can improve your listening immediately.

Get Ready to Listen

The first step to improved listening is to get yourself ready to listen. What is characteristic of being ready? An outward sign is whether you look as if you are listening. Poor listeners often slouch in their chairs. Their eyes wander from place to place. They appear

[1] Paul Tory Rankin, "The Measurement of the Ability to Understand Spoken Language," doctoral dissertation, University of Michigan, 1926, University Microfilm, 1952, Publ. No. 4352; cited by Ralph G. Nichols and Leonard A. Stevens, *Are You Listening?* (New York: McGraw-Hill Book Co., 1957), p. 6.

to be bored by the proceedings. On the other hand, good listeners sit upright—sometimes almost on the edge of their chairs. They rivet their eyes on the speaker. These physical signs of attention are indicative of mental attention. By sitting upright and looking at the speaker you may be able to keep from thinking about lunch, about your date for the evening, about a test you have the next hour, or about how you feel. Peaks of attention come in spurts and last only momentarily. Attention lags of a split second occur whether you want them to or not. If you maintain a listening posture, however, you can help keep the distracting thoughts from capturing your attention and you can improve your listening.

Withhold Evaluation

A second step to improved listening is to withhold evaluation of what you hear until comprehension is complete. This recommendation involves both the control of arbitrary judgments about a subject and control of emotional responses to content. It is a human reaction to listen attentively only to what we like or what we want to hear. Such an attitude is self-limiting and self-defeating. We should listen to learn and to gather data for evaluation. Neither of these goals is possible if we refuse to listen to anything outside our immediate interests. Analyze your listening habits very carefully. If during the first sentence or two of a speech you find yourself saying, "I don't think I am going to be interested in this topic," remind yourself that judgment must *follow* and not precede the presentation of information. Poor listeners make value judgments about the content after the first few words; good listeners approach their listening objectively. Since it is easier to pay attention to a speech if it is well presented, the theory in this book is directed to making speeches so clear and interesting that good and poor listeners alike will pay attention. Nevertheless, some of the speeches you hear, in or out of class, will be poor. In such instances, you will have to work to make the most of the experience. Your attitude affects your perception of information. The more you allow your emotions to intrude into the listening process, the more distorted will be your recollection of what was said.

Listen Actively

The third and final step you can take is to become an active listener. Communication should be a dialogue. The psychology of learning shows that a listener learns better and faster and makes sounder judgments about what he hears when he is mentally and physically active—

when he is involved. A speaker talks at about 140 to 180 words per minute. You think at between 300 to 600 words per minute. Whether you are listening effectively or not depends a lot on what you are doing with the time difference. Some listeners do nothing; others think about eating, sleeping, a test the next hour, and other things that eventually capture their attention. The active listener uses his extra time to weigh and to consider what the speaker has said. He may attempt to fill in examples, repeat key ideas, or ask questions related to the topic. When the speaker says, "One activity that provides vigorous exercise of most muscles is tennis," the active listener might also think of handball, squash, and basketball. When the speaker says, "The first major election reform bill was passed in England in 1832," the active listener might mentally repeat "reform bill," "England, 1832," two or three times each. When the speaker says, "Napoleon's battle plans were masterpieces of strategy," the active listener might ask mentally, "What were the characteristics of his strategy?" Each of these forms of involvement helps the listener master the ideas.

Earlier we mentioned that the first step toward improved listening was to get ready to listen. Those characteristics of alertness are forms of physical activity. But, in addition to sitting up straight, looking at the speaker, and responding facially to content, being physically active can also mean taking notes. Whereas the poor listener fidgets, doodles, or looks about the room, the good listener often writes down what the speaker said. Perhaps he notes words or phrases denoting key ideas; perhaps he writes out main ideas in complete sentences. In either instance, the physical activity reinforces the content. If, as the speaker says to you, "The first artificial orbiting satellite was launched by Russia in 1957," you write it down, the act of writing, coordinated with thinking the country and the year, will provide both a better chance of mental recall and the written record to refer to later.

So, good listening requires work. You must get ready to listen, you must withhold evaluation until comprehension is complete, and you must be mentally and physically an active listener.

Criteria for Evaluating Speeches

If you know the criteria for evaluating speeches, careful listening will help you identify a speaker's strengths and weaknesses. In addition to listening to the content, you should also listen to *how* the speaker develops his purpose sentence, *how* the speaker organizes his material, *how* the speaker words his ideas, and *how* the speaker delivers the speech. With each speech given in class, you should make a complete analysis of content and method. As we said before, the results of this analysis can be used to make your speeches better. The following questions are applicable to all kinds of speeches. Each of the points mentioned will be explained, discussed, and amplified in the next five chapters. When you have finished Part Two on fundamental principles of speech, refer back to this questionnaire. When you have mastered these questions, you should have a sound basis for speech criticism and an awareness of the criteria for effective speaking.

Evaluation Questionnaire

Content:
  Topic:
        Was the topic a good one for this class?
        Did the speaker seem to have sufficient knowledge of and interest in the topic?
  Specific purpose:
        Did the purpose conform with the general purpose expected of the speech?
        Was the specific purpose clear? meaningful?
  Developmental materials:
        Was the development clear? meaningful? interesting?
        Did the development really explain or support the key ideas?
Organization:
  Introduction:
        Did the introduction gain attention?
        Did the introduction lead into the body of the speech?
  Body:
        Were the main points clear, substantive ideas?
        Were the main points limited in number and scope?
        Was there an identifiable order to the main points?
  Conclusion:
        Did the conclusion tie the speech together?
        Did the conclusion leave the speech on a high note?
Style:
        Was the speech delivered in an oral style?
        Were the ideas clear?
        Were the ideas vivid?
        Were the ideas emphatic?
Delivery:
        Did the speaker have a positive attitude?
        Did the speaker look at his audience?
        Was the delivery spontaneous?
        Did the speaker show sufficient variety and emphasis?
        Was articulation satisfactory?
        Did the speaker show sufficient poise and have a good posture?

**Fundamental
Principles**

Part Two

Selecting Topics and Determining Purposes

2

Principle 1   Effective speaking requires a carefully selected topic phrased to convey a predetermined purpose.

Have you ever listened to a friend, relative, minister, or politician without knowing what he was driving at? Have you ever remarked about such a speaker, "He didn't say anything"? You didn't mean that no words were pronounced. What you probably meant was that no clear idea on a particular subject was expressed in a way that you could profit from it. In essence, the speaker had violated the first and perhaps the most important principle of speechmaking; that is, effective speaking requires a carefully selected topic phrased to convey a predetermined purpose. Although it is often difficult, if not impossible, to determine whether topic or purpose comes first in our preparation (under certain circumstances they may well occur as one process), we will first consider selection of speech topics, then consider determination of speech purposes.

Selecting a Speech Topic

As a speaker you must communicate an idea. How do you select that idea? In daily conversation you don't consider the selection of a topic as a conscious effort—often, it may seem that you just start talking. Yet, if you analyze your speaking more carefully, you should see that you are quite selective in topic and purpose, whether you are conscious of the process or not. When you come out of the classroom, you may say to a friend, "Let's go eat—I'm starved"; when you get involved in a deep discussion, you may say, "I wonder whether the space program is worth the money"; when you are at a party, you may say, "What did you think of Saturday's game?" or "I wish the Board of Education would get with it." Although these responses of conversation (spontaneous, informal communication) were seemingly instantaneous, each one required that you weigh many factors and analyze many conditions before you responded. What seemed like instantaneous response was only relatively so. When you said, "Let's eat—I'm starved," you were verbalizing a felt need. You were testing your friend's reaction to see whether he would agree and perhaps accompany you, whether he would disagree, or whether he would suggest a place to eat. When you said, "What did you think of Saturday's game?" you showed enough interest to mention the game and you thought that others present would be likely to respond. If your analysis was correct, discussion flowed freely; if not, the subject was dropped and another introduced. In both of these instances the determining features of what you said and how you said it were the interest of the speaker, the nature of the audience, and the occasion.

Speaker Interest

By far the most important of these three determinants is speaker interest. You talk best, most interestingly, and most meaningfully when you talk about subjects that interest you. Thus your foremost test is to see whether your prospective speech topic grows from or relates to one of *your* major interests. As a student, your interests probably center on your major or prospective vocation, your hobbies or activities, and those subjects that enrich your life or give it meaning and purpose. For instance, you may spend much of your time on the golf course; cooking; making clothes; working with your church; looking for fossils; reading historical fiction; evaluating advertising techniques; studying stock market trends; working with underprivileged children; or pondering such problems as air pollution, conservation, space exploration, and race relations. Activities that absorb your time, energy, and attention are subjects you should be talking about.

Although topics for everyday conversation may just "come to you," a specific topic needed for a speaking assignment may not emerge so readily. Moreover, for a formal speech you will not have the trial-and-error opportunity for evaluation that you have in informal conversation. But there are ways to overcome this problem. Speakers arrive at the best possible topic by first going through a process known as "brainstorming," which is an uncritical, nonevaluative attempt at verbalizing responses to given stimuli. You know the old word-association process: when you think the word "snow," associatively you may think of "sled," "cold," "shoveling," and "snowman." Likewise, when you suggest a word or idea related to your major areas of interest, you can often associate twenty, thirty, or even fifty other related ideas and concepts. The procedure is valuable because it allows you to get a multitude of related ideas about an interest area down on paper; and since it is easier to select a choice from among several options than it is to phrase a new option, the brainstorming process makes sense.

The related ideas listed under the headings of "Speech" and "Football" by no means exhaust the possibilities.

Speech

rhetoric	vocal process	communication	criticism
discussion	preparation	listening	textbooks
sophists	famous speakers	articulators	standards
debate	theories of	controversy	speech education
major	principles of	stage fright	amplification
originality	campaigns	sounds	evidence

Football

players	equipment	officials	leagues
defenses	positions	kicking	teams
offenses	unions	passing	Hall of Fame
safety	salary negotiations	running	exhibition games
stadium	the football	history	training
player draft	isometrics	expansion	scoring

After you have listed twenty to thirty items for each heading, select the one, two, or three that seem most interesting to you. On another sheet of paper, break each of those topics down into its various aspects. For instance, under football, "offenses," could be broken down into "T-formation," "I-formation," "double wing," and the like; under speech, "debate" could be broken down into "tournaments," "history," "types," "principles," and so on. Topics for many of your speeches should come from items mentioned on this second list.

Exercise 1

1 Divide a sheet of paper vertically into three to six columns. Head the columns with your college major or prospective vocation, your principal hobbies or activities, and a current event, social problem, or other subject area that interests you. Beginning with any of the columns, construct a list of every word, idea, or concept that comes to mind. Try to fill the entire column for each heading. If you cannot within a few minutes list at least twenty items for each, put the list aside for a while and come back to it later.

2 Select one, two, or three items from *each* of your lists. Break each of those down into specific topics encompassing single goals.

Audience Consideration

Once you have established a list of subject areas that meet the test of speaker interest, the next step is to consider the object and receiver of your communication, your audience. In both conversation and speechmaking, you direct your ideas to a receiver. In conversation, your audience is composed of one individual or a small, often homogeneous group. In the speech situation, however, your audience is composed of many individuals and is more complex—so much so that the problem of audience analysis becomes a vital factor in your potential success. When you and a friend walk from one class to another, you have no difficulty introducing a topic because you know each other's knowledge and interests and are able to relate to each other. But as a group gets larger, it becomes more difficult to relate to everyone in the group. The next time you are at a party and more than eight persons are present, note how many times the groupings of individuals change depending upon the subjects being considered. People "drop out" of the conversation when the subject no longer relates to them. Everyone lives in many worlds at the same time. Each world reflects different interests, degrees of knowledge, and attitudes. The interrelationship between speaker interest and audience orientation should determine the scope of your speech topics and, in later stages of preparation, the nature of your speech development.

Systematic analysis of audience composition is a two-part process. First, you gather essential data about your audience; and second, you draw generalizations about the data that will affect your preparation.

Essential Data

The data you are looking for concerns age, sex, occupation, socioeconomic level, and religion of your audience.

Age   Although the specific age of each member of your audience need not be known, you should determine the average age and the age range that are represented. For instance, your class may be typical, in that the members' ages range from 18 to 22 with the average age depending upon the year most students take the course. If, however, your audience is an evening class, the age range and average age might be significantly different.

Sex   The exact number of males and females is not as important to the selection or development of your topic as the balance between the sexes. You should determine whether the audience is all or predominantly male, all or predominantly female, or balanced between male and female.

Occupation   Again the specific occupation of everyone in the audience is not so important as the general nature of the audience. Your classroom audience will be composed of students who may be further classified according to majors or prospective occupations. Outside the classroom, your audience may be composed predominantly of members of particular groups, such as doctors, laborers, professional men, businessmen, or teachers.

Socioeconomic Level   Is your audience rich, poor, of average means? Is your audience from a "culturally deprived," a high society, or a middle-class background? An audience's socioeconomic level can be important in determining its knowledge and interests.

Religion   The individual religion of each member of the audience is not important. You want to find out whether your audience is predominantly one religion or whether there seems to be a balance of religions. Even though this information will affect only a small number of topics, it is extremely important for those topics.

Drawing Conclusions
about Knowledge and Interests

By examining the age, sex, occupation, socioeconomic level, and religion of your audience, you can draw conclusions about audience knowledge and audience interests that are essential to the final phrasing of your speech topic. Specifically, you want to answer the following questions: (1) Is my audience's knowledge of the subject area sufficient to allow them to understand my topic? (2) Would the explanation of my topic provide new information to most of the audience? (3) Does my audience already have an immediate interest in the topic? (4) If not, can I relate my topic to their interests? Although the fourth question will be considered in detail in later chapters, a tentative answer should be made now. If the answer to (1), (2), or (4) is "No," you should consider one of the other aspects of the topic or select a different topic altogether.

In order to see how the essential data can be used to arrive at the answers to these questions, let's examine a few specific situations:

1   Subject area: plastics.

Possible choices: uses, properties, moulding, history, future, inventors.

Choice under consideration: uses.

Audience: age—8 to 14; sex—boys; occupation—school children (scouts); socioeconomic level—middle class; religion—mixed.

Is audience's knowledge of the subject area sufficient to allow them to understand the topic? Yes. They are old enough to understand fairly detailed explanations, as long as the information relates to their interests. Their middle-class background is probably broad enough so that no special problems of adaptation would be needed.

Would the topic provide new information? Yes. Their knowledge of plastics is probably restricted to their recognition of its uses in toys and to some of its properties.

Does my audience already have an immediate interest? Questionable.

Can I relate the topic to their interests? Yes. Since most boys have plastic toys and since boys have inquiring minds, the topic could be adapted to their interests.

Conclusion about topic: "uses" would be satisfactory.

2   Subject area: diamonds.

Possible choices: polishing, mining, cutting, formation of, uses in industry.

Specific choice under consideration: cutting.

Audience: age—22–50; sex—women; occupation—housewives (local gardening club meeting); socioeconomic level—middle class plus; religion—mostly Protestant and Catholic.

Is audience's knowledge of the subject area sufficient to allow them to understand the topic? Yes. Women would know about diamonds.

Would the topic provide new information? Yes. Unless some were wives of jewelers or had made some special effort to study the topic, their knowledge of cutting would be minimal.

Would the audience have an immediate interest? Yes. Most women are interested in diamonds. Their socioeconomic level indicates that they probably own or want to own one or more diamonds.

Conclusion about topic: "cutting" would be satisfactory.

3 Subject area: cigarettes.

Possible choices: history; how to quit smoking; manufacturing; grading tobacco; medical harm.

Choice under consideration: history.

Audience: age—30–50; sex—mixed; occupation—craftsmen, skilled laborers, housewives; socioeconomic level—lower class, lower middle class; religion—mixed.

Is audience's knowledge of the subject area sufficient to allow them to understand the topic? Yes.

Would the topic provide new information? Yes. Few would know much about the history of cigarettes.

Would the audience have an immediate interest? No.

Can I relate the topic to their interests? Perhaps.

Conclusion about topic: Since history is a questionable topic for this audience, it might be better to consider "how to quit," "grading tobacco," or "manufacturing."

Although the conclusions about audience knowledge and interests may not be completely accurate, your consideration of the key questions will enable you to approach further preparation with considerably greater confidence.

Exercise 2

Complete an analysis of audience age, sex, occupation, socioeconomic level, and religion. Select the topic under "major" that you think would best meet the tests of audience knowledge and interest.

The Occasion

The third variable to be considered in selection of speech topics is the occasion. Inaugurations, commencements, and building dedications are all commemorated with speeches appropriate to those occasions. Perhaps a given holiday, anniversary, or special event will inspire you to speak on a related topic. Perhaps the occasion will affect the development of your speech, even if it doesn't help you select the topic itself.

For your classroom speeches, adapting to the occasion will mean following the directions outlined by your professor about the kind of speech, the time limits, and points to be emphasized. For every assignment, he will stipulate such things as "visual aids required," "use three library sources," "speech should be a demonstration," and "speech should define a word." You should make sure that your topic adapts to these directions.

Determining Speech Purposes

Your list of prospective topics, your audience analysis, and your assessment of the speech occasion provide you with the material needed for the final and perhaps most crucial aspect of the first step of speech preparation; that is, phrasing a clear, meaningful purpose sentence that reflects both the general purpose of the speech and the specific goal of the speech.

General Purpose

The general purpose is the kind of response you expect. Speech is a complex act that may serve a multipurpose function; nevertheless, one purpose usually takes a paramount position, with the other purposes appearing subordinately. Speeches may be classified according to their dominant purpose as entertaining, informative, or persuasive. Entertaining speeches seek to amuse or divert the audience. Although this may be accomplished by making your audience laugh, humor is only one form of entertainment. Informative speeches transmit new information, greater insight, or fresh interpretations of ideas. "The construction of the pyramids," "the principle of a jet engine," and "the major causes of juvenile delinquency" are all informative speech topics. Persuasive speeches are concerned with strengthening a belief, changing a belief, or bringing about a desired action. The goal of a persuasive speech is to affect your audience's attitude about an object or idea. "Capital punishment should be abolished," "students should be more involved in community activities," "television is a bad influence on children," and "federal poverty programs are ineffective" are examples of persuasive speech topics. Since you will be concentrating on informative and persuasive speeches during this term, the materials in this book are primarily directed to those two goals.

Specific Purpose

In contrast to the general purpose which indicates the kind of response you expect, the specific purpose states your goal. Think of the specific purpose as a single sentence that summarizes exactly what you want to do in the speech. For instance, "juvenile delinquency" is a subject area; "the causes of juvenile delinquency" is a topic; and "I want to inform the audience about the three major causes of juvenile delinquency" is an acceptable purpose sentence. "Clothing" is a subject area; "the way clothing reflects attitudes" is a topic; "I want to inform the audience that our clothes tell a great deal about our society" is an acceptable specific purpose sentence.

Because phrasing the specific purpose requires you to put together your ideas concerning topics, audiences, and occasions, it is the first really artful aspect of speech preparation. Your goal is a complete, declarative sentence that incorporates the general purpose and clarifies the boundaries of the information to be presented. The process of determining your specific purpose sentence may be outlined as follows: (1) select from your list of topics completed in Exercise 1 the word or idea that has the greatest appeal to *you;* (2) decide whether your speech is to inform or to persuade; (3) consider your topic in terms of audience knowledge and interests; (4) consider your topic in terms of the occasion; (5) work the topic into a complete sentence that incorporates general purpose and boundaries of the information.

Since this complete process is a very important one requiring time and understanding, consider the following hypothetical illustration carefully.

1   Subject area: football.

Brainstorming list: see p. 13.

Item reflecting speaker's interest: passing.

Further breakdown of "passing": "roll-out pass," "how to throw a pass," "basic patterns," "screen pass," "characteristics of a passer."

Specific topic under consideration: "screen pass."

2   General purpose indicated by assignment: to inform.

3   Analysis of audience: age—18 to 22; sex—slightly more men than women; occupation—students (mostly business administration, arts and sciences, and education majors); socioeconomic level—middle class; religion—mixed.

Is audience's knowledge of the subject area sufficient to allow them to understand the topic? Yes. Most men know basic rules of football. Most women have minimal knowledge of the game, enough to allow them to understand basic information.

Would topic provide new information? Yes. Men could define "screen pass," but unless they had played organized football recently, they probably wouldn't be familiar with all the moves and timing. For the women the topic would provide new information.

Would audience have an immediate interest? No. Most men might, but most women would not.

Could I relate topic to interests? Yes. Even women who won't care for football can be interested in the strategy, deception, and timing involved. Women's interests must be kept in mind, however.

Conclusion: "screen pass" would be a suitable topic.

4   Occasion: five-minute visual aids speech. The screen pass can be explained in five minutes. Use of visual aids would be fundamental to the explanation of this topic.

5   Working topic into complete sentence form:

"How to throw a screen pass." (No direction)

"How a screen pass develops." (Better)

"The steps required for execution of a screen pass." (Better)

"I want to inform the audience of the four steps required for successful execution of a screen pass." (Acceptable)

"I want to inform the audience that a successful screen pass depends upon the deception created by the players, the positioning of key players to form the 'screen,' the timing of the receiver, and the blocking after the pass is completed." (A more complete statement of the same idea)

Although the above material relates to informative speeches, the selection of the persuasive speech purpose is essentially the same. Since your first few speeches will probably be informative rather than persuasive, a complete comparison of persuasive and informative purpose sentences will be reserved until Chapter 15.

Exercise 3

Using the lists of ideas written for Exercise 1, frame three informative purpose sentences that meet the tests considered in this chapter. For each one, write out a complete five-step analysis leading to the final wording.

Establishing a Body of Speech Materials

3

Principle 2   Effective speaking is dependent upon quality material.

Once you have arrived at a clearly stated purpose sentence, you can begin to gather material for the speech, a process that involves knowing where to look, what to look for, and how to record what you have discovered.

Locating Material

Although you are surrounded by speech materials, you should establish a systematic procedure for discovering them. Speakers usually find that most of their materials come from their prior knowledge and observations and from written sources.

Speaker's Prior Knowledge

What do you know? At times you may have questioned the extent and the accuracy of your knowledge; yet, when you test yourself, you discover that you really know quite a lot, especially about your major interests. For instance, athletes have special knowledge about their sports, coin collectors about coins, detective-fiction buffs about detective fiction, do-it-yourself advocates about house and garden, musicians about music and instruments, farmers about animals or crops and equipment, and camp counselors about camping. As a result of the special knowledge, you should be your first, if not your best, source of information for the topics you have selected. After all, firsthand knowledge of a subject enables the speaker to develop unique, imaginative, original speeches. Regardless of what topic you have selected, take the time to analyze and record your knowledge before you go to any other source.

Of course, you must not accept every item you know or remember without testing its accuracy. Our minds play tricks on us, and you may well find that some "fact" you are sure of is not really a fact at all. Nevertheless, you should not be discouraged from using your prior knowledge. Verifying a fact is far easier than discovering material in the first place.

Observation

In addition to your prior knowledge, you should take advantage of one of your best resources, your power of observation. Many people are poor observers because they just don't apply their critical powers. Any reading of courtroom case studies will show the unreliability of untrained eye-witness reports. In contrast, law enforcement officers who have been trained to use their powers are excellent observers. That their lives may well depend upon their observations undoubtedly increases their motivation for observing accurately. But you, too, can be a better observer if you will only try. Get in the habit of seeing and not just looking. Pay attention to everything about you. The development of nearly any topic you select can profit from the utilization of materials gained by observing. Description is only the verbalization of careful observation; facts and opinions can be verified by observation; and comparisons and contrasts can be based upon observation. On your way to or from class today, try to use your powers to their maximum. List a few of the sights, sounds, and smells you never noticed before. Describe some object, person, or scene along the way. Compare one side of a street with the other. From your observation alone, try to draw valid conclusions about the neatness of the street, socioeconomic level of a neighborhood, or age of a building. Remember, observation, like speaker knowledge, can help to make a speech more imaginative and interesting.

Source Material

Perhaps the first few speeches you prepare can be developed exclusively through prior knowledge or observation. Once you get beyond short speeches of description, narration, and demonstration, however, your topics will require more material than is available to you first-hand. Experience has shown that the most effective speakers are also effective researchers. Whether your library is large or small, well equipped or poorly equipped, its contents are of little value to you unless you know how to find what you need. This section is intended to acquaint you with the sources that will provide most of the developmental materials you will need for speeches in or out of the classroom.

Card Catalog   The card catalog indexes all your library's holdings by author, title, and subject. Your principal use of the card catalog will be to locate the best books on your topic.

Periodicals and Magazines   Periodicals are publications that appear at fixed periods: weekly, biweekly, monthly, quarterly, or yearly. The materials you get from weekly, biweekly, and monthly magazines are more current than you will find in books. Of course, some magazines are more accurate, more complete, and more useful than others. Since you must know where and how to find articles before you can evaluate them, you should know and use three indexes: *Readers' Guide to Periodical Literature, Education Index*, and *International Index*.

By far the most valuable source for topics of current interest, *Readers' Guide to Periodical Literature* is an index of articles in some 125 popular American journals. Articles, indexed by topic, come from such magazines as *The Atlantic, Ebony, Business Week, New Yorker, Life, Reader's Digest, Vital Speeches*, and *Yale Review*.

If your purpose sentence is related directly or indirectly to the field of education, including such subject areas as school administration, adult education, film strips, intelligence, morale, tests and scales, Project Head Start, or ungraded schools, *Education Index*, a cumulative subject index to a selected list of some 150 educational periodicals, proceedings, and yearbooks, will lead you to the available sources.

In contrast to *Readers' Guide*, which will lead you to articles in popular journals, the *International Index*, a guide to some 150 periodicals in the social sciences and humanities, will lead you to articles in such scholarly journals as *American Journal of Sociology, Economist, Modern Language Quarterly*, and *Philosophical Review*.

Encyclopedias   Not only do encyclopedias give you an excellent overview of many subjects, but also they offer valuable bibliographies. Nevertheless, because the articles could not possibly cover every topic completely, relatively few are very detailed. In addition, because of the time lag, an encyclopedia is seldom of value for the changing facts and details needed for contemporary problems. Most libraries have a recent edition of *Encyclopaedia Britannica*, *Encyclopedia Americana*, or *Collier's Encyclopedia.*

Biographical Sources   When you need biographical details, from thumbnail sketches to reasonably complete essays, you can turn to one of the many biographical sources available. In addition to full-length books and encyclopedia entries, you should explore such books as *Who's Who* and *Who's Who in America* (short sketches of British and American subjects respectively) or *Dictionary of National Biography* and *Dictionary of American Biography* (rather complete essays about prominent British and American subjects respectively).

Statistical Sources   When you need facts, details, or statistics about population, records, continents, heads of state, weather, or any of a hundred other subjects, you should refer to one of the many single-volume sources that report such data. Three of the most noteworthy sources in this category are *World Almanac and Book of Facts* (1868 to date), *Statistical Abstract of the United States* (1878 to date), and *Statesman's Yearbook: Statistical and Historical Annual of the States of the World* (1867 to date).

Newspapers   Despite the relatively poor quality of reporting in many of our daily newspapers, newspaper articles should not be overlooked as sources of facts and interpretations of contemporary problems. Your library probably holds both an index of your nearest major daily and the *New York Times Index.*

Since the holdings of libraries vary so much, a detailed account of other bibliographies, indexes, and special resources is impractical. To locate additional sources, you should consult your reference librarian. He will be able to lead you to special sources and indexes in your interest areas. If, however, you take full advantage of those listed above, you will find an abundance of material for your prospective topics.

Exercise 4

For each of the three purpose sentences you wrote for Exercise 3, compile a partial bibliography, including books, articles, and notations from at least three categories mentioned in the preceding section.

What to Look for

Although tapping your own knowledge, observing, and discovering useful library sources will facilitate the research process, these sources will yield speech material only if you know what you are looking for. Rather than unsystematically reading all materials before you, you should attempt to discover items of information that will amplify or prove the points you wish to make. In addition, you should be alert for the most interesting developmental material available. Examples, illustrations, comparisons, statistics, and quotations are some of the forms of material that are most adaptable to speeches.

Examples

A common response to a generalization is "Give me an example." The example, a single instance that represents or illustrates a generalization or an assertion, is perhaps one of the most useful of speech materials. Your intellect allows you to generalize—to draw conclusions from your experiences and observations. Yet your listeners may not have had the benefit of those experiences, and they will not be impressed by the assertions or generalizations alone. The example really serves two functions: (1) it helps to test assertions and generalizations and (2) it helps to illustrate them for others. Examples make reading matter easier to comprehend or more persuasive, and they will serve the same purposes for your listeners.

The examples you find will be of three kinds: *real* examples that indicate actual specifics; *fictitious* examples that allude to instances that are or have been made up to explain the point; and *hypothetical* examples that suggest what would happen in certain circumstances. For instance:

Real: Automobile companies are making some effort to make their cars safer. Disc brakes are being used more frequently. Sharp or extended pieces of chrome on the interior are being eliminated.

Fictitious: Just because a person is slow does not mean that he is or should be considered a loser. Remember the story of the tortoise and the hare: the tortoise who was much slower still won the race.

Hypothetical: Dogs do very poorly on simple tests of intelligence. If a 10-foot section of fence were put between a dog and a bone, he would try to paw through the fence rather than go the 5 feet or so it would take to get around that fence.

Because examples are such excellent aids to clarity and vividness, you should keep a constant lookout for them and employ them frequently.

Illustration, Anecdote, and Narrative

Illustrations are verbal explanations; anecdotes are brief, often amusing stories; and narratives are accounts, tales, or lengthier stories.

In essence, each of these means about the same thing, the detailed relating of material, often in story form. Because interest is so important to any kind of communication and because our attention is always focused by a story, illustrations, anecdotes, and narratives are worth looking for. Actually, illustrations are very closely related to examples. If you will think of illustrations as extended examples or as examples in story form, you will appreciate that relationship. By adding details, dialogue, or elements of plot, each of the three examples noted above could be made into an illustration. For a two-minute speech, in which you do not have the time to develop a very detailed illustration, one or two examples would be preferable. In longer speeches, however, the inclusion of at least one illustration will pay dividends in audience attention. Remember the last time one of your professors said, "That reminds me of a story"? Probably more people listened to the story than to any other part of the lecture. The following illustration shows how the example about the intelligence of dogs can be developed into story form.

> Dogs usually do very poorly on simple intelligence tests. In one test, our faithful dog Rover was given a problem. A 10-foot section of fence was placed between Rover and his favorite bone. Now, Rover wanted that bone. With a little growl here and a little whimper there, Rover tried to solve the problem. First, he just sat and barked, hoping apparently that the fence would go away. Second, he began to paw at the fence. Two or three times, Rover took a step to the left or right, and just when everyone thought he was going to hightail it around the fence to get his bone, he went back to the very spot from which he started, to begin pawing and growling once more. Was Rover a particularly dumb dog? Probably not. The simple truth is that our beloved friend Rover, man's best friend, is just not very bright.

Comparison

Since you will need to discuss new ideas in terms that can be understood, you will probably learn what many successful communicators have learned before you: the value of giving meaning to a new idea by comparing it with a familiar concept. Comparison involves showing the similarities between two entities. Although you will be drawing your own later in speech preparation, you should still keep your eye open for comparisons in your research.

Comparisons may be figurative or literal. A figurative comparison expresses one thing in terms normally denoting another. We may speak of a person who is "slow as a turtle." We don't mean that he actually moves as slowly as a turtle, only that he is extremely slow in comparison to other persons. A literal comparison is an actual comparison. We may describe a ball as being about the same size as a tennis ball. In this instance, we mean that both balls are about 2½ inches in diameter.

Comparisons may be cast as metaphors or as similes. A metaphor is a figure of speech in which a word or phrase literally denoting one kind of object or idea is used in place of another. "He's a tiger" and "Their line is a stone wall" are both metaphors. A simile is a figure of speech in which a thing or idea is likened to another. "He walks like an elephant" and "She smiles like a Cheshire cat" are both similes.

Occasionally a comparison is cast as a contrast which focuses on differences rather than on similarities. "Unlike last year when we did mostly period drama, this year we are producing mostly comedies and musicals," would be a contrast. As you do your research, try to find comparisons that will help you express your ideas more meaningfully and more interestingly.

Statistics

Statistics are a systematic compilation of instances. You may know that Jack, Joe, Charles, and Susan voted in a student election. On the basis of these four instances alone, however, you would not be able to draw any meaningful conclusions about the voting. Later you find that of 16,240 students, 3,400 (approximately 20 percent) voted. If you checked last year's figures and found that 6,200 voted, you could conclude that this year's turnout was exceptionally bad. Statistics enable you to pack a great deal of information into a small package. When statistics are well used they can be very persuasive or very informative; when they are poorly used, they may be boring and, in some instances, downright deceiving. For now, it is important that you learn to recognize useful statistics so that you can record them for later evaluation.

Quotable Explanations and Opinions

When you find that a writer's explanation or opinion is valuable either for what was said or the way it was said, you may record the material precisely as stated. If you use the material in the speech, you should remember to give credit to your source. Use of any quotation or close paraphrasing that is not documented is plagiarism, an unethical procedure that violates scholarly practice. Many of our most notable quotations are remembered because they have literary merit. Winston Churchill's "I have nothing to offer but blood, toil, tears, and sweat," included in his first speech as Prime Minister in 1940, and John F. Kennedy's "Ask not what your country can do for you—ask what you can do for your country," from his 1961 Inaugural Address, are examples from speeches that are worth remembering and repeating. At other times, you will find that the clear, concise manner in which ideas were stated is worth repeating, even if the words themselves have no literary merit. In your speeches you have an opportunity and a right to use the words of others, as long as you keep quotations to a minimum and give credit where it is due.

How to Record Material

In your research (including observation and prior knowledge as well as printed sources), you may find a variety of examples, illustrations, quotations, statistics, and comparisons that you want to consider for your speech. How should you record these materials so that they will be of greatest value? You will be able to use only a fraction of the material you find. Moreover, you can never be sure of the order in which you will use the materials in the speech. Therefore, you need a method of recording that will allow you to use or select the better materials and to order the materials to meet your needs. The note card method is probably the best that is available to you. As you find materials, record each item separately on 3 x 5 or 4 x 6 cards. Although it may seem easier to record materials from one source on a single sheet of paper or on a large card, sorting and arranging material is much easier when each item of that material is recorded on a separate card. In addition to recording each item separately, you should indicate the name of the source, the name of the author if one is given, and the page number from which it was taken. You will not necessarily need this material, but should you decide to quote directly or to reexamine a point, you will know where it came from. The following illustrates a useful notecard form:

> *Topic:* Unemployment in the United States
>
> "The rate of nonparticipants in the labor force—those who have given up looking for work—of men in their prime years, increased from 4.7 per cent in 1953 to 5.2 per cent in 1963. For Negroes the nonparticipation rate leaped from 5.3 per cent to 8.2 per cent over the same period. Of those who will enter the labor force in the late sixties and in the seventies, perhaps ten million will not have completed elementary school. For them, our technology will have no room."
>
> Ben Seligman, "Automation and the Work Force," from *Guaranteed Income*, edited by Robert Theobald, p. 75.

In light of all that has been said so far in this section, you may be wondering how much source material is required for a speech. A rule-of-thumb answer is to have at least two or three times the amount of developmental material that you could use in the speech. If your speech is a three-minute assignment and you can read aloud all the material you have discovered in two to three minutes, you don't have enough. If, on the other hand, you have eight to ten minutes of material for a three-minute speech, the volume of material is probably sufficient. In addition, you should never use fewer than three sources. One-source speeches often lead to plagiarism; furthermore, a one-source or two-source speech just doesn't give you sufficient breadth of material. The process of selection, putting material together, adding, cutting, and revising will enable you to develop an original approach to your topic. How you go about organizing, developing, and adapting material to your audience will be considered in the next two chapters.

Exercise 5

For one of the purpose sentences you plan to use for a speech this term, gather three examples of each kind of developmental material discussed above: example, illustration, comparison, statistics, and quotation. Make sure that you draw your material from at least three and preferably from four or more sources.

Arranging, Developing, and Adapting Speech Materials

4

Principle 3 Effective speaking involves arranging, developing, and adapting material to the needs and interests of the audience.

Now that you have enough material to enable you to talk for the required time limit, your next step of preparation is to organize the material meaningfully. Effective speech organization (arranging, developing, and adapting speech materials) is achieved through a systematic preparation of the body, the introduction, and the conclusion of the speech; and it is tested by means of a speech outline.

Preparing the Body of the Speech

Since the body of the speech contains the essence of the content and since the introduction and the conclusion relate to it directly, the body should be prepared first. Its preparation involves selecting and stating main points and selecting and adapting developmental materials.

Selecting and Stating Main Points

If you think of your prospective speech as a series of ideas, some more important than others, you should begin to understand the principle of subordination that underlies the theory of speech organization. The purpose sentence states the goal of the speech; the main points divide the purpose sentence into its key parts; and the rest of the body of the speech develops, explains, or proves the main points. Since the main points anchor the structure of the speech and since they are next in importance to the purpose of the speech, they should be carefully selected and phrased.

As a rule, main points are complete sentence statements that best develop the purpose sentence. Let's consider the practical application of this rule to informative speech preparation. For the purpose sentence "I want to inform the audience that the three major causes of juvenile delinquency are poverty, broken homes, and lack of discipline," what would be the main points? The answer can be expressed in complete-sentence outline form:

I. One cause of juvenile delinquency is poverty.

II. A second cause of juvenile delinquency is broken homes.

III. A third cause of juvenile delinquency is lack of discipline.

Likewise, the main points for the purpose sentence "I want to inform the audience of the five steps in the production of stereophonic records" would be the sentence statements of each of the five steps. Remember, there is nothing mysterious, unusual, peculiar, or tricky about selecting main points. Each of the stated or implied areas of the purpose sentence will be one of the main points of the speech.

Actually, the ease with which you can determine your main points may prove to be an excellent test of the soundness of your purpose sentence. For if you cannot determine what your main points are, the purpose sentence is probably too vague and should be revised. For instance, what would be the main points for the purpose sentence "I want to inform the audience about airplanes"? Since the phrase "about airplanes" gives no clue to the intended line of development, the main points cannot be determined.

Once you have selected the main points, you need to consider whether you have phrased them in clear, specific, complete-sentence form. Vague, meaningless main points will have the same effect on the speech development as a vague purpose sentence. If you don't know exactly what your main points mean, you can't expect your audience to understand them. To illustrate careful phrasing, let's examine three different sets of main points, one composed of labels, a second composed of carelessly phrased sentences, and a third composed of complete, substantive statements:

Purpose: to inform the audience that our clothes tell us a great deal about our society.

Set 1	Set 2	Set 3
I. Casual	I. They are casual.	I. Our clothes indicate our casual outlook.
II. Youthful	II. They are youthful.	II. Our clothes indicate our emphasis on youthfulness.
III. Similarities	III. There is a similarity between men's and women's.	III. Our clothes indicate the similarity in men's and women's roles.
IV. Little distinction	IV. There is little distinction between rich and poor.	IV. Our clothes indicate the lack of visual distinction between rich and poor.

The labels in the first column indicate the subject areas only. Although the words "youthful," "casual," "similarities," and "little distinction" relate to the purpose and indicate the subject areas of the main points, the nature of the relationship is unknown. In the second set, the complete-sentence main points are more meaningful than the labels. Nevertheless, the use of "they" and "there" along with the copulative verb "to be" makes the statements vague, indirect, and generally unclear. The speaker might get his point across, but any effectiveness would be a result of speech development rather than a result of clear statement of main points. The third set is considerably better. The main points include each of the classifications; moreover, they explain the relationships of the categories to the purpose sentence. If the audience remembers only the main points of Set 3, they would still know exactly what our clothes tell us about our society.

As you begin to phrase prospective main points, you may find your list growing to five, seven, or even ten that seem to be main ideas. If you will remember that every main point must be developed in some detail and that your goal is to help the audience retain the subject matter of each main point, you will see the impracticality of more than two, three, four, or at most, five main points. More than five is usually a sign that your purpose needs to be limited or that like ideas need to be grouped under a single heading.

Stating main points is also a matter of order. Effective speakers have found that their ideas blend together better, will be more easily phrased, and will be more easily understood if they follow one of the three major speech patterns of time order, space order, or topic order.

Time Order   Time order is a kind of organization in which each of the main points follows a chronological sequence of ideas or events. It tells the audience that there is a particular importance to the sequence as well as to the content of those main points. This kind of order often evolves when you are explaining how to do something, how to make something, how something works, or how something happened. For each of the following examples notice how the order is as important to the fulfillment of the purpose as the substance of the points.

Purpose: to inform the audience of the four simple steps involved in antiquing a table.
   I.   Clean the table thoroughly.
   II.   Paint on the base coat right over the old surface.
   III.   Apply the antique finish with a stiff brush, sponge, or piece of textured material.
   IV.   Apply two coats of shellac to harden the finish.

Purpose: to inform the audience of the steps involved in the course of office of the Roman citizen.
   I.   Before he was eligible for office, a young Roman needed 10 years' military experience.
   II.   At age 28, he was eligible for the office of Quaester.
   III.   The office of Aedile, next in line, could be skipped.
   IV.   After serving as Aedile, or Quaester, if he skipped Aedile, a Roman could become a Praetor.
   V.   Finally, at age 42, the Roman could obtain a Consulship.

Purpose: to inform the audience of the major events leading to the Great War.
   I.   Between 1904 and 1910, a series of entangling alliances committed the major nations of Europe to the defense of almost any nation in Europe.
   II.   In 1912, several Balkan wars affected relationships among Turkey, Serbia, Greece, and Bulgaria.
   III.   In 1914, the assassination of Archduke Francis Ferdinand precipitated a series of ultimatums eventuating in Germany's invasion of Belgium.
   IV.   Once Germany moved, nearly every nation in Europe became involved.

Space Order   Space order is a kind of organization in which each of the main points indicates a spatial relationship. If a speaker's intent is to explain a scene, place, object, or person in terms of its parts, a space order will allow him to put emphasis on the description, function, or arrangement of those parts. Because we remember best when we see a logical order of items, the speaker should proceed from top to bottom, left to right, inside to outside, or any constant direction that will enable the audience to follow visually. For each of the following examples, notice how the order proceeds spatially.

Purpose: to inform the audience of the arrangement of the tower dormitory.
  I. The first floor contains the administrative offices, meeting rooms, and student lounges.
 II. The next 15 floors contain 12 four-man rooms each.
III. The top floor contains two penthouse apartments for the resident counselors.

Purpose: to inform the audience about the three layers that comprise the earth's atmosphere.
  I. The troposphere is the inner layer of the atmosphere.
 II. The stratosphere is the middle layer of the atmosphere.
III. The ionosphere is the succession of layers that constitute the outer regions of the atmosphere.

Purpose: to inform the audience of the function of the parts of a golf club.
  I. The grip allows the golfer to hold the club securely.
 II. The shaft provides leverage.
III. The head affects the nature of the drive.

Topic Order   Topic order is a kind of organization in which each of the main points arbitrarily develops a part of the purpose sentence. Although the points may go from general to specific, least important to most important, or some other logical order, the order is still at the discretion of the speaker and is not a necessary part of the topic. With this kind of order, the content of the topics and not their relationship to each other is of paramount importance. The following illustrate the use of topic order in informative speeches:

Purpose: to inform the audience that extrasensory perception is usually concerned with telepathy, clairvoyance, and precognition.
  I. Telepathy refers to the communication of an idea from one person to another without benefit of the normal senses.
 II. Clairvoyance refers to seeing events and objects that take place elsewhere.
III. Precognition refers to the ability to know what is going to happen before it happens.

Purpose: to inform the audience of the nature of the Presidency.
  I. The President is the chief of foreign relations.
 II. The President is commander-in-chief of the armed forces.
III. The President is the head of his party.
 IV. The President is the head of the executive branch.

Purpose: to inform the audience of the three major pressures that determine the selection of our clothing.
  I. Clothing is selected for physical comfort.

II. Clothing is selected in conformity with our attitudes about modesty.
III. Clothing is selected to make us more appealing.

Exercise 6

For each of the purpose sentences you wrote for Exercise 3, construct a skeleton outline including purpose sentence and main points. Apply the following tests to each:

1. Is the purpose sentence clear and concise?
2. Do the main points support the purpose sentence directly?
3. Are the main points in an identifiable pattern?
4. Are the main points limited in number to a maximum of five?
5. Are the main points stated as meaningful, substantive sentences?

Caution: Do not try to complete any more of your speech preparation until you can meet the above tests. Sound structure is a prerequisite of effective speaking.

Selecting and Adapting Developmental Materials

Taken collectively, your main points outline the structure of your speech. Whether your audience understands, believes, or appreciates what you have to say will usually depend upon the nature of your development of those main points. In Chapter 3, you learned that examples, illustrations, statistics, comparisons, and quotations were the materials you should be looking for; now you must select the best of that material, and you must think about whether it relates to the needs and interests of your audience.

If you have done adequate research, you will have plenty of material to choose from, so that as your outline evolves, you should be able to develop each main part rather completely with little difficulty. The more interesting and more challenging aspect of speech development is adapting what you have found to the needs and interests of your audience. Since an audience responds most favorably when the material relates to its needs, interests, and knowledge, you should consider the potential for adaptation of every item of information you plan to use. The following three suggestions will guide you in the evaluation and selection of your developmental material.

1. If you have a choice between two kinds of material, use audience adaptation as the major criterion for making the selection. If two

examples are equally informative and one of them relates more directly to the audience, choose it.

2. If you have a variety of developmental material that supports your point, but none of it relates to your audience, create an adaptation. Remember, comparisons, hypothetical examples, and narratives can be invented by the speaker if he will think creatively.

3. If most of your developmental material is composed of statistics, detailed explanations, or elaborate quotations, make a special effort to find additional material that has built-in audience appeal. Illustrations, anecdotes, narratives, comparisons, and contrasts are inherently more interesting. Their novelty alone will often earn audience attention.

Now, let's see how these three suggestions can be applied to a typical problem of idea development. Suppose you were working on the main point "Japan is a small, densely populated nation." This sentence calls for you to show Japan's area and population. Using material from any reputable almanac, you could say:

Japan is a small, densely populated nation. Her 97 million people are crowded into a land area of 142,000 square miles. The density of her population is 686 persons per square mile.

The essential statistics about population and area have been given. Although the statistics are accurate and the unit is clear, the development is neither as interesting nor as meaningful as it could be. Now compare the following development, which incorporates the suggestions listed above:

Japan is a small, densely populated nation. Her population is 97 million—about one half that of the United States. Even though her population is nearly half that of our nation, her people are crowded into a land area of only 142,000 square miles—roughly the same land area as the single state of California. Just think of the implications of having one half of the population of the United States living in California. To further show the density of population, Japan packs 686 persons into every square mile of land. We in the United States average about 60 persons per square mile. Japan then is about eleven times as crowded as the United States.

This second development was built upon an invented comparison of the unknown, Japan, with the familiar, the United States and California. Even though most Americans don't have the total land area of the United States (let alone California) on the tip of their tongue, they know that the United States covers a great deal of territory and they have a mental picture of the size of California compared to the rest of the nation. It is through such detailed comparisons that the audience is able to visualize just how small and crowded Japan is. In addition to audience adaptation, the speaker can improve idea development using elements of oral style that will be considered in detail in Chapter 5.

If you were trying to explain the size and population of Japan to your class, what kinds of materials would you use to make those ideas meaningful? Suppose a Frenchman was trying to make the same point to a French audience? How could he adapt that content to his audience? When you get in the habit of asking yourself *why* you are developing ideas in a particular way, you will begin using your research material artfully. Remember, speech development is not just putting together ideas and facts you have researched. Not only must you have enough material, but also you must consider how you will adapt the material to your audience.

Exercise 7

Select one main point from the skeleton outlines you completed for Exercise 6. List three details you could use to develop that point. How would you adapt those details to your classroom audience?

Preparing the Introduction of the Speech

After the body of the speech is planned, you can think about how you will begin and end your speech. In oral communication, it is especially important to get the audience listening attentively early, before you move into the body of the speech. By motivating them to listen during the first ten or twenty seconds of a short speech or within the first minute or so of a longer one, you can be reasonably assured that they are psychologically prepared to listen to the heart of the speech. Your major goals are to get audience attention and to focus that attention on the subject matter. These two goals are not synonymous. A speaker who begins by pounding on the stand will get attention; the speaker who begins by shouting "Listen!" will get attention; the speaker who begins by telling a very funny joke will get attention. The question is whether any of these three approaches will prepare the audience for the body of the speech. If the attention does not relate to the speech topic, it is usually short-lived.

How you go about meeting these goals and how much time you spend is entirely up to you. Much depends upon the length and complexity of the speech, the knowledge and attitudes of your audience, and the nature of the occasion. For some audiences and occasions, the bold statement of the topic is all that is needed to get them interested enough to listen. In other cases, you may have to spend as much as 20 percent or more of your total speaking time preparing them for what you have to say. Speakers have discovered numerous ways for accomplishing their goals. The following are four of the most common:

The Question or Startling Statement

In a short speech, attention must be obtained and focused on the topic quickly. Although the burden appears to be great, the goal can be accomplished with one or more questions or startling statements along with any explanation that seems appropriate. Consider the following two short openings:

> Do you know what compels you to buy the clothing you wear? Many pressures are busily at work when we walk into a clothing store. Today I'd like to talk with you about a few of them.

> Look at the glass jar I'm holding. It appears to be empty. It isn't. What it contains is the air we breathe. Be wary—it could kill you. Let's see why.

Quotation

In your research you may well have discovered several quotable statements that are appropriate to your speech. If a particular quotation is especially vivid or thought provoking, you may decide to use it to open your speech. A quotation is best suited to a speech introduction when it is short, concise, and attention getting. The speaker then usually works from the quotation itself to the subject of the speech. Notice how the following short, familiar quotation was used for a speech on cigars:

> It was about 100 years ago that Thomas Marshall said, "What this country needs is a good five-cent cigar." What with one hundred years of inflation, it is rather amazing to find out that today you can buy one for five cents! Let's examine cigar production to see how modern science and technology enable the cigar manufacturer to produce a smokable cigar for as little as five cents.

Anecdote, Narrative, Illustration

Earlier, we talked about how eyes open and ears perk up when someone says, "Did you hear the one about...?" Nearly everyone enjoys a good story. You should be aware, however, that anecdotes, narratives, and illustrations can be the best or the worst ways of beginning a speech, depending upon how they relate to the topic. Some speakers who are so taken with the notion that a story is worth telling may begin with one whether it relates to the topic or not, with the result that the audience enjoys the story and ignores the speech. Since most good stories take time to tell, they are usually more appropriate for speeches of eight to ten minutes or longer. The following illustrates the use of a story to begin a speech on "The Communication Gap":

> A plumber wrote to a government agency, saying he found that hydrochloric acid quickly opened drain pipes. Was this a good thing to use? A scientist at the agency replied that "the efficacy of hydrochloric acid is indisputable, but the corrosive residue is incompatible with metallic permanence." The plumber wrote back, thanking him for assurance that hydrochloric acid was all right. Disturbed by this turn of affairs, the scientist showed the letter to his boss—another scientist—who then wrote to the plumber: "We cannot assume responsibility for the production of toxic and noxious residue with hydrochloric acid and suggest you use an alternative procedure." The plumber wrote back that he agreed, hydrochloric acid worked fine. Greatly disturbed by this misunderstanding, the scientists took their problem to the top boss. He wrote to the plumber: "Don't use hydrochloric acid. It eats hell out of the pipes." I think it's fair to say that this story illustrates a communication gap. All of us are subject to misunderstandings of this kind. Today I'd like to talk with you for a few minutes about four things that we can do to narrow this communication gap with our audiences.

Personal Reference

Since the audience is the object of all communication, a direct reference to the audience or occasion may help achieve your goals. Actually, any good opening has an element of audience adaptation to it. The personal reference is directed solely to that end. Although we have learned to be suspect of insincere use of this method made by individuals who are only after our votes, proper use of the personal reference is particularly effective. The following opening would be especially appropriate for a speech on essay exams:

> Each of us is well aware that final exams start next week. Now, whether we believe in final exams or not isn't too important—we're going to take them anyway. If your professors' tests are anything like mine, you will probably have at least one essay question to answer on any test. You know, many students are really afraid of essay questions, but if you will keep just a few hints in mind, you will find your grades going significantly higher on essay tests.

Although each has been discussed individually, the various types of introductions may be used alone or in combination, depending upon the time you have available and the interest of your audience. The introduction is not going to make your speech an instant success, but an effective introduction will get an audience to look at you and listen to you. That's about as much as you have a right to ask of an audience during the first minute of your speech.

Exercise 8

For any topic that you might use during this term, prepare three separate introductions that would be appropriate for your classroom audience. Which is the better one? Why?

Preparing the Conclusion of the Speech

Inexperienced speakers often end their speeches abruptly after they have completed the body, or they ramble on aimlessly until they find a place that allows them to go sit down. The result of such practices is that the speaker may lose much of the effect he nurtured so carefully during the speech. Like the introduction, even the best conclusion cannot do much for a poor speech; but it can help to heighten the effect of a good speech and, equally important, it can tie the speech together into a compact, concise package for the audience. Look at it this way: you may have talked for five minutes, twenty minutes, or an hour—regardless of the length of time, when you get near the end you have only one last chance to focus upon the main points. Therefore, even though the conclusion is to be a short part of the speech, seldom more than 5 percent, it may have great importance.

By far the easiest way to end a speech is by summarizing the main points. Thus, the shortest appropriate ending for a speech on the causes of juvenile delinquency would be, "In conclusion, the three major causes of juvenile delinquency are poverty, broken homes, and lack of discipline." The virtue of such an ending is that it restates the main points, the ideas that are after all the three main ideas of the speech. Although such a conclusion is appropriate, easy, and generally satisfactory, it isn't very stimulating. A better one would lead up to the summary more interestingly. Notice how the following conclusion improves the over-all effect:

Each of us is concerned with the problem of juvenile delinquency; likewise, each of us realizes that no real dent can be made in the problem until and unless we know the causes. I hope that as a result of what I've said you have a better understanding of the three major causes of juvenile delinquency: poverty, broken homes, and lack of discipline.

Whether the speech is informative or persuasive, the summary type of conclusion is always appropriate. But even when you are using a summary, you may want to supplement it in some way so that your message is impressed upon the audience. Speakers have found that quotations, illustrations, anecdotes, and narratives may be used with a summary or alone to increase emotional impact of the conclusion. Furthermore, when the purpose is persuasive, speakers have found that an appeal—a direct, straightforward request for audience action—will get the desired response. For instance, in a persuasive speech about dry cleaning, a speaker might conclude: "So, the next time you are about to take your clothes to the dry cleaner, take them to Gilmore's—they'll do a better job, with greater care, and save you money besides."

Exercise 9

For the same topic used in Exercise 8, prepare a short summary conclusion. Is there any way that you can supplement the summary to give the conclusion greater impact?

Evaluating the Speech Structure—The Complete Outline

A speech outline is a short, complete-sentence representation of the speech that is used to test the logic, organization, development, and over-all strength of the structure before any practice takes place. It should contain the purpose, the main points, some of the development, and an indication of a prospective introduction and conclusion. Furthermore, the outline should be written in complete sentences and should use a consistent set of symbols to show idea subordination. So that the outline will be a representation and not a manuscript with letters and numbers, it should seldom contain more than one third [1]

---

[1] Because a lengthy outline can inhibit spontaneity, you should be very careful with your first few outlines to be sure that they are of a suitable length. One way of testing the length of an outline is by computing the total number of words that you could speak during the time limit and then limiting your outline to one third of that total. Since approximate figures are all that are needed, you can assume

the number of words that could be spoken within the time limit. The substance of the outline will be included in every practice—the methods of development, the audience adaptation, and the language will and should vary during each practice and during the speech itself.

The following example illustrates the various rules, parts, and tests of an informative speech outline. Study it closely and try to make your early outlines conform as nearly as possible to the form of this example. The first column contains the outline; the second column contains a detailed analysis:

Outline for a Speech
(4–6 minutes)

Outline	Analysis
Specific Purpose: to inform the audience of the three major pressures that determine the selection of our clothing.	The purpose sentence is not a part of the speech per se. It reminds the speaker of his goal and should be used to test whether everything in the outline is relevant.

Introduction

I. Do you know what compels you to buy the clothing you wear?	The word "introduction" sets this section apart as a separate unit. The content of the introduction is devoted to getting attention and preparing the audience for the speech topic. The introduction may be modified considerably before the speaker is ready to give his speech.
II. We are not aware of it at the time, but many pressures are busily at work when we purchase clothing.	

Body

I. Clothing is selected for physical comfort.	The word "body" sets this section apart as a separate unit. Main point *I* reflects a topical relationship of main ideas. It is stated as a complete, substantive sentence.
A. Temperature changes ranging from hot to cold dictate the type of garment that needs to be worn at that particular time.	The main point could be developed in many ways. These two subdivisions, shown by consistent symbols (*A* and *B*) indicating the equal weight of the points, consider the type and the amount of clothing that will yield physical

---

that your speaking rate is about average—160 words per minute. Thus, for a two- to three-minute speech, which would include roughly 320 to 480 words, the outline should be limited to 110 to 160 words. The outline for an eight- to ten-minute speech, which will contain roughly 1,200 to 1,500 words, should be limited to 400 to 500 words.

B. Weather conditions such as snow or rain decide for us how much or how little clothing is needed for our comfort.

   1. A trench coat seems fitting enough for damp, rainy days.
   2. Then naturally we consider ear muffs for snow and ice in January.
   3. On a hot, muggy day in July, we try to wear as little as we can.

comfort. Each of the subdivisions of *B* relate directly to the subject of *B,* the amount of clothing needed.

II. Clothing is selected to conform to our attitudes about modesty.

Main point *II* continues the topical relationship. The sentence is a complete, substantive statement paralleling the wording of main point *I*. Furthermore, notice that each of the main points considers one major idea.

A. Our dress is in accordance with our Puritan heritage.

B. Certain religious precepts influence some people as to what is modest and what is not.

C. Our culture influences our standards of modesty.

   1. In the early 1900s a bare calf was considered indecent.
   2. Today, short skirts and two-piece bathing suits have become standard.

Since main point *II* considers the determinants of "modesty," the major subdivisions are related to those terms. The degree of subordination is at the discretion of the speaker. Ordinarily, subordination is shown by the following set of symbols: major points—*I, II, III,* etc.; subdivisions of major points—*A, B, C,* etc.; subdivisions of subdivisions—*1, 2, 3,* etc.; further subdivisions—*a, b, c, etc.* Although greater breakdown can be shown, an outline will rarely be subdivided further. After the first two stages of subordination, words and phrases may be used in place of complete sentences in further subdivisions.

III. Clothing is selected to make us more appealing.

Main point *III* continues the topical relationship, is parallel to the other two in phrasing, and is a complete, substantive sentence.

A. Women take great pride, expend energy, and spend money in their clothing decisions.

   1. They dress to please and to attract members of the opposite sex.
   2. They dress to get group approval from their contemporaries.

In this case the subdivisions classify on the basis of men's motives and women's motives, as opposed to direct topical development of all the motives that are present. Throughout the outline, notice that each statement is an explanation, definition, or development of the statement to which it is subordinate.

3. Yet at the same time, they wish to remain distinctive and individualistic.

B. Men also take pride in their appearance when dressed.
   1. They want to look appealing and distinctive.
   2. They put less emphasis on status.

The substance of the outline should be tested by asking the following questions:
1. Is the purpose sentence a clear, concise, statement of intent?
2. Are the main points stated as clear, substantive sentences?
3. Do the main points develop the purpose sentence directly?
4. Are the main points in an identifiable pattern?
5. Does each main point consider only one idea?
6. Are the main points limited to a maximum of five?
7. Do the various subpoints really support the division they are subordinate to?
8. Can each of the points be developed with examples, quotations, comparisons, and other forms of amplification?

Conclusion

I. The next time you are driven to making a clothing decision, ask yourself honestly what has determined your decision.
II. It may be physical comfort, it may be an attitude about modesty, or it may be to make you more appealing.

The word "conclusion" sets this apart as a separate unit.

The content of the conclusion is a form of summary tying the key ideas together. Although there are many types of conclusions, a summary is always acceptable for an informative speech.

Exercise 10

Complete an outline that could be used for your first speech assignment. Test the outline to make sure that it conforms to the assignment.

Developing
Speech Style

5

Since ideas are communicated in part by language, the way they are phrased is every bit as important to communication as their content and organization. Broadly defined, style is the personal use of language. Because a complete analysis of style would be inappropriate for our purposes, in this highly selective chapter we shall discuss only those aspects of style deemed fundamental to effective speech. Your goal then is to test your style against the standards of effectiveness and to improve it where necessary. Maximum value can be gained by learning the characteristics of oral style that allow the speaker to adapt his ideas to audience and occasion and by studying the standards of clarity, vividness, and emphasis.

Characteristics of Oral Style

We communicate ideas symbolically through speech and through writing. Although speech and writing have many things in common (in fact under some circumstances good speech and good writing are essentially the same), a comparison of your own conversation with your themes, essays, and term papers shows that certain differences do exist. Notably, oral style is more informal, more personal, and more repetitious. Instead of focusing on these differences, we often tend to proceed as if we were about to write a theme. Our past conditioning controls our word choice, so that what is produced is not a speech, but an essay that will be spoken. Speech is for the ear; writing is for the eye. Every rule governing writing has to do with perception by the eye. But as a speaker, you must affect the ear. Charles James Fox, a great British Parliamentary debater once remarked, "Does it read well? Then it's not a good speech." What he said contains a great deal of truth. Although some material is equally good read or heard, most is not. Let's focus on the three differences that will make your language more appealing to the ear.

Informal

Because oral communication should be conversational, informality is an important element of oral style. Perhaps the key to informality is naturalness. Once someone is assigned a speech, he often attempts to phrase ideas counter to his natural tendency. Such an attempt breeds stiltedness, excessive formality, and occasionally affectation. Yet familiar words, contractions, short sentences, and even sentence fragments are all characteristic of good oral style. Of course, informality does not mean sloppiness. Poor grammar, slang, and excessive colloquialism may appear in conversation, but they should be avoided in public speeches. Perhaps the best way of describing the goal is to say that your language for speechmaking should exhibit the characteristics of informality of your best conversational style.

Personal

Oral style is far more personal than most written style. When you write an essay, a theme, or a short story, you are talking to your audience rather indirectly. Even though a theme may be written for a professor or an article may be written for *The Atlantic Monthly* or *The Reader's Digest* audience, the writer is not around to see or hear the audience reacting to the message. A speaker, on the other hand, has an audience in front of him and the audience feedback is instantaneous. Since your communication in class is face to face, you have the opportunity and perhaps the obligation to convey the personal nature of the communication. What are some of the characteristics of a personal style? Two useful ones are the personal pronoun and the audience question. Although you may have been encouraged to avoid personal pronouns in theme writing, you should use them in speeches. Get used to talking in terms of "us," "we," "our," "you," "your," and the like. In addition, get used to asking rhetorical questions. Although you don't expect an audience to answer verbally, these questions will encourage an audience to think with you. You want to do what you can to convey the impression that you are talking with the audience and not at them. A personal style helps to achieve that end.

Repetitive

Oral style is far more repetitive than written style. A speaker may express the same idea two, three, or even four different ways, until he is sure that the audience has the point. Yet, a key idea may not have hit the mark on first statement; for one reason or another various members of the audience may have missed a point or may not have been impressed by the point. Repetition may be exact duplication or it may be a restatement. If you want the audience to remember the exact words, you should use repetition. If you want the audience to remember the idea, restatement is probably preferable. For instance, the explanation "Even a three hundred hitter only gets three hits in every ten times at bat—That means for every three hits he gets, there are seven times he is put out," reiterates the idea and not the words.

In summary, written and oral style are similar. Nevertheless, by making your speeches informal, personal, and repetitive, you will be appealing to the ear of the audience. Now let's consider the standards of oral style: clarity, vividness, and emphasis.

Clarity

Clarity is achieved by using language that can be understood by an audience as it is spoken. As with so many of the standards of speech-making, the audience determines the relative clarity of the communication. As a result, much of the discussion within this chapter is based upon the assumption that your audience will be a typical college audience. In order to illustrate relative clarity, suppose a speaker, describing a near accident said, "the big thing almost got me." The audience would have only a vague idea of what happened—the communication would not be very clear. Suppose he said, "As I was crossing the street I was almost run over by a big Cadillac that was turning the corner." Phrased this way, the idea is much clearer. Suppose, however, he had said, "Yesterday about 3:00 P.M., I was almost run over by a large red Cadillac sedan, license AB 34456, turning right at the corner of Center and Main, while I was approximately two fifths of the way across the street." In this case, the clarity would be obscured by the excessive detail. Clarity, then, consists of saying specifically and concretely all that needs to be said in order to communicate the idea and no more. Let's consider each of these aspects of clarity separately.

Specificity

In ordinary conversation, under the pressure of having to talk with little or no previous planning, we tend to speak in general terms. But general and vague language inhibits clear communication. For purposes of improvement, the time to test whether or not your language is specific is during your practice periods after the speech has been planned, but before the actual delivery. Listen critically to yourself to see which list of words below illustrates your word selection:

things	characteristics or objects or sayings
large stick	baseball bat
car	red sedan
five trees	three elms and two maples
writing instrument	pen or pencil
a container	a square, cardboard box
selected fruit	apples and oranges

If the words in the left-hand column represent your style, then your language may be vague, general, and unclear. If the words in the right-hand column represent your word selection, then your style is specific. A good method of practice is to recall objects, places, and events and try to describe them. If you have a tape recorder, record your statements. If not, perhaps a friend or relative could help you with your analysis. After each sentence, reexamine every word to see whether your language was specific enough to communicate clearly. If not, try for a more specific statement of the general words and phrases.

Concreteness

Just as we tend to speak in general rather than specific terms, we also tend to speak in abstract rather than concrete terms. Although use of some abstract language is unavoidable (in fact, high-level abstraction may be a sign of high intelligence), abstraction often substitutes for lack of concrete knowledge. You want to use words that communicate to the audience the same meaning you intended. With overuse of abstractions, clear communication becomes nearly impossible. For instance, in the 1968 presidential campaign, Richard Nixon, George Wallace, and Hubert Humphrey all talked about justice. Probably 100 percent of their audiences concurred that justice is a desirable goal. But what did Wallace mean by "justice"? What did Nixon mean? And Humphrey? Or equally important, what did their audiences think they meant? What does "justice" mean? Could you write a one-sentence definition? Ask your roommate what he thinks "justice" means. Ask three or four other persons for their definitions. Experiments of this kind reveal how the use of abstract terms can block communication. Whenever you hear yourself using an abstract word, ask whether your meaning would be clearer if you used a concrete expression. Increased use of the expressions in the right-hand column would make your speech more clear:

Honesty	Returning a five dollar bill to someone who dropped it in the street.
Equality	Being able to buy a home in the suburbs if you can afford to.
Loyalty	Defending a friend's character when it is being attacked in his absence.
Justice	Equal application of the law regardless of your color, whether you have long hair, or whether you are poor.

Economy of Words

Not only must language be specific and concrete, it should also be free from the senseless repetition, extraneous words, and excessive qualification and detail that creep into our speech. In several parts of this text we will have occasion to recommend repetition of key ideas for emphasis. Unfortunately, we often repeat words, phrases, and occasionally entire sentences for no apparent reason. The speaker who says, "Yesterday, ah, yesterday we went to the store," probably hadn't decided what he was going to say. In order to give himself some time to think, he repeated "yesterday." You may repeat words and phrases for this reason occasionally. Minimal repetition of this kind will not hinder communication. In fact, without memorizing speech, it is nearly impossible to avoid some repetitions. If, however, you find yourself repeating words and phrases constantly, for no apparent reason, you should take steps to check the bad habit.

In addition to senseless repetition, some people clutter their speech with extraneous words. On the printed page, breaks in thought are noted by commas, periods, semicolons, dashes, and other punctuation. While speaking, you can punctuate effectively with pauses of varying lengths. An unacceptable way is with extraneous, meaningless words and sounds used to fill the pauses. Most individuals have their own pet fillers. Are you one who says, "uh," "er," "well uh," "you know uh"? Although we accept these irritating expressions from our friends, we do not accept them from public speakers. The speaker who turns the extraneous words and sounds on, turns the audience off. If your professor calls such uses to your attention, you must learn to listen to your speech. Once you hear what you are doing, correction of the habit is rather easy. Of course, you shouldn't be too hard on yourself for a few lapses. Not many speakers can talk for five to ten minutes without using an occasional extraneous filler—the test is whether you can keep these to an absolute minimum.

Economy of words also refers to the number of words it takes you to get a point across. The sentence "Yesterday at about 3:00 P.M. I was almost run over by a very large, red Cadillac sedan, license AB 34456, turning right at the corner of Center and Main, while I was approximately two fifths of the way across the street" is ludicrous, because it is so cluttered with excessive detail. Such excessive detail, use of endless qualifiers, and reliance on that overused admission of lack of clarity, "in other words," all hinder effective communication. Examine your communication to make sure that you say all that is necessary—but only what is necessary. Once you learn selectivity, the ability to tell what is important enough to say and what should be left out, you will increase your clarity.

Vividness

Clarity of language allows you to secure understanding; vividness of language allows you to arouse and sustain interest in what you are saying. Literally, vividness means creating pictures or evoking lifelike mental images. A visual aid allows the audience to see details; vividness allows an audience to picture the details *in their imaginations*. This vivid imagery makes it possible for an audience to gain immediate understanding. Perhaps more important, this vivid imagery makes it possible for an audience to recall the experience itself. Since the imagery you are attempting to create is based upon sensory impression, you should try to heighten the image of the sensory impression. For instance, when you think vividly about pizza, you can see the round, flat pie, about 15 inches in diameter, with the crust cooked to a golden brown; you can hear the crackling of the crust and the popping of the sauce as it cooks; you can smell the savory tomato sauce, the pungent aroma of the pepperoni; you can taste the plump, juicy mushrooms, the spicy anchovies, the subtle flavor of oregano, the tang of the tomato sauce; you can feel the firm crust as you bite into it. And just as you can imagine these impressions, you can create them for an audience in your speech. As with clarity, some economy of words (especially adjectives) is appropriate. Too many will wear your audience out or give an artificiality to your speech. Judicious use of vivid words is the key.

Vividness of speech must begin with vividness of thought. You must have a mental picture before you can communicate one to your audience. If you can't feel the bite of the wind and the sting of the nearly freezing rain, if you can't hear the thick, juicy T-bone steaks sizzling on the grill, if you can't feel that empty yet exhilarating feeling as the jet climbs from takeoff, you won't be able to describe these sensations to your audience.

Vividness is not solely the product of speaker imagery. It can also be achieved by selecting appropriate examples, illustrations, comparisons, and contrasts. Anything that you can do to bring about mental pictures in the minds of your audience will help make your speech more effective.

Emphasis

In a 500-word speech, all 500 words are not of equal importance. We neither expect nor necessarily want an audience to retain the memory of every word uttered. Thus, throughout your speech preparation you are concerned with ways of emphasizing those words and ideas that are more important than others and should therefore be remembered. In Chapter 4, we studied emphasis through idea subordination; in Chapter 6, we will talk about emphasis through voice and bodily action. In this chapter, we are concerned with emphasis through language itself. Actually, it is impossible to separate emphasis from clarity and vividness, for both make ideas stand out.

In addition to repetition, which was discussed earlier, emphasis may be achieved by transitions. Transitions are words, phrases, or sentences that show the relationship between and among other words, phrases, and sentences. Transitions usually summarize, clarify, or forecast, and in almost every case, emphasize. In essence, transitions tell the audience the kind of relationship the speaker wants them to see. They may be in the form of enumeration: "The first step is . . ." or "The second step is . . ." They may be in the form of summary-forecast: "Now that we have all the materials, we can begin construction." They may be prods to our attention: "Now get this point, it's important" or "Here we come to the key idea of the speech." Further examples and a more complete discussion of the use of transition for emphasis are included in Chapter 9.

Exercise 11

Select an event or a scene from your recollection of the past 48 hours. Describe the event or scene aloud. Pretend that you are relating the material to your classroom audience. If you have a tape recorder, analyze the playback. If not, have a roommate listen to you. Analyze what you've said for specific, concrete, vivid, emphatic language. Note extraneous words or useless detail. See whether the language is informal, personal, and where necessary, repetitive.

Practicing
the Delivery
of the Speech

6

**Principle 5   Effective speaking depends upon careful speech practice
based upon the characteristics of effective speech delivery.**

The final step of speech preparation is to practice the delivery of
the speech. The old saying "practice makes perfect" can be especially
applicable to speech delivery. If you learn the standards of good speech
delivery and practice the characteristics that will achieve those standards, then practice will help you considerably; if, on the other hand,
you just repeat bad habits over and over again, practice can make
those bad habits "permanent" and your speeches worse. In order to
make the most of your speech practice periods, you need to consider
the modes of speech delivery, the standards of effective delivery, and a
program of speech practice that will help you achieve those standards.

Modes of Delivery

Speeches may be delivered impromptu, by manuscript, by memorization, or extemporaneously. Impromptu speaking is done on the spur
of the moment without previous specific preparation. Although nearly
all of our conversation is impromptu, most people prefer to prepare
their thoughts well ahead of time before they face an audience. Regardless of how good you are at daily communication, you would be fool-

hardy to leave your preparation and analysis for formal speeches to chance. Audiences expect to hear a speech that was well thought out beforehand.

A common and often misused mode is the manuscript speech. Because the speech is written out in full (and then read aloud), the wording can be planned very carefully. Although Presidents and other heads of state have good reason to resort to the manuscript (even the slightest mistake in sentence construction could cause national upheaval), most speakers have little need to prepare a manuscript. Often their only excuse is the false sense of security that the written speech provides. As you can attest from your listening experience, however, few manuscript speeches are very interesting. Because manuscript speeches are not likely to be very spontaneous, very stimulating, or very interesting and because of the natural tendency to write a speech in written style devoid of audience adaptation, you should avoid manuscripts.

A memorized speech is merely a manuscript committed to memory. In addition to the opportunity to polish the wording, memorization allows the speaker to look at his audience while he speaks. Unfortunately for beginning speakers, memorization has the same disadvantages as the manuscript. Few individuals are able to memorize so well that their speech sounds spontaneous. Since a speech that sounds memorized affects an audience adversely, you should also avoid memorization.

The ideal mode is one that has the spontaneity of impromptu, yet allows for careful preparation and practice. The extemporaneous speech (the goal of most professional speakers) is prepared and practiced, but the exact wording is determined at the time of utterance. Most of the material in this text relates most directly to the extemporaneous method. Later in this chapter, we will discuss how a speech can be carefully prepared without being memorized.

Standards of Delivery

Delivery is the use of voice and body to help convey the message of the speech. Although the best delivery will not save the poorly prepared speech, particularly poor delivery may well harm your speech so much that even exceptional content and organization are negated. Speech delivery may be the deciding factor in the audience's estimation of your effectiveness. What then are the minimum common elements of delivery that you should master? Effective speakers convey a desire to communicate, a sense of audience contact, and a spontaneity, all con-

tributing to a conversational quality. If you master these three characteristics and meet minimum standards of voice, articulation, and
bodily action, your speech delivery will contribute to your effectiveness.

Desire to Communicate

Audiences are very perceptive about speaker attitude. When you
want to communicate, your voice will have a quality in it that audiences will recognize and respond to. If you really, honestly care about
your topic and your audience, your voice will usually reflect that
attitude. And if you really want to communicate, your audience will
usually listen.

Chances are that the preceding short paragraph is enough to get
you on the right track. Since the ability to show enthusiasm does vary
with individuals, however, you should consider two of the realities
of speaking: the effect of personality on delivery and the degree of
nervousness that all speakers possess. As individuals, each of us exhibits personality traits that make him distinct. These traits combine
to make some of us more outgoing than our neighbors and some of
us more reserved. The relationship to our speechmaking is that if
you are outgoing, you may find it easier to project your attitude
about your topic. If, however, you are rather reserved, the audience
may not be able to pick up the cues showing your attitude so readily.
If you seldom show much overt responsiveness to your feelings, you
must do a little more than "what comes naturally." Whereas the
extrovert shows emotional responsiveness even when his feeling is not
very strong, the introvert registers the same level of expressiveness
only when he has reached a high degree of emotion. If you tend to be
more reserved, you must intensify your feelings about what you are
doing in order for the emotions to be communicated. Make sure your
topic pleases you; get involved with the developmental material; and
constantly remind yourself that what you are planning to say will
benefit the audience. Audiences do not listen without some motivation;
they will expect some effort on your part.

Audience perception of your actual attitude about a topic may also
be affected by your nervousness about speaking in public. This nervousness is often called stage fright. Now, let's be realistic—everyone,
beginner and experienced alike, exhibits degrees of nervousness about
speaking. Before your speech, your palms may perspire, your stomach
may feel queasy, and your mouth may get dry. Such reactions are
normal. In fact, it would be quite abnormal if you did not show some
nervousness. The question, then, is not whether you will be nervous,
but how you will cope with your nervousness. Speakers past and
present have lessened their nervousness by recognizing the following

three realities: First, if you are really well prepared, you will be less nervous than if you are only partially prepared. Nervousness is based in part on expected audience reaction. If you know you have nothing of value to say or that you haven't prepared fully enough, you will and should be nervous. If you have prepared and practiced five to ten hours for a five-minute speech, there's no need to be nervous. Second, if you will try to think about communicating the subject and not about yourself, you will be less nervous. Speakers who become an active part of the communication process don't have the time to worry about themselves. Third, and perhaps most important, once you realize that you can succeed (and you can), you will be less likely to be concerned about your nervousness. Success breeds confidence. You will begin with easy speaking tasks—as you succeed with them you will build confidence for the next task. Eventually you will have enough confidence to attempt and accomplish very complex speaking assignments. So even if you are rather nervous about your first speech, as long as you are well prepared and as long as you think about the speech and not yourself, you will be amazed to find that each time you speak you will be better able to control your nervousness.

Audience Contact

Although perception of speech communication seems to be primarily auditory, we concentrate better on the message when a visual bond is established between speaker and audience. In fact, in face-to-face communication we expect the speaker to look at us while he is talking. If the source of the sound, the speaker, does not look at us, we will lose our need to look at him, and, thus, our desire to pay attention to him. The result is a break in the communication bond and a proportional loss of attention. As a speaker then, you have a certain amount of control over your audience's attention simply by looking at them.

Not only does good eye contact help attention, it also increases audience confidence in the speaker. What do you think of an individual who will *not* look you in the eye when he speaks with you? Your attitude toward him is probably negative. On the other hand, when a speaker does look you in the eye, you are probably more willing to trust him. Eye contact is not material evidence of a speaker's sincerity. We do, however, regard it as psychological evidence.

But as you gain skill in speaking you will become aware of the most beneficial aspect of good eye contact; that is, your ability to study audience reaction to what you are saying. Communication is two-way. You are speaking with an audience, and they in turn are responding to what you are saying. In daily conversation, their response would be verbal; in public speaking, their response is shown by various cues they give. An audience of people who are virtually on the edges of their seats with their eyes upon you is paying attention. An audience of people who are yawning, looking out the window, and slouching is not paying attention. You can determine what adjustments, what additions, changes, and deletions you need to make in your plans by being aware of audience reaction. As you gain greater skill, you will be able to make more and better use of the information learned through eye contact.

How do you maintain audience eye contact? It is, of course, physically impossible to look at your whole audience all at once. What you can do is to talk with individuals and small groups in all parts of the audience throughout your speech. Don't spend all of your time looking front and center. The people at the ends of aisles and those in the back of the room are every bit as important as those right in front of you.

Spontaneity

The third quality or characteristic that is fundamental to effective speech delivery is spontaneity, the impression that the idea is being formed at the time it is spoken. At some time in your academic career, you may have had the opportunity, or the misfortune, to memorize some bit of prose or poetry. Remember when you were working on the assignment, you were not nearly as concerned with the meaning of the words as you were with the process of memorizing the flow of words. If you or other classmates had to recite, you will remember that the class was seldom inspired by the presentations. Why? Since the words sounded memorized, any semblance of meaning was lost. Spontaneity, the particular characteristic of voice that makes an idea sound new, fresh, and vital even if it has been practiced for days, was missing. Although our best actors and actresses can make lines they have spoken literally thousands of times sound original, most of us do not have the ability or the know-how. Have you ever wondered why a public official often sounds so much better in off-the-cuff interviews than he does when reading a speech? Once the word is memorized or written down, it is no longer spontaneous communication and the speaker is then required to become somewhat of an actor to make the idea sound spontaneous.

How can you make a planned speech seem spontaneous? The answer lies in the utilization of characteristics of your own conversational method. Since there is a tremendous difference between knowing ideas and memorizing them, you need to have a mastery of content, not words. If I asked you to tell me how to get downtown, you would be able to tell me spontaneously because you have made the trip so many times the knowledge is literally a part of you. If I asked you to tell me about the handball game or the field hockey game you just finished, you could do it spontaneously because key parts of the game would be vivid in your memory. If, on the other hand, I asked you to tell me a little about the material you studied for a history class, your ability to do it spontaneously would depend upon the quality of the effort you had made to master the material. If you had weighed and considered the material, if you had tried to understand the concepts rather than just memorize the details, you would have enough understanding to discuss the content spontaneously. Spontaneous presentation of prepared materials requires experience with the facts, vivid images of the facts, and true understanding of the facts.

Students will often say that they can speak so much better on the spur of the moment than when they try to give a prepared speech. What they mean, of course, is that given a topic about which they have had experiences, vivid images, and understanding they can communicate reasonably well on the spur of the moment. Since you have the opportunity to weigh and consider your subject matter, there is no reason why you should not be equally spontaneous with the prepared speech. How to show spontaneity will be considered further when we examine speech practice later in this chapter.

These three concepts—desire to communicate, eye contact, and spontaneity—when taken together, give a speaker what has come to be called a conversational quality. Speechmaking and conversation are not really quite the same. However, by utilizing the best characteristics of conversation in the formal speech situation the speaker will give the audience the feeling that he is conversing with them. These three characteristics of conversational quality are so important that their presence will guarantee good delivery for the speaker whose voice is acceptable, who articulates clearly, and who is physically responsive to his own ideas.

Voice

Speech is a product of breathing, phonation, resonation, and articulation. During inhalation, air is taken in through the mouth or nose, down through the pharynx (throat), larynx, trachea, bronchial tubes, and into the lungs. We get the power for speech from exhaling the air we breathed. As air is forced from the lungs back up through the trachea and larynx by controlled relaxation of the diaphragm and contraction of abdominal and chest muscles, the vocal folds that help protect the opening into the trachea are brought closely enough together to vibrate the air as it passes through them. This vibration is called phonation, the production of sound. The weak sound that is emitted (like the sound made by vibrating string) travels through the pharynx, mouth, and in some cases the nasal cavity. Each of these three cavities helps to resonate the sound. This resonated sound is then shaped by the articulators (tongue, lips, palate, and so forth) to form the separate sounds of our language system. These individual sounds are then put together into words, or distinguishable oral symbols. We call the sound that we produce voice. Now let's examine the major characteristics of voice that work together to give us the variety, expressiveness, and intelligibility that assist communication.

Pitch   Pitch refers to the highness or lowness of the voice. As mentioned above, voice is produced in the larynx by vibration of the vocal folds. In order to feel this vibration, put your hand on your throat at the top of the Adam's apple and say "ah." Just as the change in pitch of a violin string is brought about by making it tighter or looser, so the pitch of your voice is changed by the tightening and loosening of the vocal folds. Although you have no conscious control over the muscles that change the tension in the vocal folds, you can feel the change of position of the entire larynx by placing your hand on the Adam's apple again and saying "ah" first at a very high pitch and then at a low pitch. The pitch that a speaker uses most frequently is called the "key" of his voice. Fortunately, most people talk in a pitch that is about right for them. Occasionally a person talks in a pitch that seems abnormally high or low. If you have questions about your pitch, ask your professor. If you are one of the very few persons with a pitch problem, he will refer you to a speech therapist for corrective work. Since for most of us our normal pitch is satisfactory, the question is whether we are making the best use of the pitch range that we have at our disposal.

Volume   Volume is the loudness of the tone we make. When we exhale normally, the diaphragm relaxes, and air is expelled through the trachea. When we wish to speak, we need to supplement the force of the expelled air on the vibrating vocal folds by contracting our abdominal muscles. This greater force behind the air we expel increases the volume of our tone. To feel how these muscles work, place your hands on your sides with your fingers extended over the stomach. Say "ah" in a normal voice. Now say "ah" louder. Now say "ah" as loud as you can. If you are making proper use of your muscles, you should have felt the stomach contraction increase as you increased volume. If you felt little or no muscle contraction you are probably trying to gain volume from the wrong source, resulting in tiredness, stridency, and lack of sufficient volume to fill a large room. Under ideal circumstances, you should be able to increase volume without raising pitch. Each of us, regardless of size, is capable of a great deal of vocal volume. The problem is that most of us don't use our potential. If you have trouble getting sufficient volume, work on exerting greater pressure from the abdominal area.

Rate   Rate is the speed at which we talk. As mentioned earlier, a normal rate is somewhere between 140 and 180 words per minute. Rate, like pitch, is an individual matter. There is no one rate that is best for everyone. Since some people talk more rapidly and some more slowly than others, the test is whether an audience can understand what a speaker is saying.

If your professor believes you talk too rapidly or too slowly, he will tell you; and before improvement in normal conversation is possible, you must adjust your ear to a more appropriate rate. The most effective method is to read passages aloud, timing yourself to determine the exact number of words per minute you speak. Then you must make a conscious effort to decrease or increase the number of words per minute accordingly. At first, a different speech rate will sound very strange to your own ear. But if you practice daily, within a few weeks you should be able to hear an improvement and you should be able to accustom your ear to the change.

Quality   Quality is the tone, timbre, or sound of your voice. Voices are characterized as being clear, nasal, breathy, harsh, hoarse, strident, and by other such adjectives. If your voice has too great a degree of some undesirable quality, consult your professor. Although you can make some improvement on your own, improvement requires a great deal of work and a rather extensive knowledge of vocal anatomy and physiology. Severe problems of quality should be referred to a speech therapist.

Vocal Variety and Expressiveness   In determining effectiveness of delivery, these variables are not nearly so important individually as they are in combination. It is through the variety of pitch, volume, rate, and occasionally quality that you are able to give the most precise meaning to your words. An expressive voice is not flawed by the two most common faults of speech melody: monotone and constant pattern.

A monotonous voice is one in which the pitch, volume, and rate remain constant, with no word, idea, or sentence differing from any other. Although very few people speak in a true monotone, many limit themselves severely by using only two or three tones and relatively unchanging volume and rate. The effect of an actual or near monotone is that the audience is lulled to sleep. Without vocal clues to help them assess the comparative value of words, an audience will usually lose interest. To illustrate what proper vocal emphasis can do for meaning, say the sentence, "I want to buy ice cream," in such a way that the pitch, rate, and volume are held constant. Such a delivery would require the auditor to decide what the sentence meant. Now say "buy" in a higher pitch, louder, or perhaps more slowly than the other words in the sentence. Through this vocal stress alone, you are communicating the idea that you want to buy ice cream rather than making it or procuring it in some other way. With this sentence, meaning can be changed significantly by changing only vocal emphasis of "I," "want," "buy," or "ice cream." During an actual speech, you should give such vocal clues in almost every sentence to insure audience interest and understanding.

The other prevalent fault detracting from expressiveness is the constant vocal pattern in which vocal variation is the same for every sentence regardless of meaning. The resulting vocal pattern is nearly as monotonous as a true monotone. For instance, a person may end every sentence with an upward pitch, or he may go up in the middle and down at the end of every phrase. Vocal variety is of little value unless it is appropriate to the intended meaning. The best cure for a constant pattern is to correlate changes in voice with meaning. If you suffer from a relatively severe case of monotone or constant pattern you should set up a work program that you can pursue every day. One method is to read short passages aloud to a friend. Ask your friend to tell you which words were higher in pitch, or louder, or faster. When you find that you can read or speak in such a way that your friend will recognize which words you were trying to emphasize, you will be showing improvement in using vocal variety to clarify meaning.

Articulation

Articulation is the shaping of speech sounds into recognizable oral symbols that go together to make up a word. Articulation is often confused with pronunciation, the form and accent of various syllables of a word. Thus in the word "statistics," articulation refers to the shaping of the ten sounds (*s, t, a, t, i, s, t, i, k, s*); pronunciation refers to the grouping and accenting of the sounds (*sta-'tis-tiks*). If you are unsure of a pronunciation, look it up in a dictionary. Constant mispronunciation labels a person as ignorant or careless or both.

Although true articulatory problems (distortion, omission, substitution, or addition of sounds) need to be corrected by a speech therapist, the kinds of articulatory problems exhibited by most students can be improved individually during a single term. The two most common faults among college students are slurring sounds (running sounds and words together) and leaving off word endings. "Wutcha doin" for "What are you doing" illustrates both of these errors. If you have a mild case of "sluritis," caused by not taking the time to form sounds clearly, you can make considerable headway by taking ten to fifteen minutes a day to read passages aloud, trying to over-accentuate each of the sounds. Some teachers advocate "chewing" your words; that is, making sure that you move your lips, jaw, and tongue very carefully for each sound you make. As with most other problems of delivery, you must work conscientiously every day for weeks or months to bring about significant improvement.

Bodily Action

Ideas are not communicated by voice and articulation alone. A speaker may supplement what he says by appropriate movement of face, arms, hands, and body.

Facial Expression   The eyes and mouth communicate far more than some people realize. You need only recall the icy stare, the warm smile, or the hostile scowl that you received from someone to validate the statement that the eyes (and mouth as well) are the mirror of the mind. Facial expression should be appropriate to what we are saying. We are impressed by neither deadpan expressions nor perpetual grins or scowls; we are impressed by honest and sincere expression reflecting the thought and feeling being communicated. Think actively about what you are saying and your face will probably respond accordingly.

Gesture   By gesture we mean the movement of hands, arms, and fingers. Gestures are usually descriptive or emphatic. When the speaker says "about this high" or "nearly this round," we expect to see a gesture accompany the verbal description. Likewise, when the speaker says "We want you" or "Now is the time to act," we look for him to point a finger, pound his fist, or use some other gesture that reinforces his point. If you gesture in conversation, you will usually gesture in a speech; if you do not gesture in conversation, it is probably best not to force yourself to gesture in a speech. As aids in helping you "do what comes naturally," I would suggest that you try to leave your hands free at all times. If you clasp them behind you, grip the sides of the speaker's stand, or put your hands in your pockets, you won't be able to gesture even if you want to. If you wonder what to do with your hands at the start of the speech so that they won't seem conspicuous, you may either rest them on the speaker's stand partially clenched or hold them relaxed at your sides, or perhaps with one arm slightly bent at the elbow. Once you begin the speech, forget about your hands—they'll be free for appropriate gestures. If, however, you discover that you have folded your arms in front of you or clasped them behind you, put them back in one of the two original positions. After you have spoken a few times, your professor will suggest whether you need to be encouraged to be more responsive or whether you need to be somewhat restrained.

Movement   Some speakers stand perfectly still throughout an entire speech. Others are constantly on the move. In general, it is probably better to remain in one place unless you have some reason for moving. Nevertheless, because a little movement adds action to the speech, it may help you maintain attention. Ideally, movement should occur to help focus on transition, to emphasize an idea, or to call attention to a particular aspect of the speech. Avoid such unmotivated movement as bobbing and weaving, shifting from foot to foot, or pacing from one side of the room to the other. At the beginning of your speech, stand up straight and on both feet. If during the course of the speech, you find yourself in some peculiar posture, return to the upright position standing on both feet.

With all kinds of bodily action, be careful to avoid those little mannerisms that often are so distracting to the audience, like taking off or putting on glasses, smacking the tongue, licking the lips, or scratching the nose, hand, or arm. As a general rule, anything that calls attention to itself is bad, and anything that helps reinforce the idea is good.

A Program of Speech Practice

All that we have discussed so far is concerned with the standards of delivery, or what you should practice. Now we can apply the theory showing *when* and *how* you should practice your delivery. Novice speakers often believe that preparation is complete once the outline has been finished. Nothing could be further from the truth. If you are scheduled to speak at 9:00 A.M. Monday and you have not finished the outline for the speech until 8:45 A.M. Monday, the speech is not likely to be nearly as good as it could have been had you allowed yourself sufficient practice time. Try to complete your outline a day in advance of a two- to five-minute speech and two or even three days in advance of longer speeches. The only way to test the speech itself is to make proper use of the practice period. Practice gives you a chance to revise, evaluate, mull over, and consider all aspects of the speech.

Like any other part of speech preparation, speech practice must be undertaken systematically. In order to make the practice period as similar to the speech situation as possible, you should stand up and practice aloud. The specific procedure may be outlined as follows:

1. Read through your outline once or twice before you begin.
2. Put the outline out of sight.
3. Look at your watch to see what time you begin.
4. Begin the speech. Keep going until you have finished the ideas. If you forget something, don't worry about it—complete what you can.
5. Note the time you finish.
6. Look at your outline again.

Now the analysis begins. Did you leave out any key ideas? Did you talk too long on any one point and not long enough on another? Did you really clarify each of your points? Did you try to adapt to your anticipated audience? Unless you are prepared to criticize yourself carefully, your practice will be of little value. As soon as you have completed the analysis of your first attempt, go through the six steps again. After you have completed two sessions of practice and criticism, put the speech away for a while. Although you may need to practice three, four, or even ten times, there is no value in going through all the sessions consecutively. You may well find that a practice session right before you go to bed will be extremely beneficial. While you are sleeping, your subconscious will continue to work on the speech. As a result, you will often note a tremendous improvement at the first practice the next day.

How many times should you practice? This depends upon many variables including your experience, familiarity with subject, the length of the speech, and so on. What you don't want to do is to practice the speech the same way each time until you have it memorized. An effective speaker needs to learn the difference between learning a speech and memorizing it. One has to do with gaining an understanding of ideas; the other has to do with learning a series of words.

When a person memorizes, he repeats the speech until he has mastered the wording. Since emphasis is then on word order, any mistake requires backtracking or some other means of getting back to the proper word order. Unfortunately, this kind of practice does not make for mastery of content, it does not give additional insight into the topic, and it does not allow for audience adaptation at the time of presentation. Another way that speakers memorize is to say the speech once extemporaneously and then repeat the same wording over and over again. The result is about the same in both instances.

When a person stresses the learning of ideas, he practices his speech differently each time. Utilizing the principles of proper speech practice, a description of the shaft of a pencil would take the following forms:

1. The shaft is a cylindrical piece of wood about 6 inches in length. Its color is yellow. It houses a piece of graphite of about $\frac{1}{16}$ of an inch in diameter.

2. It's the shaft that houses the graphite. The yellow shaft is about 6 inches long and is cylindrical in shape. The piece of graphite that does the actual writing is about $\frac{1}{16}$ of an inch in diameter.

3. The main part of the pencil is made out of a soft piece of wood. Its shape is cylindrical. Its color is yellow. Its length is about 6 inches long. It houses a $\frac{1}{16}$-inch piece of graphite that runs the entire length of the shaft—and of course, it's the graphite that leaves the imprint on paper.

4. The main part of the pencil is a cylindrical shaft that houses the graphite writing compound. The shaft, painted a bright yellow, is about 6 inches long. The graphite runs the length of the shaft and is about $\frac{1}{16}$ of an inch in diameter.

Notice that in all four versions the same essential facts were included: the shaft is a cylindrical piece of wood; it is about 6 inches long; it is painted yellow; it houses a $\frac{1}{16}$-inch piece of graphite. These are the facts that would appear on the outline and that the speaker would attempt to include in every practice and in the speech itself. An interesting phenomenon is that each practice usually gets a little better. As a result, more often than not the actual speech will be similar to the best practice period rather than to the worst. Because the speaker would not be tied to a particular phrasing, he could adapt to audience reaction at the time of delivery.

Exercise 12

Make a diary of your program of practice for your first formal speech. How many times did you practice? At what point did you feel you had a mastery of substance? How long was each of your practice periods?

**Informative
Speaking**

Part Three

Requirements of Informative Speaking

7

In the five chapters of Part Two, we considered the major principles that underly the preparation and presentation of any and all speeches. Even though these principles do not change from speech to speech, their application and emphasis may vary. In this chapter, we want to examine the goals, the materials, and the types of informative speaking.

The Goal of Informative Speaking

Although the goal of informative speaking, to relate information to an audience, is apparently obvious enough, many speakers fail to achieve it because they misunderstand its implications. A careful analysis reveals that most of us require that information have both newness and depth. Technically, any fact is information to someone. We think of the fact as information, however, only when it adds to our knowledge or gives new insights into the knowledge we already possess. For instance, the statement "the earth is a planet" is a fact. Since we already know that the earth is a planet, time spent by a speaker in explanation would be time wasted. Two key tests of "information," therefore, are whether it has added to our present knowledge or has given us a clarification in the form of deeper insight into knowledge we already possess. A third test is whether it is meaningful or relevant to our experience.

The test of relevancy explains some reactions to various classroom lecturers. If one professor's lecture consists of a summary of the chapter he assigned last time, a chapter that the students had read before coming to class, they may reject his attempts with the comment, "He's just a book follower." On the other hand, if a professor gives a highly factual but theoretical fifty-minute lecture based upon entirely new material, his students might say, "That was too deep for me" or "He just bored us with a mountain of facts," meaning that the content did not relate to their prior knowledge or interests. However, if a professor emphasizes selected areas of a chapter, gives new examples and illustrations to explain vague portions, or offers supplemental material; or if a professor talks for fifty minutes on new material, but relates its relevancy to the class, he is characterized as a stimulating lecturer. In summary then, an informative speech is one that relates information to an audience—information that is new, that gives new insights, or that adapts to the knowledge and interests of the audience.

Because of these tests of informative speaking, subject selection is extremely important to your potential success. Your goal as stated in Chapter 2 is to select a topic that meets the needs of the speaker, the audience, and the occasion. Although careful analysis on your part should allow you to select suitable topics, you should be very cautious about topics that exemplify the most common deficiency of student informative speeches, superficiality. For some reason, many novices are satisfied with the most obvious, least demanding topics. For instance, in a round of speeches requiring the use of visual aids, almost every section has at least one girl who tells us how to make brownies, cookies, or a cake and at least one boy who tells us how to swing a baseball bat or a golf club. Assuming the validity of the subject areas for those particular speakers, the topics are still questionable. Although they may appear to meet the tests cited above, they are not nearly so good as a half a dozen other possibilities drawn from the same subject areas. An audience is paying for every speech it listens to—it is paying with the most valuable of treasures, time. Almost every member of every audience is likely to ask himself whether he got five minutes of value for every five minutes he listened. Many of your classmates will already know the fundamentals of such skills as how to make a cake and how to swing a golf club; those who don't are not likely to learn how from the speech alone.

This does not mean that speeches on cake or golf swings must be avoided; it does suggest that the speaker should resist the obvious, the banal, and the superficial. Let's reexamine the subject of making cakes for a moment. Although most of us like to eat cake, we might not like every cake. In fact, even if we ordinarily like chocolate cake we might not like all chocolate cakes. What is it that makes one cake better than another? Why do we show a preference for a particular cake? How do experts judge the quality of cakes? Why is it that a package cake can taste almost as good as an entirely homemade cake? Which ingredients are crucial in making cakes? Questions such as these lead to some topics that have great informative potential. Thus, "the major criteria for determining the quality of a cake" would be a better topic than "how to bake a cake." Similarly, a speech on "how to swing a golf club" is not nearly so good as one on "the three most common faults that golf pros see in their students' swings," "the components that make for a power golf swing," or "the common characteristics found in the swings of most pro golfers." Each of these topics allows for greater depth and more stimulating development.

Before you make a hasty decision about a topic, go back to that list of items you made during your brainstorming session. Judge the list in terms of questions raised in this section. If you do, you will come up with topics that will allow the audience to say, "Yes, that five minutes was well spent—I really learned something!"

Informative Speech Development

Although the materials of informative speaking include all of the kinds of speech development discussed in Chapter 4, you should pay special attention to the kinds of development that are best suited to making audiences more receptive to your information or are more likely to encourage your audience to remember. In many ways, your intent is much the same as that of the classroom teacher. You are both trying to teach your audience something. How and when do audiences learn? Both individuals and audiences learn when they want to and when it is easy for them. If you can keep an audience awake and interested, they will learn; if you can put the information in a way that will make retention easy, they will learn. Three of the effective ways of stimulating retention and interest are repetition, emotional impact, and association.

Repetition

When you meet someone for the first time, you will be more likely to remember his name if you repeat it a few times immediately after being introduced; when you are trying to learn a new definition, a formula for a compound, or a few lines of poetry, you will master them only after you have repeated them often enough to remember. And as we all know, some of the most effective, as well as the most irritating, television commercials are based upon the simple device of repetition.

As a student of public address, you should learn when and how to take advantage of this potent device. Unfortunately for beginning speakers, the words that are most often repeated are of the nature of "uh," "well," "now," and "you know." The artful speaker will determine the two, three, four, or five most important words, ideas, or concepts in his speech, and he will think of ways that he can repeat them for emphasis.

Exact duplication is called repetition; duplication of idea but not of words is called restatement. If you want the audience to remember the exact word, repetition is the proper device to use; if you want the audience to remember the idea, restatement is probably better. Thus a speaker who wants you to remember a telephone number would say: "The number is 365–4217—that's 3, 6, 5, 4, 2, 1, 7." In contrast, a speaker who wants you to remember the approximate size of a city would say: "The population is 497,000—that's roughly half a million people." A speech with artful use of repetition and restatement will be remembered longer than a speech without them.

Emotional Impact

Think back over your life and recall what stands out most vividly about the past. What you recall is probably some happening, event, experience, or incident that had highly emotional impact. Was it your first date? The day you fell out of the apple tree? The spanking you got for rolling the new car into the telephone pole? The artful speaker can simulate this emotional impact through anecdotes, illustrations, and examples. A speaker trying to explain "permissive parent" to an audience might say:

> A permissive parent is one who tolerates or goes along with any request or demand of his children. A classic case of the permissive parent was Henry Fox, father of Charles James Fox, the famous English parliamentary speaker. Allegedly, Henry went along with anything his son wanted—stories about the extremes of this indulgence have become classics. For instance, once when Charles raved that his father had broken a promise and had a wall removed from the estate in his absence, his father had it rebuilt so that it could be blasted in Charles' presence.

The more vivid you can make your development, the more powerful the emotional impact will be. Repetition can become boring when used to excess, but audiences seldom tire of amplification that has sensory impact. A speech that is devoid of illustrative material will seldom arouse an audience or leave an enduring impact.

Association

A third way we learn or remember is by association. Psychologically, association is defined as the tendency of a sensation, perception, or thought to recall others previously coexisting in consciousness with it or with states similar to it. That means when one word, idea, or event reminds you of another, you are associating. Effective speakers take advantage of this tendency by building association through vivid comparisons and contrasts. If I were trying to show you how a television picture tube worked, I would try to build some association between the unknown of the television tube and some knowledge you had. The metaphor "a television picture tube is a gun shooting beams of light" would be an excellent association to develop. The image of a gun shooting is a familiar one. A gun shooting beams of light is easy to visualize. If the association were made strikingly enough, every time you thought of a television picture tube, you would associate it with guns shooting beams of light. If you can establish one or more associations during your speech, you are helping to insure audience retention of key ideas.

The Kinds of Informative Speeches

You have considered the goal of informative speaking and some of the materials that create a climate for learning. Now you should be ready to work on some informative speeches. The following chapters explain and illustrate typical informative speech assignments. During the term you may prepare some or all of the assignments discussed. You may be asked to utilize certain combinations of assignments to meet a new assignment suggested by your professor. Or you may be asked to prepare an informative speech in which you incorporate two or more types in one assignment. The next seven chapters, which progress from the easiest to the most difficult of assignments, include discussions and examples of speeches illustrating organization, speeches illustrating audience adaptation, speeches of definition, visual aids speeches, descriptive speeches, expository speeches, and research reports.

Speeches Illustrating Organization

8

Audiences have an almost instinctive need for clearly organized speeches. We are all painfully aware of the coughing, shuffling, and generally uncomfortable reaction that greets the speaker who rambles on interminably, getting nowhere. In this chapter, we want to concentrate on the characteristics of speech organization that increase audience understanding and recall. The assumptions that underlie this discussion are (1) that clear organization significantly improves audience recall of ideas and (2) that speakers can, through organization, determine which ideas the audience will recall. In order to take advantage of the power of speech organization, you must understand both inherent and perceptible speech organization.

Inherent Organization

By inherent organization we mean the logic of the communication. If a speech has a beginning, a middle, and an end that achieve their goals; if the speech follows internally from point to point; and if each point is in turn developed by material that follows logically, then that speech is inherently well organized. In Chapter 4 you learned how to test the internal order, the logic, and the development of your speeches with a sentence outline. If you completed the exercises in Chapter 4 and if you understand those principles of speech organization, you are ready to work on making that organization apparent to your audience.

Perceptible Organization

Perception is prerequisite to understanding. Although a speech must begin with a solid inherent organization, since your audience is going to be receiving and perceiving your speech by means of the ear, you must transfer the inherent organization of the speech to the mind of the audience by way of the ears of that audience. You must provide clues to help the audience answer such questions as "What are the important points?" "What should I remember?" and "What should I be listening to most carefully?" Three means available to you are placement, proportion, and transition.

Placement

Placement refers to the positioning of the main points in your speech. If your speech follows a time order, the first main point must be the first step of that process, and each succeeding point must correspond to the time sequence. With time order, placement is built into the structure itself. If your speech follows a space order, the direction you want the eye to follow determines placement. With space order, placement follows logically once you determine the most suitable direction for that particular topic. If your speech follows a topic order, and by far the majority of all informative speeches utilize some kind of a topic order, placement is at your discretion.

How to take best advantage of placement has been a question for considerable debate in speech literature. Even with the benefit of contemporary experimentation, speech theorists have been able only to indicate that the most favored position is either first or last. Those who advocate putting the most important point first argue that audiences perceive the first things that a speaker says to be the most important. Those advocating putting the most important point last argue that audiences will remember longest that which comes last in the speech. Whichever the position for the most important point, other points should come in the middle of the speech—and weak points are best omitted.

Of course, this advice will help you only if you are able to recognize which points are the most important or the best. To the uncritical speaker, everything is of equal importance. After you have finished a tentative outline, ask yourself honestly which of your main points is the most important. Then decide what order would best communicate your intent.

Proportion

A second way of calling attention to importance of ideas through organization is called proportion, the amount of time spent on each of the ideas in the speech. The psychological importance of proportion can be illustrated by a hypothetical example. Assuming for a moment that proportion can be considered independently, if in a ten-minute speech on the causes of juvenile delinquency, the three main points (poverty, broken homes, and permissiveness) were discussed for about three minutes each, the audience might perceive the ideas as having equal weight. If, however, the speaker spent five minutes on poverty and only two minutes on each of the other two causes, the audience would perceive poverty, the five-minute point, as the most important one in the speech. Now, if poverty was indeed the most important cause, proportion would be well used as an organizational device; if, however, broken homes was really a more important cause of juvenile delinquency, audience perception would differ from speaker intent.

You will probably find that your ideas have the greatest effect if proportion is correlated with position. Thus, in a ten-minute speech, if you put the most important point first, it should be the one you spend four or five minutes on. If you put the second most important point last, spend three or four minutes on it. The remainder of the time should be divided among the points you put in the middle. Since audiences are likely to remember best those points that were discussed in greater detail, the artful speaker takes care that the most important points receive the greatest amount of discussion.

Proportion is brought about by amplification. If a point is important but is not receiving proper development, you should add a few examples or illustrations to build its strength. Remember, don't add words for the sake of words. If a point really is important, you should have valuable information to include. If you find that you have to invent "padding," you might want to reevaluate the importance of that particular point.

Transition

Transitions are the words, phrases, and sentences that show idea relationships. Transitions summarize, clarify, forecast, and in almost every case, emphasize. Of the three methods of making organization perceptible, transition is perhaps the most effective, yet is the least used. If you understand both internal and external transitions you can increase audience recall.

Internal Transition   Internal transitions grow from the relationships between the ideas themselves. Our flexible language provides us with numerous words that show relationships. Although the following list is not complete, it indicates many of the common transition words and phrases that are appropriate for speech.[1]

Transitions	Uses
also and likewise again in addition moreover	You will use these words to add material.
therefore and so so finally all in all on the whole in short	You will use these expressions to add up consequences, to summarize, or to show results.
but however yet on the other hand still although while no doubt	You will use these expressions to indicate changes in direction, concessions, or a return to a previous position.
because for	You will use these words to indicate reasons for a statement.
then since as	You will use these words to show causal or time relationships.
in other words in fact for example that is to say more specifically	You will use these expressions to explain, exemplify, or limit.

Because these particular words and phrases give the oral clues needed to perceive idea relationships, you should accustom yourself to their use.

External Transition   External transitions call special attention to words and ideas. Since internal transitions can be missed if the audience isn't paying close attention, both for the sake of variety and for additional emphasis you can utilize direct statements to call atten-

[1] After Sheridan Baker, *The Complete Stylist* (New York: Thomas Y. Crowell Co., 1966), pp. 73–74.

tion to shifts in meaning, degree of emphasis, and movement from one idea to another. These statements tell the audience exactly how they should respond. Consider the following list:

> Now I come to the most important idea in the speech.
> If you haven't remembered anything so far, make sure you remember this.
> Pay particular attention to this idea.
> Remember, this is the second step of the process.
> Are you sure you have this point? It is one of the most important.
> But maybe I should say this again, because it is so significant.

These examples represent only a few of the possible expressions that leave the flow of ideas and interject subjective keys, clues, and directions to stimulate audience memory or understanding. Although these are not very subtle, experimental studies have indicated that they are effective in helping audiences to recall information.[2]

Assignment

Prepare a two- to four-minute informative speech emphasizing speech structure. Outline required. Criteria for evaluation will include (1) whether introduction gains attention and leads into the speech; (2) whether main points are clear, concise, and follow an identifiable order; (3) whether position, proportion, and transition are used effectively; and (4) whether the conclusion ties the main ideas of the speech together.

**Outline: Speech Illustrating Speech Structure
(2–4 minutes)**

Since this outline is for a speech illustrating structure, notice the way it is written. Test each part against the recommendations for outlining on pages 42–44. Also note that this outline contains only 211 words, a good length for the assigned speech.

Purpose Sentence: To inform the audience of three aspects of dining with a Spanish family.

---

[2] Ronald Stingley, "An Experimental Study of Transition as a Means of Emphasis in Organized Speeches," unpublished Master's thesis, The University of Cincinnati, 1968, p. 36.

Introduction

I. Have you ever been ravenously hungry, but no dinner until 10:00 P.M.—or faced enough food for two people at one meal—or tasted nothing but olive oil while eating?

II. Then you've been to Spain!

Body

I. The dining hours of Spanish families are completely different from an American household.
   A. Breakfast is served at 10:00 A.M.
   B. Lunch is eaten at 2:00 or 3:00 P.M.
      1. People take a siesta during the hottest part of the day.
   C. Dinner is served late at night, around 10:00 or 11:00 P.M.

II. The amount of food served at the various meals is not at all in balance with the way I am accustomed to eating.
   A. Breakfast consists of a roll and coffee or tea.
   B. Lunch is normally the big meal of the day.
   C. Dinner is also a large meal.

III. The taste of food in Spain is entirely different from what I expected.
   A. There is an erroneous belief that Spanish food is spicy.
   B. The Spanish women use a lot of tomato sauce in their cooking.
   C. Due to the heavy use of olive oil, the food tasted quite different.

Conclusion

I. People expecting to live and dine in Spain should be prepared to face different dining hours, larger amounts of food, and no spices.

II. If you can adjust to this situation—*Bien Viaje.*

Read the speech in the left-hand column through aloud in its entirety.[3] After you have judged the quality of its organization, read the speech again noting the criticism included in the right-hand column.

Dining in Spain

Speech	Analysis
Have you ever been ravenously hungry at 10:00 P.M. with no dinner in sight until 11 or so? Have you ever	One way to begin a short speech is with a series of questions. These three questions are particu-

[3] Speech given in Fundamentals of Speech class, University of Cincinnati, 1968. Printed by permission of Susan Woistmann.

eaten enough food for two at one meal daily? Or have you ever sat down and eaten food that tasted as bland as Cream of Wheat every meal? If you have, then you have eaten in Spain.

The visitor soon finds that in Spain the dining hours are quite different from an American household. In Spain breakfast is served at approximately ten in the morning—I guess mostly because the people don't go to bed until two, three, and sometimes four o'clock. Of course, there's no need to get up at six o'clock and rush around to make it to work on time or to school by eight. Lunch isn't served until two o'clock. It's eaten during the hottest part of the day, and the hottest part of the day in Spain is from about two until four. So, they have a long lunch hour. Dinner, as I mentioned, is served at about ten or eleven in the evening. If you are lucky, your family will give it to you by twelve. At dinner time, they just sort of take the time to relax and talk over what happened during the day, and afterwards they just let the dishes go until morning.

Just as the dining hours are quite different from an American household, the amount of food is just absolutely out of balance with what you are accustomed to here. For breakfast, you may eat scrambled eggs, bacon, or whatnot. There you get a roll, coffee, or milk and that's all. Then for lunch you get a four-course meal. A big, huge, heaping plate of potatoes or rice is your first course. Your second course usually consists of a large dinner-sized plate full of potatoes, vegetable, and meat, fish, or chicken. Dinner is also a large meal, but the food isn't as heavy. Rather than having a first

larly good because they relate to student experiences and they forecast the main points of the speech. The final sentence is a short but effective lead into the body.

This one-sentence transition and main point move satisfactorily into the first area to be considered. The first point is developed with the particulars of when the meals are served. The speaker has tried to draw comparisons and contrasts to emphasize the explanations.

Here is another effective use of transition. By summarizing the first point and forecasting the second, the speaker has let us know that we are leaving a main point, she has reminded us of the substance of the point we are leaving, and she gives us a clue about what we should be listening for. This kind of transition will help even a poor listener to follow the flow of ideas.

Again the speaker supports her generalization with specific examples. As a result of economy of words, she gets quite a lot of information into only slightly more than a minute's worth of speech.

plate of potatoes and rice, you'd be served a bowl of soup. And for dessert, you usually get a fruit.

Perhaps more than even the contrast in dining hours or the amount of food, the taste of Spanish food is quite different from what you expect. There's an erroneous belief that Spanish food is very, very spicy. Well, it's just not true. During the entire three months while I was in Spain, I didn't find one pepper shaker, either in my house, a hotel, or a restaurant. No pepper shakers! And the only thing that I really found to be spicy was the lettuce salad, and it was so salty you had to choke it down—you couldn't even taste the lettuce. And the Spanish people use a lot of tomato sauce, mostly for its coloring, but you can taste it. That's about the only really special thing that you can have. And due to the heavy use of olive oil, your digestive system has quite a lot to get used to. They cook everything in olive oil. All the way from boiling the rice, which I didn't believe at first, down to frying the chicken or meat—they even boil their potatoes in olive oil.

People who expect to live and dine in Spain should learn how to become accustomed to the dining hours, to the amount of food, and also to the taste. So, if you can become adjusted to this situation, *Bien Viaje!*

This particular transition serves two important purposes. First it takes us smoothly from the second to the third main point of the speech. In addition, it conveys the idea that this is the most important contrast of the three. And, since this most important point is put last, it conforms with the placement theory discussed in the chapter. The latter part of this development doesn't support the main point as well as it could. Notice, she is trying to show that the Spanish food is bland. Her experience with the absence of pepper shakers develops the idea of blandness. But when she speaks of the excessive salt on salads, the use of tomato sauce, and the olive oil, we wonder whether bland was really the most descriptive term. This part of the speech needs some reevaluation.

The speaker elects to end her speech with the simple summary. When the assignment is a short, informative speech, this is perhaps the best choice available. The final sentence of the speech gives the conclusion a necessary life.

Speeches Illustrating Audience Adaptation

9

Nearly every chapter in this text has alluded to audience adaptation, the relating of speech material to the knowledge and interests of your audience. Since it is so important to your success as a speaker, you should get in the habit of adapting your material directly to your audiences in your first speeches. Audience adaptation is a product of two separate but interrelated kinds of activities: knowing the frame of reference of your audience and utilizing characteristics of adaptation.

Knowing the Frame of Reference of Your Audience

A portion of Chapter 2 showed you how to analyze the age, sex, occupation, socioeconomic level, and religion of your audience in order to determine their knowledge and interests. After making that analysis, you can select your purpose sentence and determine the kinds of examples, comparisons, statistics, illustrations, quotations, and explanations that your audience would understand and respond to. But just as organization can be inherent or perceptible, so can audience adaptation. Now that we have considered the frame of reference, let's consider the conscious efforts that show audience adaptation.

Characteristics of Audience Adaptation

During the speech, you want the audience to believe that you are talking with them. Although no device will give the impression if you are not sincere, there are ways to emphasize your sincere interest to your audience. Each of the following recommendations will help you reinforce your interest.

Use Personal Pronouns

Personal pronouns by themselves are a form of direct audience adaptation. Saying "you," "us," "we," "our," whenever possible will give the audience a verbal clue to your interest in them. Too often, speakers ignore this simplest of devices by stating ideas impersonally. Suppose you wanted the audience to consider buying a house. You could say: "When an individual eventually gets enough money for a down payment on a house, he needs to ask himself some very serious questions." Notice the psychological difference if you were to phrase the same idea this way: "When you eventually get enough money for a down payment on a house, you need to ask yourself some very serious questions." In one sentence you would be able to show *three* times that you are thinking about your audience. Although this may seem a very small matter, it may make the difference between audience attention and audience indifference.

Use Audience Questions

One of the secrets of audience adaptation is inducing audience involvement. Asking audience questions is an easy way of gaining involvement. In her speech explaining man's reasons for wearing clothing, a girl said: "There are certain decisions you must make and there are factors affecting these decisions. One reason we wear clothing is to protect our body from any visible harm." Although she included personal pronouns, she might have augmented the directness of the statement and improved the adaptation by saying:

> There are certain decisions you must make and there are factors affecting these decisions. Why do we wear clothes at all? What is a motivation for anyone to wear clothes? I'm sure some of you thought of a reason that has been of prime importance since clothes were invented. To keep warm or dry or comfortable. Thus we can say that one of the decisions for wearing clothing at all is to protect our body from visible harm.

Audience questions generate audience participation; and, of course, once an audience is participating, the content will be even more meaningful to them. Because direct audience questions seeking verbal audience responses may disrupt your flow of thought (and sometimes yield unexpected answers), the rhetorical question, a question seeking a mental rather than a verbal response, is usually safer. Rhetorical questions encourage the same degree of involvement and they are easier to handle. Furthermore, audience questions need not be restricted to the speech introduction. Questions are appropriate at any place in the speech where special emphasis is needed.

Despite their value, one caution about the use of questions is in order: Unless the speaker is really interested in asking a question, his delivery will sound artificial. Get used to asking questions naturally and sincerely.

Incorporate Audience Experience

Incorporating audience experience also brings about audience involvement. You can incorporate audience experience by relating an anecdote, narrative, or illustration that might well be common to many if not all the members of the audience. For instance, if you were expressing the idea that a store in a shopping center often doesn't have a person's size or color, you might say:

> I'm sure you've all had the experience of going to a shopping center for some item that you had particularly in mind only to find when you got there that either the store didn't have the color you wanted or they didn't have your size.

You want the audience to identify with the experience. Identification stimulates thought. If an audience is thinking with you, they will be listening to you.

Build Hypothetical Situations

Since audience involvement is so important to audience attention, you can often simulate involvement by placing the audience into a hypothetical situation. The hypothetical situation can incorporate the entire framework for the speech, or it can be utilized to reinforce a single item of information. Suppose you wanted to show the audience how they could turn a cast-off table or chair into a fine piece of refinished furniture. You could start the speech by placing the audience into the following hypothetical situation:

> Many times we relegate our cast-off end tables, a desk, a record cabinet to the land of the lost—the storage room of our basement.

We know the piece of furniture is worth saving—but we don't know why. That cast-off is probably a lot heavier and a lot more solid than most furniture being made today. So, what are we going to do with it? Why not refinish it? Let's assume for this evening that you have just such a piece of furniture in your basement. Let's take it out of that storage room and go to work on it. Where do we start? Well, first of all, we have to gather the right material to do the job.

Whether members of the audience actually have such pieces of furniture is somewhat irrelevant. Because of the hypothetical situation, they can involve themselves in the procedure.

The hypothetical situation can also be used to illustrate a single portion of the speech. In your speech on the same topic, refinishing furniture, you might explain the final step, putting on the varnish, by saying:

The final step in the process is to varnish the piece of furniture. Now, varnishing appears to be a very simple task—and it is if you do it the right way. Let's assume that you've got a good-quality 2-inch brush in your hand, with a good quality of transparent varnish open and ready to go. Now, how are you going to apply that varnish? Many of you may be used to the paintbrush method, you know, back and forth until the piece is covered. But in varnishing, this may well lead to a very poor finish. Instead, start about 4 inches from the edge with the grain, and move your brush to the edge. Now, don't go back the other way. Pick the brush up and make another stroke adjacent to the first—always keep the stroke in the same direction. After you've covered the width go back another 4 inches (now 8 inches from the edge). Move the brush in one direction and continue right over the part you did first. If you will continue doing it in this way you will leave no brush marks in your work and you will have a smooth, even finish.

Whether you used a visual aid or not to visualize the procedure, the hypothetical example would involve each member of the audience in the actual varnishing. The hypothetical situation is just another way of inducing audience involvement.

Show the Relationship of the Topic to the Audience

As human beings, we are interested in *our* appearance and *our* welfare. Although self-interest can be carried to an extreme, a degree of vanity is innate with all of us. Suppose that at the start of the next class period, your professor took a class picture with his Polaroid camera. After waiting the required fifteen seconds to develop it, suppose that he passed the picture around the class. When it came to you, whom would you look for first? In all probability, you would look for yourself. Later, perhaps you would look for that boy or girl who had caught your eye; but first, you would look for yourself.

Because of this degree of self-interest, each member of a listening audience expects a speaker to say something that will relate to him. If he sees some relationship between the subject and himself, he will listen; if he sees no relationship, he may not listen. Since a successful speaker does not leave the decision to listen or not to chance, at every opportunity you should attempt to demonstrate the need for the audience to listen. Sometimes this is very easy. In talking to a classroom of young ladies on the topic "how to protect yourself if you are attacked," your topic itself would probably hold the attention of most girls. Even those who already know some of the suggestions for self-defense would probably listen for new pointers. Suppose, however, that you are talking about "air pollution," "the stock market," or "emerging nations of Africa." Before you give the speech, you must think of some way that you can make the topic relate to individual members of the audience.

The major thrust of showing audience relevance may come in the speech introduction—but it should be reinforced at various places in the speech. A speaker might start his speech on the stock market by saying:

> Many of you, I'm sure, are very happy whenever you see that bank interest rates have gone up. The difference between say 4 percent and 5 percent can amount to a lot of money over a few years. What if banks gave 6 percent or even 7 percent interest per year? You'd probably be standing in line with your money. But you know if you've got a little money to work with there's no reason at all for being content with even 6 percent or 7 percent. With a little time, effort, and care, you can be getting a 10 percent or more return on your money every year. How? By learning about the stock market and then by investing your money in it.

This would be a good opening for your speech because everyone in the class would see a reason for learning more about the stock market. If at the conclusion, members of the audience still felt that the entire speech was relevant to them, attention and retention would be excellent. Remember what happens to a student's attention when the professor mentions casually, "You'd better make note of this point, it will be on the test." The students see the relevancy, and they listen. Now, of course you can't threaten your audience with a test. But you can stress relevancy enough to keep motivation high.

Associate the Most
Important Points of the Speech with a Story

In various places in this textbook, we have spoken of the importance of anecdotes, narratives, illustrations, and other forms of idea development that are storylike. A story may be a good form of audience adaptation even if it doesn't relate to the individual. We all like to tell and listen to stories. When a story is relevant to the topic or audience, it is even better.

We have discussed some of the direct and indirect methods of audience adaptation that will emphasize your concern for the audience. Whether you use them individually or in combination, your speech will profit by their use.

Remember, however, that the time to begin working on audience adaptation is after you have completed your speech outline. Audience adaptation does not necessarily affect the speech structurally: you could discuss three rules for investing in the stock market before your class, the women's gardening club, the Young Democrats, and the local Kiwanis; and the outlines for speeches to all four of these audiences might be nearly the same. After you are satisfied with the structure, you can determine how you will use the methods of audience adaptation.

Assignment

Prepare a three- to five-minute informative speech. Outline required. Criteria for evaluation will include how well the speech was adapted to the audience. The speech should include at least three of the following: use of personal pronouns, audience questions, audience experience, hypothetical situation, relationship of topic to audience, and storylike idea development.

Outline: Speech Illustrating Audience Adaptation
(3–5 minutes)

Notice that the following outline contains a structural weakness that should have been avoided. The flow of ideas, as represented by the development subpoints, reflects a time order. Yet the main points are not clear statements of a time-order pattern. The outline (and the subsequent speech) would be improved with revision of both main points II and III.

Purpose Sentence: I want to inform the audience that unidentified flying objects have been reported throughout recorded history.

Introduction

I. Recently, Dave Withrow gave a talk on contemporary UFO sightings.

II. Today, I'd like to talk about UFO sightings in history.

Body

I. Reports of UFO sightings go back as far as the very beginning of man himself.
   A. Chinese scientists discovered a cave with carvings of strange beings and cylindrical objects dating to 4500 B.C.
   B. The walls of Egyptian tombs contain hieroglyphic reports of UFOs.
   C. The Bible is also a source of possible UFO sightings.
      1. In the story of Moses' exodus from Egypt, the pillar of fire by night and dark cloud by day has been construed by some as a UFO.

II. These UFO reports in history aren't confined to any particular place on the globe.
   A. Sightings have been made in Scotland.
      1. In the years 60 and 763, objects flying over Scotland were seen by the king himself.
      2. In 966, luminous vertical cylinders were seen at sea.
   B. Sightings have been made over Japan.
      1. In 1015, a large sphere was seen giving birth to two small spheres.

III. During the eighteenth and nineteenth centuries, documented sightings were reported by competent observers.
   A. In 1716, Halley saw a UFO bright enough to read a manuscript by.
   B. In 1798, John Martin described a UFO as a flying saucer.
   C. A Captain Brace described a sighting in 1880.
   D. A mysterious planet, Vulcan, appeared and disappeared in the 1870s.

Conclusion

I. There have been at least 10,000 reports of UFOs before the twentieth century.

II. The question is whether they are a physical phenomenon of our atmosphere or actual extraterrestrial visitors.

Study the following speech (recorded in the left-hand column) in terms of audience analysis.[1] Underline every word or idea that you believe helps adapt the speech to the audience. After you have read

[1] Speech given in Fundamentals of Speech class, University of Cincinnati, 1968. Printed by permission of David Schmit.

the speech at least once aloud and after you have studied the use of audience adaptation, read the detailed analysis in the right-hand column.

Unidentified Flying Objects

Speech

About a week ago, we heard our classmate Dave Withrow give a talk on contemporary sightings of unidentified flying objects. Today, I'd like to give you a historical perspective.

The history of reports of UFOs might go back as far as the very beginning of man himself. The earliest report of a UFO that I was able to find was brought to life recently by a Chinese scientist from the University of Peking, who discovered a cave in northern China which dates back to 4500 B.C. On the walls of this cave, he found carvings of strange beings with small heads and large bodies and large cylindrical objects in the air above them, upon which similar types of beings were seen standing. On the walls of many Egyptian tombs containing hieroglyphics are also reports of UFOs. These usually take the form of spherical objects at which the people are seen staring as if they really didn't understand what they were. The Bible is also a good source of UFOs, especially the Old Testament, which is primarily a history book. In the Bible, people tended to explain things either with religious implications or in terms of things they knew, such

Analysis

In this opening, Mr. Schmit adapts to audience knowledge by referring to a previous speech. If you find during this term that a classmate gives a speech on a topic you have selected, instead of saying "Oh no, he gave my speech," refer to some of the previous speaker's material in your speech. Rather than "wrecking" your speech, a previous speaker's analysis can be used as orientation material, or as in this speech, it can pave the way for a contrasting approach.

The first main point of the speech is clearly stated. Interjections like "the earliest report I was able to find" add a personal touch and speaker credibility through research to the speech. An audience will usually "warm up" to the speaker who is really talking *with* his audience. In addition to using personal pronouns and incorporating audience experience throughout the speech, Mr. Schmit presents many clear, descriptive examples that, because of their interest value, serve as audience adaptation.

as they might describe a UFO as being a flying ship or something of this sort. We're all familiar with the story in the Bible of Moses' exodus from Egypt, when he's followed by a pillar of fire by night and a dark cloud by day. This has been construed by some authors as a UFO.

Throughout history, these UFO reports came from all parts of the globe. For example, in the year 60 A.D. and again in the year 763, numerous objects described as flying ships were seen over Scotland, and several of these were seen by the king himself. Later, on July 29 or 30 of the year 966—and these dates are believed to be fairly accurate—several luminous vertical cylinders were seen at sea. Later, in 1015, over Japan, a large sphere was seen giving birth, as it was described, to two smaller spheres. Incidentally, this report has its counterpart many times in modern history when one large UFO is seen emitting several smaller UFOs. This large UFO is easily referred to as the mother ship and the smaller ones as scouts.

During the eighteenth and nineteenth centuries, documented sightings from competent observers continued to be reported. In 1716, the astronomer Halley who discovered Halley's Comet saw a UFO which he described as being bright enough to read a manuscript by. Late in the eighteenth century, in the year 1798, a ship captain, John Martin, described a UFO that he saw as a flying saucer. And this is where that term first originated, and it has stuck to this day. In May of 1880, a ship captain, Lee Forrest Brace, of the ship *Pavna*, saw an object at sea which he described like this: "An enormous wheel whirling around, the spokes of which seemed to brush the airship along. The wheels must have been 500 or 600

Here is one of the places in the speech where Mr. Schmit adapts to the audience by alluding to audience knowledge or experience.

Considered independently, this main point is clearly stated; however, the examples of sightings over Scotland and Japan don't really advance the point very well. Perhaps a statistic about the number of different countries in which sightings were made, preceding the examples, would have strengthened the main point. As it is, these seem like a few more historical examples following the chronology established in main point *I*.

The wording of this main point returns to the chronological pattern begun with the first main point.

yards in diameter." And this is as long as five or six football fields. One of my favorite television shows is *Star Trek*, and one of the prominent characters on this show is Mr. Spock, who is reportedly from the planet Vulcan. During the last part of the nineteenth century a planet named Vulcan did exist in our solar system, and it was located inside the orbit of Mercury which is now the closest planet to the sun. This planet suddenly appeared in the year 1877, and disappeared just as suddenly a year later, in 1878, leaving no trace as to where it had gone. This has become a classic in UFO history. This chronology brings us up to the beginning of the twentieth century, and this is where Dave's speech began.

From the small smattering of detail that I've given you today, and this is by no means the whole story for there are at least 10,000 different reports of UFO sightings before the twentieth century, you can see that UFOs have been a source of controversy throughout history. The question that now must be answered is —are these UFOs some type of physical phenomenon that occurs only in our atmosphere, or are they actual extraterrestrial visitors?

This comparison to football fields is a good one.

The first three examples develop the point quite well, but this Vulcan example is irrelevant to the main point as stated. Yet, the allusion to a popular television character from the mythical planet represents such good audience adaptation that what Mr. Schmit loses in logical development, he may gain in interest.

This final sentence of the main point reinforces the adaptation to the previous speech.

This is a good conclusion for the speech. Mr. Schmit alludes to the entire historical development and then asks the provocative question that alludes to the importance of the subject.

This speech exemplifies the value of use of personal pronouns, allusions to audience experience, and storylike development. Furthermore, the speech illustrates how a speaker can make use of information provided by a previous speaker. The only weakness of the speech is its structure. Although the organization is clear, the main points and the content don't correlate as well as they might. Mr. Schmit had two choices for improving structure: (1) He could have used a time order describing sightings under the headings of "Biblical," "Classical," "Medieval," and "Nineteenth Century"; or (2) he could have emphasized history of sightings, geographical spread, and competence of reporters. Balanced against all the superior qualities of the speech, this is a minor point of criticism.

Speeches of Definition

10

Definition is an invaluable aid to informative speaking. Every time we use a dictionary, we are reminded that our working vocabularies are relatively small compared to the total number of words in the English language. Moreover, anyone who has attempted to answer small children's constant refrain "What does that mean?" is well aware that even those words we use everyday are often difficult to explain. As a result of our problems with vocabulary, our attempts at relating to others often fail—sometimes because we don't know the meaning of a word and sometimes because we accept one meaning when the communicator intended another. Yet, since we cannot solve problems, learn, or even think without meaningful definitions, the ability to define clearly, emphatically, and vividly is essential for the effective communicator. To gain the best insight into definition, we should know how words may be defined and how a speech of definition may be developed.

How Words Are Defined

Although individuals have used numerous methods to define words for their audiences, you can improve your communication by mastering the following four.

Classification and Differentiation

When you define by classification and differentiation you give the boundaries of the particular word and focus on the single feature that gives the word a different meaning from similar words. For instance, a dog may be defined as a carnivorous, domesticated mammal of the family Canidae. "Carnivorous," "mammal," and "family Canidae" limit the boundaries to dogs, jackals, foxes, and wolves. "Domesticated" differentiates dogs from the other three. Most dictionary definitions are of the classification-differentiation variety.

Synonym and Antonym

Synonyms are words that have the same or nearly the same meanings; antonyms are words that have opposite meanings. When you use synonym or antonym, you are defining by comparison or contrast. For instance, synonyms for "sure" are "certain," "confident," "positive." An antonym would be "doubtful." Some synonyms for "prolix" would be "long," "wordy," or "of tedious length." Antonyms would be "short" and "concise." Synonyms and antonyms are often the shortest, quickest, and easiest ways to clarify the meaning of a new word. Of course, the use of synonym and antonym presupposes that the audience is familiar with the synonyms and antonyms selected.

Etymology and Historical Example

Etymology is the derivation or an account of the history of a particular word. Depending upon the word being defined, etymology may or may not be a fruitful method of definition. Since words change over a period of time, origin may reveal very little about modern meaning. In many instances, however, the history of a word reveals additional insight that will help the audience remember the meaning a little better. Consider the following definition: "A sophist is an individual who is more concerned with ingenuity and specious effectiveness than he is with soundness of argument." In this case, the following explanation of the history of the word adds considerable insight to the rather barren classification definition:

> In ancient Greece there were professional teachers who distinguished themselves for their teaching of practical politics, language, and speech. These men became some of the most renowned men in Greece. Although most of them were dedicated, intelligent, and valuable contributors to their cultures, some of them became so entranced with their powers of persuasion that they regarded belief as more important than truth. Plato was so incensed by the power of these men who could "make the worse case appear the better" that he devoted large segments of many of his dialogues to destroying the reputation of the sophists. He was so successful that today

when we refer to someone as a sophist, we do not mean an excellent teacher of practical politics; instead we mean a rather slippery individual who is more interested in effectiveness than in truth.

Under certain circumstances, etymology and historical example can give an excellent assist in the definition of a word.

Uses and Functions

A fourth way to define is to explain the use or the function of a particular object. Thus when you say, "A plane is a hand-powered tool that is used to smooth the edges of boards," you are defining the tool by indicating its use. Since the use or function of an object may be more important than its classification, this is often an excellent method of definition.

Regardless of the kind of definition you select, it should always differentiate, meet all circumstances, include all that is necessary, and, perhaps most important, be understandable.

Developing a Speech of Definition

Definition can be applied to your informative speeches in at least two basic ways: either as a form of support or as the framework for a major speech. Since this chapter is concerned with an assignment of a speech of definition, we need to see how such a speech may be developed. One method is to adopt a standard definition found in a dictionary or other authoritative source and expand it. The other method is to develop an original definition.

Adopting a Standard Definition

Webster's Seventh New Collegiate Dictionary defines "jazz" as "American music characterized by improvisation, syncopated rhythms, contrapuntal ensemble playing, and special melodic features peculiar to the individual interpretation of the player." Like most dictionary definitions, this is of the classification-differentiation variety that requires an understanding of the various terms used within the definition. Before its meaning would be clear, most people would have to look up "improvisation," "syncopation," "contrapuntal" (which refers to "counterpoint"), and "ensemble." Nevertheless, such a dictionary definition makes for a very good purpose sentence for an informative speech. By utilizing each aspect as a prospective topical development of the speech, a potentially sound organizational structure is provided with very little effort on your part. Assuming that you had the background to attest to the accuracy of the definition and to understand the various topics mentioned, your structural outline would look like this:

Purpose Sentence: To inform the audience of the four major characteristics of jazz.

  I. Jazz is characterized by improvisation.
 II. Jazz is characterized by syncopated rhythms.
III. Jazz is characterized by contrapuntal ensemble playing.
 IV. Jazz is characterized by special melodic features peculiar to the individual interpretation of the player.

With this method, then, the organization is suggested by the definition itself. The inventive process determines how you enlarge upon each aspect of the definition. Your selection and use of examples, illustrations, comparisons, personal experiences, and observations would give the speech original distinctive flavor. Furthermore, you would have the option of utilizing other methods of definition to reinforce various parts of the speech.

Developing a Definition

The second procedure, to evolve a definition, allows for a slightly different methodology. A purpose sentence, instead of utilizing an existing definition, is evolved from the various existing definitions and from individual analysis of the subject. Suppose you wished to define or clarify the concept "a responsible citizen." A dictionary would indicate that "responsible" means "accountable" and "citizen" means a "legal inhabitant who enjoys certain freedoms and privileges." But this definition does not really tell what a "responsible citizen" is. As you think about citizenship in relation to responsibilities, you might begin to list such categories as social, civic, financial, and political. From this analysis, you could evolve the following subjective definition: "A responsible citizen is one who meets his social, civic, and financial obligations." Once you are satisfied with the soundness of your definition, you may proceed in much the same way as the person who has adopted a dictionary definition. Your organization, developed topically, would look like this:

Purpose Sentence: To inform the audience that a responsible citizen is one who meets his social, civic, and financial obligations.

   I. A responsible citizen meets his social responsibilities.

  II. A responsible citizen meets his civic responsibilities.

III. A responsible citizen meets his financial responsibilities.

This second method allows you to talk about concepts that have connotative or subjective meanings that are not usually found in dictionaries.

For the following assignment you are of course not restricted to either of these procedures. Your goal is to give the clearest, most meaningful definition possible, utilizing any of the methods of definition suggested above.

Assignment

Prepare a two- to four-minute speech of definition. Outline required. Select a word or concept that is not readily definable by most members of the class. Criteria for evaluation will include the clarity of the definition, organization of main points, and quality of the developmental material.

Outline: Speech of Definition (2–4 minutes)

Notice the clear statement of purpose and clear elucidation of the three main points, insuring a clearly organized speech. Also notice that each main point is an essential of the definition. This 170-word outline is within the recommended limits for a two- to four-minute speech.

Purpose Sentence: To inform the audience of the three major points in the definition of the word fossil.

Introduction

   I. Haven't we all at some time picked up an object and thought it was a fossil?

  II. The common concept of a fossil is not clear.

III. Any fossil must possess three qualities.

Body

   I. A fossil must be the remains of a plant or animal.

     A. This rules out all objects that never lived.

       1. Examples of commonly mistaken objects.

B. This aspect of the definition would still seem to include recently living animals and plants.

   1. Recently living animals and plants are rejected as fossils because of the second aspect of the definition.

II. The remains must be preserved in rock by natural means.

  A. Imprints are not natural means.

  B. Chemical replacement is the chief natural means.

    1. Examples and/or comparisons.

III. The remains must be old.

  A. Our usual definitions of old aren't very useful.

    1. Anecdote.

  B. A fossil implies a degree of antiquity older than historic times.

Conclusion

I. Thus, a fossil can be described as the remains of a plant or animal, preserved in rock by natural means, and having a degree of antiquity older than historic times.

Study the following speech in the left-hand column in terms of organization, clarity of definition, and means of developing the aspects of the definition.[1] Before you attempt to evaluate, read the speech at least once aloud. After you have read and analyzed the speech, turn to the detailed analysis in the right-hand column.

A Definition of Fossils

Speech

Haven't we all at some time picked up an object of some sort and thought it was a fossil? Perhaps you found an old arrowhead or a petrified cow's horn and thought it was a fossil. Then you've got some people who like to refer to teachers or professors as fossils. So as you can see there is a great diversity as to what people commonly think fossils are. But there are three basic qualities which all fossils must possess.

Analysis

The speaker begins with a question that states a reasonable assumption. With the very first sentence he has been able to get audience agreement. He continues to adapt to the class by alluding to objects that they might have thought were fossils. With his allusion to the professors as fossils, the speaker got the laugh he wanted without detracting from the subject matter. Well-used humor that grows from the content will usually contribute to a speech. His forecast of the organization at the end of the introduction is a good idea. It prepares the audience to listen for each of the three main points.

[1] Speech given in Fundamentals of Speech class, University of Cincinnati, 1966. Printed by permission of Frank Ettensohn.

First, they must be preserved remains of a plant or animal. Well, this right away will cast out all things that never have lived, such as people finding Indian arrowheads, pretty stones, or crystals. Some people think these things are fossils but they aren't. What about the animals that die in the woods and their bones are left lying around, aren't they preserved? Well, to a certain extent they are, but this example I think we'll find will be cast out by the next part of the definition which is that the fossil must be preserved in rock by natural means.

Well, now, I can go and stick my foot or drop a leaf in some concrete and get a nice print. Fine. I can put my hand in some mud and make a nice imprint and watch it fill over. And, sure, maybe after the concrete or the mud hardens you might think you have a fossil, but you don't because it wasn't preserved by natural means. Now, what is natural means in relation to fossils? Well, specifically it's chemical replacement, and I can draw a rough contrast to chemical replacement by what happens to this class after it leaves out. Now, I call it student replacement. As soon as the bell rings, some of us are kinda slow, we take our time getting our books together, and some of us get out very quickly. Well, as we go out, other students come in and take our places—gradually the whole class is replaced. And if I were standing up here, I would see the exact same arrangement of chairs, but the composition would be different. There'd be different people, their clothes would be different colors. So we have the same exact shapes, but we have a different composition. And this is what happens with fossils when they're replaced. The animals die or fall into the sea. The com-

This first main point is clearly stated. Enumeration is a satisfactory transitional device, for it lets the audience know what point is being considered. The phrasing "all things that never lived, such as people..." illustrates the kind of grammatical problem that often creeps into extemporaneous speaking. Throughout this section and the rest of the speech, the speaker tends to overuse "well." Extraneous words of this kind seldom serve any useful purpose. In the speaker's favor, notice that throughout most of the speech his word choice is specific and concrete.

Notice that even though the second main point was introduced at the end of the first section, some of the emphasis is lost. Perhaps part of the problem is the abandonment of the enumeration. Speakers, especially beginners, tend to begin series with such statements as "the first..." The device is self-defeating, however, if "one" is never followed by "two," "three," and "four." In this case, for purposes of consistency as well as clarity, it would have been better for him to introduce the second part by saying: "The second characteristic of a fossil is that it must be preserved in rock by natural means." "Now, what is natural means..." represents a very good use of rhetorical question. Well-phrased and well-presented questions interspersed throughout the speech encourage the audience to think along with the speaker. His explanation of chemical replacement is a very interesting invented comparison. Since it explains the most difficult concept in the speech and since it is clear, vivid, and easy to follow, it is perhaps the most effective part of the speech. It certainly represents excellent use of originality and audience adaptation.

pounds within the shell are very unstable. So we have another compound that comes in and replaces them. And one by one we get a completely new object in the same shape but different composition.

Now the last criterion, one that's sort of a new point in geology, is how old is the fossil. Well, they have to be extremely old. I once heard a little story that says if it stinks, it belongs to zoology; if it doesn't, it belongs to the study of fossils. Well, most geologists will concede that a fossil must have a degree of antiquity older than historic time, and this will roughly go back to, say, 7000 B.C. or something like this. It's ah, they're not quite sure when.

So, grouping all these things together, we can say that a fossil is the remains of a plant or animal, preserved by natural means in rock, and possessing a degree of antiquity older than historic times. Thank you.

Unlike the introduction of the second main point, this transition and statement of the main point are quite good. Notice, however, that the speaker has given up his enumeration. The story about the difference between zoology and geology is a good one. Although something may well stop "stinking" within a few months, the story adds another touch of humor to the speech. The final two sentences in this section are rather weak. It would have been better for the speaker to state his material more authoritatively.

A good summary. At the end of the speech, however, the "thank you" is unnecessary. If the speech was good, the audience will be appreciative anyway; if the speech was not good, the "thank you" has no real effect on the quality of the speech. During the speech, the speaker mentioned the three aspects in the introduction, discussed each in detail during the body, and drew the definition together in the conclusion. Despite some questionable word selection and a few grammatical lapses, this is a worthy model for a speech of definition.

Speeches Utilizing Visual Aids

11

The visual aid is a unique form of speech amplification, for it gives the speech a new dimension. Speech, being primarily verbal, appeals to the ear; visual aids appeal to the eye. With the use of visual aids, the ideas of the speech gain a double sensory impact. Because of this unique feature, speakers have come to regard visual aids as one of the most impressive forms of speech amplification. Yet, their misuse can hurt and can even destroy an otherwise carefully presented speech. In this section, we will consider the kinds and uses of visual aids in informative speeches.

Kinds of Visual Aids

By definition, anything other than the speaker himself that is used to appeal to the visual sense of the audience is a visual aid. In the classroom, the most common types of visual aids are objects; models; pictures, drawings, and sketches; maps, charts, and graphs; and, occasionally, films, slides, and overhead and opaque projections.

Objects

Objects are usually excellent visual aids in that they eliminate most of the possible distortions of size, shape, and color. If you talk about a vase, a basketball, a braided rug, or an épée, the object itself is most suitable for display. Unfortunately, most objects are too small to be seen or too large to be carried to class, maneuvered, or shown. As a result, even though the actual object might be the best visual aid, its use may be impracticable.

Models

A model is a representation used to show the construction or to serve as a copy. When the object itself is too large to bring to class, a model will usually prove a worthwhile substitute. If you were to talk about a turbine engine, a racing car, the Great Pyramid, or a dam, a model might well be the best visual aid. Especially if you are able to obtain or construct a working model, the speech will usually benefit from its use. Your most important test is whether the model is large enough to be seen by the entire audience. Some model cars, for instance, may be only 3 or 4 inches long—too small to be used for a speech; on the other hand, a model car made to the scale of 1 inch to 1 foot (perhaps 12 to 18 inches long) would be large enough. Although models distort size, their shape, color, and maneuverability make them excellent visual aids.

Pictures, Drawings, and Sketches

Pictures, drawings, and sketches probably account for a majority of all visual aids used in speeches in or out of the classroom. Because they may be obtained or made so much more easily and inexpensively, their use is undoubtedly justified. Obviously, any picture, drawing, or sketch gives up some aspect of realism in size, shape, color, or detail. Nevertheless, the opportunities for emphasis of key features usually outweigh any disadvantages.

Pictures, of course, are readily obtainable from a variety of sources. In your selection, make sure that the picture is not so detailed that it obscures the central features you wish to emphasize. Colored pictures are usually better than black and white; and, above all, of course, the picture must be large enough to be seen. The all-too-common disclaimer, "I know you can't see this picture but ..." is of little help to the audience.

Many times you will have to draw your own visual aid. Don't feel that you are at any disadvantage because you "can't draw." If you can use a compass, a straightedge, and a measure, you can draw or sketch well enough for speech purposes. If you were making the point that a water skier must hold his arms straight, his back straight, and have his knees bent slightly, a stick figure (see p. 102) would illustrate the point every bit as well as an elaborate, lifelike drawing. In fact, elaborate detailed drawings are not worth the time and effort and may actually obscure the point you wish to make. Although actual representation is not a major problem, size, color, and neatness often are. For some reason, people tend to draw and letter far too small. Before you complete your visual aid, move as far away from it as the farthest student in class will be. If you can read the lettering and see the details, it is large enough; if not, you should begin again. Color selection may also cause some problem. Black or red on white are always good contrasts. Chartreuse on pink and other such combinations just cannot be seen very well.

Maps, Charts, and Graphs

Maps, charts, and graphs may be discovered or drawn. Although maps, charts, and graphs do not always have the eye appeal of drawings and models, they can contribute greatly to a speech. To get the most out of them, however, you should be prepared to make extensive interpretations. Since maps, charts, and graphs do not speak for themselves, you should know how to read, test, and interpret them before you use them in speeches. The obvious tests of size and color are the same as for drawings.

Films, Slides, and Projections

Seldom will you have the opportunity to use films, slides, or projections. The scheduling of projectors, the need for darkened classrooms, and the tendency for these visual aids to dominate the speaker all combine to outweigh possible advantages of their use. Beginning speakers find it difficult enough to control the speaking situation without having to cope with the problems that films, slides, and projections involve.

Using Visual Aids

Since visual aids are very powerful types of speech amplification, you should take care to use them to your advantage. The following are some of the guidelines that will enable you to get the most out of your visual aids.

1. Show visual aids only when you are talking about them. It takes a very strong-willed person to avoid looking at a visual aid while it is being shown. And while a person is looking at a visual aid, he will find it difficult to pay attention to the speaker's words if they are not related to that visual aid. So, when you show a visual aid, talk about it; when you have finished talking about it, put it out of sight.

2. Show visual aids so that everyone in the audience can see them. If you hold the visual aid, hold it away from your body and let everyone see it. Even when the visual aid is large enough, you may find yourself obscuring someone's view inadvertently if you are not careful in your handling of your aid. If you place your visual aid on the chalk board or mount it on some other device, stand to one side and point with the arm nearest the visual aid. If it is necessary to roll or fold your visual aid, you will probably need to bring transparent tape to hold the aid firmly against the chalk board so that it doesn't roll or wrinkle.

3. Talk about the visual aid while you are showing it. Although a picture may be worth a thousand words, it still needs to be explained. You should tell your audience what to look for; you should explain the various parts; and you should interpret figures, symbols, and percentages.

4. Talk to your audience and not to your visual aid. Even though most of the members of the audience will be looking at your visual aid while you are speaking, you should maintain eye contact with them. The eye contact will improve your delivery, and you will be able to see how your audience is reacting to your visual material.

5. Don't overdo the use of visual aids; you can reach a point of diminishing returns with them. If one is good, two may be better; if two are good, three may be better. Somewhere along the line, there is a point at which one more visual aid is too many. Visual aids are a form of emphasis; but when everything is emphasized, nothing receives emphasis. If you have many places where visual aids would be appropriate, decide at which points the visual aids would be most valuable. Remember, a visual aid is not a substitute for good speechmaking.

6. Don't pass objects around the class. Since we are used to professors passing out materials, we sometimes became insensitive to the great hazards of such a practice. Audiences cannot resist looking at,

reading, handling, and thinking about something they hold in their hands; and while they are so occupied, they are not listening to the speaker. More often than not, when you pass out materials you lose control of your audience—lessening your chances of achieving your purpose. Even when only two or three objects are passed around, the result may still be disastrous. Most members of the class become absorbed in looking at the objects, looking for the objects, wondering why people are taking so long, and fearing that perhaps they will be forgotten. Anytime you pass something around, you are taking a gamble —a gamble that usually is not worth the risk.

7. Use the chalk board only as a last resort. Although chalk boards are provided for a professor's convenience, they are, nevertheless, about the worst kind of visual aid. Since the board is most useful to write on while you are talking, the tendency is to talk to the board and not to your audience. In addition, since you may be nervous when you speak, your board work is not likely to be as neat or as clear as you would like. For short numbers, words, or for sketchy representations that can be written in a few seconds, the chalk board may be appropriate; however, because of the serious limitations, it should be used only after other methods have been tested in practice.

8. Discover ways to simplify demonstrations. For you, a visual aid speech may mean one in which you show how to do something, how to make something, or how something works. Under these circumstances, part or all of your speech will be in the nature of a demonstration. Since demonstrations often take longer and since motor control will be a little more difficult in front of an audience than at home (did you ever try to thread a needle with 25 people watching you?), you should consider some way to simplify your demonstrations. The following example illustrates how one speaker accomplished the goal. For her speech on flower arranging, she brought a bag containing all the necessary materials. Since her second step was to prepare the basic triangle to begin her floral arrangement, she began to put the parts together in their proper relationship. Rather than trying to get everything together perfectly in the few seconds she had available, she drew from a second bag a partially completed arrangement that illustrated the triangle. Her third point was to show how additional flowers and greenery could be added to bring about various effects. Again, she began to add flowers to give us the idea of how a florist proceeds, and then she drew from a third bag a completed arrangement illustrating one of the possible effects that could be made. Even though she did not complete either of the steps for us, we saw how a florist handles her materials. In effect, her use of visual aids was every bit as professional as the floral arrangement she showed us.

Technically, this would not be demonstration, for she did not go through all the steps in their entirety. Since discretion is the better part of valor, however, with any complex subject it is probably better to have some of the steps completed beforehand.

By carefully deciding what kind of visual aids will best serve your purpose and by using visual aids in the manner described above, you will find that visual aids can be an effective complement to your speaking.

Since visual aids can be used in almost any kind of speech and since the kind of visual aids are almost unlimited, no one assignment can meet every possible goal. The following assignment will allow you to focus on the selection and use of visual aids in informative speaking.

Assignment

Prepare a four- to six-minute informative speech in which visual aids are the major kind of speech amplification. Outline required. The speech may show how something is made, how something is done, or how something works. Criteria for evaluation will include selection and use of visual aids.

Outline: Speech Utilizing Visual Aids
(4–6 minutes)

This outline needs one minor revision to strengthen its structure. Since the purpose of the speech is to explain the four parts of a piston stroke, A, B, C, and D under II are really the main points of the speech and should be labeled as I, II, III, and IV. The idea labeled as I is really orientation and should be included in the introduction. Otherwise, the outline meets the tests included on page 44.

Introduction

I. You can have a baby without knowing what's going on for nine months; you can speak without having very much knowledge of phonetics; you can drive without knowing what's going on under the hood. But it's a little more helpful if you do understand a little bit of what's going on behind the scenes.

II. I would like to give you a little bit better understanding of where the power comes from in your engine.

Body

I. Power is transferred from your gasoline to your back wheels through an instrument called a piston.
   A. The piston moves up and down in a cylinder.
   B. A six-cylinder car has six cylinders; an eight-cylinder car has eight.
   C. A valve opens and closes.

II. This piston stroke has four parts.
  A. The first part is intake.
    1. The gas valve opens.
    2. The piston makes a down stroke.
    3. Gas is sucked into the cylinder.
  B. The second part is compression.
    1. The piston starts its upward stroke.
    2. The gasoline that's in the cylinder is mashed together.
  C. The third part is ignition.
    1. The spark plug ignites the gas.
      a. It's the same as putting a match to the gas.
      b. The gasoline explodes.
    2. The valve is closed and there's no place for the gas to go.
    3. The expanding gas pushes the piston down giving the force to drive the car.
  D. The final part is called exhaust.
    1. The exhaust valve opens.
    2. The piston moves upward.
    3. The stale gas is pushed out into the air.

Conclusion

I. The four parts are intake, compression, ignition, and exhaust.

Study the following speech transcribed in the left-hand column in terms of kinds and uses of visual aids, organization, and audience adaptation.[1] Read the speech through at least once aloud. After you have read and analyzed the speech, turn to the detailed analysis in the right-hand column.

The Automobile Piston Stroke

Speech

You can have a baby without knowing what the heck's going on for nine months. You can speak without having very much knowledge of phonetics. And in a similar manner you can drive a car without knowing what the heck's going on under the hood. But I think we'll all agree that it's a little more helpful if you do understand a little bit of what's going on behind the scenes. And don't

Analysis

This informal, slightly humorous opening proved quite effective. By adapting to the majority of the class, in this case a largely female audience, the speaker gave a real reason for listening. Notice, he is not expecting the audience to gain a working knowledge, but only to have a familiarity with the central process involved in the gasoline engine. The first sentence is well adapted to a young audience, the second sentence re-

[1] Speech given in Fundamentals of Speech class, University of Cincinnati, 1968. Printed by permission of Derek Dunn.

get the wrong idea, I'm not going to try to make you all mechanics or something in five easy steps. But I would like to give you a little bit better understanding of where the power comes from in your engine.

Now first of all, power is transferred from your gasoline to your back wheels through an instrument that's called a piston. This is what a piston looks like—now this one came out of a motorcycle, but essentially it's the same as one in a car, except for a difference in size. This is a shank. The piston head moves up and down in a cylinder, a tube-shaped object. Hence a six-cylinder car has six cylinders with one piston in each; an eight-cylinder has eight pistons and so forth.

I have a little schematic drawing [Figure A], and it is schematic because this is not exactly the way it looks. But this would be the edge of your cylinder, this is your piston, and this is to denote a valve. In this position the valve is closed, when it's not sticking out into the cylinder, and in this position the valve would be considered open. This is essentially to say that if you put a hole in a bag you can let something come in or go out. Now, basically, the piston stroke has four parts.

lates to a speech class, and the third sentence suggests the general nature of the topic. In effect, he got the audience's attention on the subject.

The speaker begins his orientation by showing an actual piston, giving us a realistic view. There's nothing wrong with using a motorcycle piston since, according to the speaker, it looks about the same. He would have been wiser to tell us which piston would be the larger. We assume the one in the automobile, but we don't know.

Here the speaker moves to his schematic drawing with movable parts, At this point, we begin to get the idea that we are actually going to see how the various parts work. He has completed the orientation; the audience is ready to follow the steps of the process. Notice that the speech contains the same minor weakness noted in the outline. The speaker thought of this section of orientation as the first main point of his speech, when in reality it is part of the introduction. Nevertheless, his wording at the end of this section leads us to believe that he knows the heart of the speech has to do with the four parts. The fault might not be so much failure to recognize which are the main points, as an uncertainty about how to represent the main points on paper.

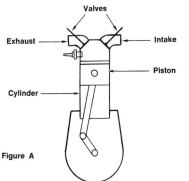

Valves

Exhaust

Intake

Piston

Cylinder

Figure A

The first part is intake [Figure B]. Your gas valve, I'll call it, opens up

The speaker states his first main point clearly. As he begins to talk (we'll get our piston in the starting position)—the gas valve opens up and the piston makes a downward stroke. Since this is a closed system, and we've opened this part here, essentially what you do is you suck your gasoline into the cylinder.

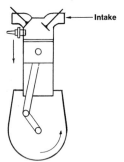

Figure B
Intake

about the first part, he notices that during the introduction he got his piston in the wrong position, so he takes a second to fix it. Although the speaker might have selected a better word than "suck" to describe the process, his phrasing certainly communicates what happens.

Now, next, after that has occurred, you close your valve, which now makes a closed system and the piston starts its upward stroke, and this is called compression [Figure C]. Now, during compression, what you've done is you've taken the gas that's been in the cylinder and you've mashed it together in compression.

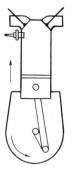

Figure C
Compression

"Now, next," serves as the transition to this second major part. Because of the way he leads into the step, a great deal of emphasis is lost. Perhaps he could have said, "After the first part of the stroke, intake, the piston starts its upward stroke. This second part is called compression." Whatever the wording, the speech would be slightly improved by some transition statement that let the audience know that compression is really the second part. Once more, the speaker uses a very graphic, if not particularly elegant expression, "mashed it together." Despite the questionable word choice, the idea is clear.

Now, at the peak of compression—this here is our spark plug—at the peak of compression, your spark plug ignites. This is done by letting the electrical charge jump across a gap. It's the same thing as putting a match into the gasoline. And what

The speaker gets into the third part with no transition at all. Notice that five sentences are spoken before the main point is suggested. This is a common fault when describing a process. The speaker tends to get so involved with the flow of the proc-

really happens is that it sets the gasoline on fire and causes an explosion [Figure D]. Notice our valve is closed, so there's not a place for the gas to push out except through this movable part, the piston. And

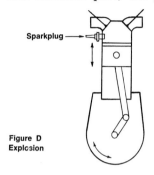

Sparkplug

Figure D
Explosion

ess that he forgets to itemize the main points. And since he made a point of saying in the introduction that there are four distinct parts, he should be careful to elucidate these parts as he comes to them. Nevertheless, his excellent use of visual aids during the speech gave a visual clarity to the process where verbal clarity was lacking. The comparison between a spark plug igniting fuel and putting a match to gasoline is quite good. Throughout the speech, the speaker has made his explanations clear and vivid. Unfortunately, "this here" and other grammatical errors, as well as some poor word selections have some negative effect.

what we have then is our power stroke or our ignition. And thus as the gas expands and pushes our piston down, we get the force that drives the car [Figure E].

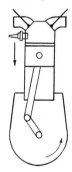

Figure E
Power

Our next and final stroke is called exhaust. And what essentially happens in exhaust is that our exhaust valve opens, the piston makes an upward movement and pushes all that stale gas out into the air and gives you smog and makes you cough and everything like that. Now, then, this valve closes and our gas valve opens, and essentially what we do is start the process over again [Figure F].

Notice that the fourth main point, exhaust, is clearly labeled. "Our next" is not the best transition, but in this case it is satisfactory. The sentence "The piston makes an upward movement and pushes all that stale gas out into the air..." was a real audience pleaser. Not only is the idea vivid, but the audience had a chance to laugh. In this instance, the laugh was planned, and it contributed to the over-all effectiveness.

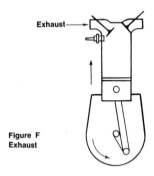

Figure F
Exhaust

Throughout the body of this speech, the speaker held his visual aids out so that we could see them. As he went through each of the parts, he moved the appropriate parts of the visual aid so that we could see the process in action. The speaker put in much time preparing his visual aids but the time was well spent. Four separate pictures would probably have done the job but giving us the opportunity to see the process in motion gave the speech action and added to the vividness of the explanation. As a result, the speech was as close to a real demonstration as would be possible with cardboard aids.

So, you can see there are four parts here seen all at one time [Figure G]. You start out with intake—we suck the gas into the cylinder. Our second stroke, the piston moves upward and compresses the gas. The third stroke, we have our spark plug setting off our power stroke ignition. And our fourth stroke begins our smog through our exhaust pipe. Now, hopefully, this little demonstration will give you a little bit better idea of where the power comes from in your car, so the next time you go to the garage, and the mechanic says, "Uh, you don't have compression," you don't have to say, "Is that something like having hiccups?" You will have a little bit better idea of what's going on. Thank you.

For the conclusion, the speaker did show a single visual aid with each of the steps drawn separately. Notice that the conclusion is rather long, but the reiteration contributed to the probability that the audience would remember the steps better. Again, the last sentence returns to the light touch that was apparent in the opening and carried throughout the speech. In this instance, the final "Thank you," was really unnecessary, the audience was visibly impressed by the speech. There's no doubt that better grammar and more careful word choice would make the speech read better. Nevertheless, the spontaneous quality, the excellent use of visual aids, and the fine audience adaptation far outweighed the speech's weaknesses.

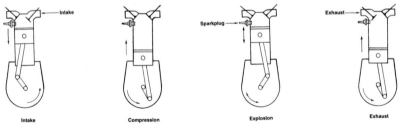

Figure G

Descriptive Speeches

12

Because description may be so important in achieving clarity and vividness in your speeches, the descriptive speech assignment provides an excellent opportunity for emphasizing language skill. The goal of the descriptive speaker is to give an accurate informative description of an object, a structure, or a place. Although animals and people may seem like obvious subjects, the tendency to describe them in terms of subjective reaction rather than objective analysis makes them less suitable topics for informative description. In preparation for a descriptive speech, you should consider subject selection, the essentials of description, organization, and language.

Topics for Descriptive Speeches

Although the first things that come to mind—the pencil sharpener on the wall, the statuette on the shelf, or the site of a summer vacation —may be acceptable, you should select your topic from the lists you compiled in Chapter 2. If you discover that your original lists do not include any subjects that would be appropriate for description, continue the brainstorming process until you have compiled several possibilities to choose from. For instance, if your hobby is "camping," you might list "turtleback campers," "campsite," "kerosene lantern," "tent trailers," "tents," "sleeping bags," and other topics associated with camping. If your major is medieval history, you might list "moats," "castles," "jousting spear," "coat of mail," or "crossbows."

In evaluating your topic selection, remember that it must meet the principal test of informative speeches—the potential for new information. Description itself is, and must be, subordinate to informative intent. You want to describe what the object, place, or building looks like, but your intent must be informative rather than poetic.

Essentials of Description

You achieve your goal in descriptive speaking by providing word pictures for your audience. In order for the auditor to reconstruct a mental image that corresponds with your perception, an amount of essential data is required. If the object is simple and familiar (a light bulb, a rocking chair), the description need not be very detailed; if the object is complex and unfamiliar (a sextant, a nuclear reactor), the description must be more detailed. Even common objects must be described vividly if you want to differentiate them from the standard. The essentials of description are size, shape, weight, color, composition, age, condition, and location of subordinate items.

Size

Size is described subjectively by "large" or "small" and objectively by dimensions. Ordinarily a meaningful description of size will contain a comparison. For instance, neither "The book is a large one," nor "The book is 9 inches by 6 inches by 3 inches," by itself creates an image. On the other hand, "The book, 9 inches by 6 inches by 3 inches, is a large one, the same length and width but twice the thickness of your textbook" would be descriptive.

Shape

Shape is described in terms of common geometric forms. "Round," "triangular," "oblong," "spherical," "conical," "cylindrical," and "rectangular" are all descriptive. A complex object is best described as a series of simple shapes. Since most objects do not conform to perfect shapes, you can usually get by with approximations and with comparisons to familiar objects: "The lake is round," "The lot is pie shaped," or "The car looks like a rectangular box," all give reasonably accurate impressions. Shape is further clarified by such adjectives as "jagged," "smooth," or "indented."

Weight

Weight is described subjectively as "heavy" or "light" and objectively by pounds and ounces. As with size, descriptions of weight are clarified by comparisons. Thus, "The suitcase weighed about 70 pounds, that's about twice the weight of a normally packed suitcase" would be descriptive.

Color

Color, an obvious necessity of description, is difficult to describe accurately. Although most people can visualize black and white, the primary colors (red, yellow, and blue), and their complements (green, purple, and orange), very few objects are these colors. Perhaps the best way to describe a color is to couple it with a common referent. For instance, "lime green," "lemon yellow," "brick red," "green as a grape," "banana yellow," or "blue as the sky" give rather accurate approximations. Just be careful with how far you carry the comparisons. Paint companies, fabric dealers, and cosmetics manufacturers stretch our imagination to the breaking point at times with such labels as "blimey blue" or "giddy green."

Composition

The composition of an object helps us to visualize it. A ball of aluminum does not look the same as a ball of yarn. A pile of rocks gives a different impression than that of a pile of straw. A brick building looks different from a steel, wood, or glass building. Sometimes you will refer to what the object seems like rather than what it is. An object can appear metallic even if it is not made of metal. Spun glass can have a woolly texture. Nylon can be soft and smooth as in stockings or hard and sharp as in toothbrush bristles.

Age

Whether an object is new or old can make a difference in its appearance. Since age by itself may not be descriptive, it is often discussed in terms of the next category, condition.

Condition

Although condition is difficult to describe objectively, it can be very important to an accurate description. The value of coins, for instance, varies tremendously depending on whether they are uncirculated or their condition is good or only fair. A 1915 Lincoln penny in fair condition may be worth two cents, whereas an uncirculated 1960 penny may be worth five cents. Books become ragged and tattered, buildings become run down and dilapidated, land is subject to erosion. Age and condition together often prove especially valuable in developing informative descriptions.

Location of Subordinate Items

If your object for description is complex, the parts must be fitted into their proper relationship before a mental picture emerges. Remember the story of the three blind men who described an elephant in terms of what each felt? The one who felt the trunk said the elephant was like a snake; the one who felt a leg said the elephant was like a tree; and the one who felt the body said the elephant was like a wall. Not only must we visualize size, shape, weight, color, composition, age, and condition, but also we must understand how the parts fit together.

Since the ultimate test of description is that it enables the audience to visualize, the speaker probably should include too much detail rather than not enough. Moreover, if some particular aspect is discussed in two or three different ways, everyone might get the mental image, whereas a single description might make the image vivid to only a few. Begin your practice sessions with more material than you could possibly get into the time limits for your speech. As you gain a mastery of the material in practice, you can begin to delete until you get the speech down to a workable length. Keep in mind, however, that with the descriptive speech perhaps more than any other you will have to resist the desire to memorize.

Organization of Description

Since at least one of the goals of a descriptive speech is to leave with the audience a visual image of your subject, arrangement of main points by space order will often prove the most workable. A description of a jet-powered racing car might go from back to front, front to back, outside to inside, or inside to outside. A description of a painting might go from foreground to background, background to foreground, left to right, or top to bottom.

Although space order organization should be used most often, when you are describing a class of objects you might use a topic order with a space order of subdivisions. For instance, in a description of your campus, you might want to speak on the topics of buildings, the walk system, and the wooded park areas. Or, in a description of Yellowstone Park, you might talk about Old Faithful geyser and the Fountain Paint Pot as the two main topics. Each of the main topics would in turn be developed with a space order arrangement of subordinate detail.

A significant benefit of a space order organization is that your decision about placement of main points is simplified. Once you determine that you will go from left to right, top to bottom, or inside to outside, every key feature that the eye encounters will become either a main point or an important subdivision of a main point.

Language

Although a descriptive speech has several goals, it derives its major benefit as a language exercise. With this assignment you can concentrate on clarity, emphasis, and vividness, the three fundamental qualities of style we discussed in Chapter 5. You want to make your description so vivid that the audience will be able to visualize your subject accurately.

As you consider your wording of the speech remember the function of description. You want your speech to be informative, not poetic. Be on the lookout for florid description, emotive words, and excessive adjectives and adverbs. A descriptive speech should not sound like a page from a literary magazine. By keeping the emphasis on the informative nature of the topic and not the beauty, by keeping the emphasis on the functional nature of the language and not the poetic, you should be able to make your speech clear, emphatic, and vivid without being affected or artificial.

Earlier you were cautioned about not memorizing this speech. Since there are unlimited ways that you can describe in any part of your speech, in each practice keep the essentials in mind, and try to use slightly different wordings to express your descriptions. By adapting to your audience and by having a true spontaneity, you will be able to avoid memorization.

Assignment

Prepare a two- to four-minute speech describing an object, a building, or a place. Outline required. For this speech only, visual aids will be prohibited. Criteria for evaluation will include clarity, emphasis, and vividness of the description.

Outline: Descriptive Speech
(2–4 minutes)

Notice that the outline follows a space order going from outside to inside. Main point II, *the inside, is further developed by means of the space order method.*

Purpose Sentence: I want to describe the Munich Hofbrau House.

Introduction

I. This past summer I accomplished in one night what I couldn't accomplish in three years in college—I enjoyed drinking beer.
II. I think the success has more to do with the hall than with the beer.

Body

I. The Munich Hofbrau House is the largest and best-known beer hall in Munich.
   A. Especially on Saturday evening, all traffic seems to lead to the Hofbrau House.
   B. You are led into the Hofbrau House through two large hand-carved doors.
      1. The wood is very old and heavy.
      2. The carvings are typically German.
II. The inside is an enormous structure with a very high ceiling.
   A. There are no windows.
   B. A small band plays German songs in the front left-hand corner of the hall.
   C. Off to your right as you walk in are numerous rows of tables and benches.
      1. The tables are long.
      2. They are completely occupied with people of all ages.
   D. On both sides of the room the walls are covered with shelves filled with various knickknacks, cuckoo clocks, and beer steins.
   E. A high ceiling is covered with beautiful wooden beams.
   F. At the rear of the room are two large doors.
      1. They are smaller than the ones through which you enter.
      2. These lead to the upper floor where much of the same is found.
      3. These also lead to the often frequented restrooms.

Conclusion

I. Everything looks the same after two litres.
II. You might as well be in the Mug Club in Cincinnati.

As you read the speech transcribed in the left-hand column, analyze the descriptions of size, shape, weight, color, composition, age, condition, and location of subordinate items.[1] Which descriptions are vivid? Which need more detail? After you have read the speech at least once aloud, read the analysis in the right-hand column.

The Munich Hofbrau House

Speech	Analysis

This past summer I accomplished in one night in a Munich beer hall what I couldn't accomplish in three years in college, and that was I actually enjoyed drinking beer. I think that the beer hall had more to do with it than the beer because I'm not drinking beer right now. I'd like to describe the beer hall to you. The Munich beer hall or better known as the Hofbrau House is the largest beer hall. And in order to find it all you really have to do is follow any crowd coming from any direction. And especially if it's a Saturday night, the crowd will probably deposit you right in front of the beer hall.

Although Miss Paul leads into her topic quite well, her statement, "I'm not drinking beer right now," should be reworded. We get the idea that she's not drinking beer while she's talking, but she means that she has not become a beer drinker.

As you are standing in front of the beer hall, you'll walk through two large doors, each about 8 feet high and nearly 4 feet wide. The wood these beautiful doors are made out of is very old and heavy, and the hand carvings on them belongs in Munich.

We probably need a little better description of the outside of the hall. Although we "see" the size of the two large, old, heavy wooden doors, we don't have a visual image of the carvings or the rest of the outside of the hall.

The hall itself is just an enormous structure, that must be nearly the size of the Topper Club, with a very high ceiling. Along the ceiling are wooden beams that run from one wall to the other, and also from the ceiling to the floor. As you enter the beer hall, off to the left in the front-hand corner of the room is an old-fashioned band playing German beer hall music from a bandstand. Benches and tables, which look very

Here Miss Paul shows size by comparing the hall to a dance hall that Cincinnati students could visualize. The order of Miss Paul's description is quite clear throughout this main point. Probably the strength of this speech is her creation of atmosphere. In addition to seeing the hall and its parts, we can imagine the sound, the activity, the gaiety. For instance, her statement about cuckoo clocks, "But if they did

---

[1] Speech given in Fundamentals of Speech class, University of Cincinnati, 1968. Printed by permission of Toni Paul.

much like picnic tables but they're much larger, are located in a line along the right-hand side of the room and the left-hand side. These tables, covered with the traditional red-checked tablecloths, are overflowing with people who are overflowing with beer. And very rarely can you find a place to sit. And that just doesn't seem to bother people because they're also sitting on top of the tables. But it makes for a very merry evening. Along the walls on both the right side of the room and the left side of the room you'll see very large shelves that are covered with cuckoo clocks that range in size. They don't cuckoo. But if they did, I doubt if anybody would hear them.

[cuckoo], I doubt if anybody would hear them," allows us to sense the degree of noise.

Also located on these shelves on the walls are steins of various designs, colors, and shapes. Now, their beer mugs are not like ours. When you order a mug of beer, you are ordering a liter, which in essence is a quart of beer. And it doesn't come any smaller. And people seem to drink them like we drink our mugs of beer. On the rear of the hall you'll find another large door that empties to a large staircase that can either take you upstairs to a room similar to the one downstairs, or to the restrooms. Now, this door's frequented quite often in the beer hall.

This is a good description of the size of the beer stein.

This allusion to the frequency of use of the door leading to the restrooms adds a light touch to the speech.

But after one or two liters of beer, you forget that you are in the Munich beer hall, and you can just assume you are in the Varsity Mug Club on Calhoun Avenue.

The conclusion, alluding to a favorite spot near the Cincinnati campus, is satisfactory. The descriptive speech may be one of the most difficult of informative speeches. You must be very observant in order to describe accurately. In addition, you must think creatively in order to make the description vivid. Although this is not an exceptional speech, it does a good job of describing size and atmosphere.

Expository Speeches

13

Although any speech of explanation is in a sense an expository speech, for purposes of this assignment an expository speech is defined as one that places emphasis on the understanding of idea and that requires outside source material to give the speech depth. For example, "the causes of juvenile delinquency," "the practice of religion in ancient Egypt," "the nature of a guaranteed annual income," "the history of the struggle for women's suffrage," and "the origin and classifications of nursery rhymes" are all examples of topics for expository speaking. Under this definition, a descriptive or demonstrative speech or a speech that can be given using only personal knowledge or observation would not be acceptable. In explanation of this assignment, we will consider some of the types of expository topics and the imaginative, original, creative development of resource material.

The Types of Expository Topics

In order to stimulate your thinking and to help you anticipate and solve some of the problems you might face, let's consider the nature, special problems, and topic possibilities of expositions of a theory, principle, or concept; expositions of political, economic, and social issues; expositions of historical events and forces; and expositions of critical appraisal.

**Exposition of
Political, Economic, and Social Issues**

Before you can hope to solve a problem, you must know something about it. Now, as perhaps never before, the ordinary citizen needs all kinds of information to help him cope with his environment. One such problem facing everyone is air pollution. Although we may believe that something should be done about it, many of us don't know enough about the complexity of the causes and we have little knowledge about existing or proposed solutions. As an expository speaker, you have the opportunity and perhaps the obligation to make us aware of the various factors that should be considered before a decision can be made. You are not charged with the responsibility of proving the harm of an existing problem, nor do you attempt to move us to a particular action —these are all within the province of the persuasive speaker. You as an expository speaker provide the facts about some phase of the problem. Your goal is understanding.

One of the special problems met in dealing with contemporary issues is objectivity. You cannot hope to speak objectively (to discuss your topic in a detached manner) unless you are also objective in your analysis of the problem. For instance, you should not begin your research with the thought "I'm going to prove to them that we've got to put more money into the solving of this problem now" or "I'm going to show them why gas-fueled transportation should be banned." What you can do is decide what aspect of the contemporary issue needs to be discussed, then go ahead and find the material that will yield understanding of that aspect. For instance, if after reading a few articles, you decide that the experts see the elimination of the internal combustion engine for automobiles as an answer to air pollution, you can speculate about alternative automotive power plants. Further research might show that the present thrust in automotive engineering is directed toward battery-driven and steam-driven automobiles. As an expository speaker, then, you may talk about why experts are considering the elimination of the internal combustion engine, or you may talk about one or both of the alternative systems. You would not attempt to prove that we should abandon the gasoline engine, nor should you attempt to convince us that either of the two alternatives is superior. So, objectivity is insured by reading widely on the topic, selecting an aspect of the topic, then presenting the information as an addition to our knowledge and not as proof of a position.

Arousing audience interest may be even more difficult than maintaining objectivity. Psychologically, you may face at least two problems: antipathy toward matters of importance and audience saturation. The first of these, antipathy, might be called the spinach syndrome. Just as some people rebel at eating spinach because it is "good for them," they also rebel at listening to speeches that will be "good for them." Since an understanding of contemporary issues is obviously important, you must think of ways to make these important topics interesting. The second related problem is our tendency to "turn off" when we reach a saturation point; at various times, all of us just get tired of hearing about riots, Vietnam, the Middle East crisis, even though these topics may be vital. The answer to the saturation problem is to consider some aspect of a contemporary issue that will be new to the audience. Although a speech on the causes of riots may get a deaf ear, a speech on the types of, or accomplishments of, black capitalism may arouse audience interest. Instead of giving the impression that you are going to give another one of the innumerable talks about a "common" problem, select some aspect that is fresh. In summary, new information presented in a fresh manner may counter both antipathy and saturation.

Although your topics should always grow from your brainstorming sheet, here and in each of the following sections several subject areas will be listed to help stimulate your thinking:

Topics for Consideration

Organized crime	Race relations
Air pollution	Balance of payments
Population explosion	Water pollution
Drugs	Conservation
Foreign aid	Indians
Labor relations	Organ transplants
School financing	Inflation
Artificial organs	Mass media

Exposition of Historical Events and Forces

It has been said that men who don't understand history are forced to repeat it. History can be fascinating for its own sake; moreover, through historical analysis we learn to appreciate the causal relationships that can help to explain or at least to illuminate contemporary society. Whether you talk about the strategy of war, mathematics, wrestling, or air pollution, you can find historical information to give an insight into the subject matter that is impossible to get in any other way.

Because history is a mirror of life, it may be dull or exciting. The most intriguing problem facing the expository speaker on historical events and forces is selecting an aspect of history that can be made interesting. Yet, by thinking historically, you can uncover fascinating topics relatively quickly. For example, let's assume for a moment that you have an interest in machines, mechanics, building, construction, or related areas. As a result, you may be fascinated by the knowledge of all that is involved in creating a skyscraper or a bridge or a high-rise apartment. Let your mind wander a bit. Think of some of the famous constructions of the past—of the Great Wall of China, Stonehenge, or the Pyramids. In ancient times, man did not have such equipment as cranes, steamshovels, and bulldozers. How were these remarkable structures built? Why were they built? What materials were used? Why have they lasted? These are just examples. Every area of study is replete with topics of historical interest that are worth exploring.

History can be made lively and interesting when you select examples, illustrations, and experiences that vivify your ideas. Re-creation of actual events, actions, and description all will help add interest to historical analysis. If you've noticed, many people who say they don't like history enjoy historical fiction. Why? Because the history is made vivid and exciting.

Relevancy is a second major problem of historical analysis. Since your audience may not share your immediate or automatic interest, you must show a relevancy to contemporary times. Building pyramids may be related to modern construction problems, medival jousts may be related to one or more modern sports, battle strategy may be related to modern warfare. As an expository speaker, you must seek out the tie between historical knowledge and our interests. Notice, I say seek out the tie. If the material has any intrinsic value or merit, it can be related to audience knowledge and needs.

Topics for Consideration

Pyramids	Oriental use of gunpowder
Greek drama	One-room schoolhouse
Roman chariots	Pirates
Circus Maximus	Establishing trade routes
Roman roads	Exploration
Genghis Khan	Napoleonic wars
Castles	Inventions
Chivalry	Battle strategy
Stonehenge	Witches

Exposition of a Theory, Principle, or Law

The way we live is determined by natural laws, physical principles, and man-made theories. Yet as important as these are to us, many of us do not understand the laws, principles, and theories, either in themselves or in how they affect us. Take gravity, for example. We know that when we drop something it goes "down." We know that all of us stand upright on earth and that "up" to people on opposite sides of the earth happens to be opposite directions. Some of us may even remember that all heavier-than-air objects drop at the same rate of speed regardless of size or weight; and we may even remember that, although they drop at the same speed, their velocity (weight times speed) differs geometrically. When astronauts reach a given height, they experience weightlessness. If you have an interest in physical laws, perhaps you could explain these and other phenomena having to do with gravity. Or you may be able to discuss applications of this law to other phases of our lives—applications that would be of tremendous informative and interest value to your audience. Because we are really so naïve about the forces around us, theories, principles, and laws make excellent expository topics.

The exposition of a theory, principle, or law brings about at least one problem that is peculiar to this kind of speech: the tendency to overuse or become dependent upon scientific terminology, formulas, and jargon. This dependence is one reason why some engineers, mathematicians, economists, and behavioral scientists find it very difficult to talk with people outside their professions. Your problem, then, is to explain scientific terms in a language that can be understood. Popularizers such as Vance Packard, Margaret Mead, and Isaac Asimov, have earned reputations for their ability to bridge the gap between the specialists and the common man. A good expository speaker must be such a popularizer. He must understand the subject, and he must be able to discuss that understanding in an intelligible manner. An effective tool of the popularizer is the example. Any theory, principle, or law can be explained by using one or more examples. The more closely the example relates to the frame of reference of the listener, the more easily it can be understood. For instance, when you learned πr^2, the formula for the area of a circle, you probably needed one or more examples to give you a mastery of the formula. When your teacher wrote $22/7 \times 7 \times 7 = 154$ on the board, you saw how the formula worked. After she wrote $22/7 \times 10 \times 10 = 2200/7 = 314\frac{2}{7}$, you may have said, "I understand." The two examples then allowed you to put the formula into practice. You can help your audience gain a mastery by using examples to put the law, theory, or principle into practice. Furthermore, you can let the use of example help you avoid a dependence upon jargon.

As with historical exposition, relevance is also a problem with theories, laws, and principles; however, one of their most exciting aspects is *how* they relate to us. The fact that plastic has the property of being molded into almost any form and the capacity for retaining that form under many stresses allows us to make many uses of plastic. The law that force is equal to mass times acceleration allows us to make jet engines. The "law" of supply and demand allows us to understand many modern business practices. And the formula $E = mc^2$ holds the key to our possible salvation or ultimate destruction. To assure your success you must show us what a particular law, theory, or principle means to us—with good topics, the challenge shouldn't be difficult.

A third problem is to avoid misleading an audience. We hypothesize about many things in this world. From our hypotheses we formulate theories. Be sure that you know whether your topic is a theory or a fact. The formula πr^2 will give us the area of a circle, pure water boils at 212° Fahrenheit at sea level, and gravity can be measured. Relativity, evolution, and multiplier effect are theories that may or may not be valid. If you keep this differentiation in mind, you can avoid confusing yourself or your audience.

Topics for Consideration

Binomial theory	Colors—complement and contrast
Boyle's law	Condensation
Archimedes' law	Light refraction
Binary number system	X-rays
Einstein's theory of relativity	Multiplier effect
Harmonics	Magnetism

Exposition of Critical Appraisal

Probably every university in the country offers courses in film, art, and music appreciation. The purpose of these and similar courses is to give insight into the standards of criticism. To appreciate means to understand *why* we respond the way we do. Because much of our pleasure and satisfaction is based upon our evaluation of paintings, musical composition, books, films, speeches, and other art forms, the exposition of critical appraisal is worth considering for your exposition speech.

A major problem with this kind of assignment is recognizing the difference between objective evaluation and persuasive intent. We should, of course, be well aware that anything we say in a speech may have a kind of persuasive appeal for an audience. The difference, however, between a persuasive speech and an informative one is the intent of the speaker. A speech in which you tried to prove to the audience that Van Gogh's "Starry Night" is a great painting or is overrated, would be persuasive. In contrast, a speech on the characteristics of the painting that help to make it popular or a study of the painting in terms of Van Gogh's mental state would be informative.

In addition, as a critic you must have an accepted critical base from which to work. You should be familiar enough with the subject area to have some confidence in your knowledge and ability to explain and not just list. For instance, in appraisal of "Starry Night," you could comment on the use of heavy brush strokes. Although this fact in itself may be interesting, it would be better for you to explain what this kind of a stroke does to or for the painting and to show what kinds of effects are possible as a result. In other words, you must be prepared to go beyond superficial analysis and to give real insight into the work.

A third and a very real problem in a short speech is to give the audience enough orientation. With a speech on a Van Gogh painting, this can be done by showing a color reproduction of the painting itself; within a few seconds, an audience can get as much knowledge as it needs about the work being analyzed. If, however, you discuss a book, a film, or a speech, you may have to familiarize your audience with the work itself before you can go into a critical appraisal. The following guidelines will help you decide how much orientation will be necessary. If you select as a subject something that can be grasped by observation, you have no major problems. If you have a subject that is well known (for example, Lincoln's Gettysburg Address), you can assume an audience understanding. If the subject cannot be grasped on observance or is not familiar, you must make sure that you can explain it in no more than two minutes. If you cannot explain it in that time, it probably is not a good topic for this class and these time limits.

Subject Areas for Consideration

Painting:
  Picasso
  Van Gogh
  Rembrandt
  Rockwell

Music:
  Jazz
  Folk rock
  Symphony
  Concerto

Film:
  Silent movies
  Foreign movies

Literature:
  Poetry
  Novels
  Short stories
  Science fiction
  Historical fiction

Speeches:
  Inaugural addresses
  Courtroom speaking
  Legislative speeches

Originality, Imagination, and
Creativity in Expository Speaking

Because expository speaking requires the use of outside sources, imagination, originality, and creativity are essential to your success. An original speech is new; it is not copied, imitated, or reproduced. To you, the expository speaker, this means that your speech must be a product of, but entirely different from, the sources you used. You find material, you put it in a usable form, then you inject your insights, your personality into the speech. Use your imagination to put the information into unique form.

Originality and imagination are both products of the creative process. To be creative, you must give yourself enough time to allow the creative process to work. Once you have prepared yourself fully (completed your outline), you need two or three days for your mind to reflect upon what you have gathered. Some people have the mistaken idea that creativity is a natural by-product of a "creative individual." Actually, we all have the potential for thinking creatively—some of us just haven't given ourselves enough time to try. Creative thinking is roughly analogous to cooking. You can't rush good cooking. Have you ever tried to make a good spaghetti sauce? It takes hours and hours of simmering tomatoes, herbs, and spices. A good cook knows that success with the best ingredients and the best recipes is dependent upon allowing the proper length of time. So it is with speechmaking. If you finish your outline an hour before the speech, you may give an adequate speech; but you won't give nearly as good a speech as one for which you had given your mind time to reflect upon the materials. You may find that the morning after a few uninspiring practices you suddenly have two or three fresh ideas for lines of development. What has happened is that while you were sleeping, your mind was still going over the material. When you awoke, the product of unconscious or subconscious thought reached the level of consciousness. Although these inspirations should be analyzed carefully, many times they are the flashes of insight that are characteristic of creativity. So, give yourself time. Even if the topic isn't new, by applying your imagination you can develop an original, creative speech that meets all of the tests of exciting, informative speechmaking.

Assignment

Prepare a five- to seven-minute expository speech. Outline and bibliography (at least three outside sources) required. Criteria for evaluation will include quality of the content and the originality, imagination, and creativity shown in the presentation. The speech should be informative and interesting.

Outline: Expository Speech
(5–7 minutes)

The following is a clear and well-organized outline.

Specific Purpose: To inform the audience of four major classifications of nursery rhymes.

Introduction

I. "Hey diddle diddle, the cat and the fiddle, the cow jumped over the moon. The little dog laughed to see such sport, and the dish ran away with the spoon."

II. Did you know that there are four major classifications of nursery rhymes?—ditties, teaching rhymes, historically based, and modern use.

Body

I. Ditties are nursery rhymes with a prophetic purpose.
   A. A fortune-telling rhyme is told while counting the white spots on the fingernails.
   B. Just as in *Poor Richard's Almanack*, by Benjamin Franklin, Mother Goose had her merry wise sayings.
   C. Traditionally, a rhyme on the topic of love fidelity is said while plucking the petals of a daisy.

II. Some nursery rhymes were used as teaching aids.
   A. "Hickory Dickory Dock" is an example of onomatopoeia, which is an attempt to capture in words a specific sound.
   B. Song rhymes helped the children with their coordination.
      1. Historical background.
      2. Children's usage.
   C. Numbers in nursery rhymes obviously retain the traces of the stages by which prehistoric man first learned to count.

III. Many nursery rhymes have historical significance.
   A. Religious problems entered into the nursery rhymes with "Jack Sprat."
   B. It became a tradition in England that some of these country rhymes may have been relics of formulas used by the druids in choosing a human sacrifice for their pagan gods.
   C. Cannibalism is quite prevalent in nursery rhymes.

IV. A modern classification of the nursery rhyme is the parody.
   A. The famous prayer "Now I lay me down..." was first published in 1737, but has now been parodied.
   B. A joke has been created out of "Mary and Her Lamb."

Conclusion

I. Every song, ballad, hymn, carol, tale, singing game, dance tune, or dramatic dialogue that comes from an unwritten, unpublished word-by-the-mouth source contributes to the future culture of our nation.

II. Remember that with your next cute saying, teaching aid in the form of a rhyme, reference to our history, or modern use of the nursery rhymes, you may become the next Mother Goose.

Bibliography

Baring-Gould, William S., and Cecil Baring-Gould, *The Annotated Mother Goose* (New York: Clarkson A. Potter, Inc., 1962).

Bett, Henry, *Nursery Rhymes and Tales—Their Origins and History* (New York: Henry Holt and Company, 1924).

Ken, John Bellenden, *An Essay on the Archaeology of Popular Phrases and Nursery Rhymes* (London: Longman, Rees, Orme, Brown, Green, and Company, 1837).

Mother Goose, *Mother Goose and the Nursery Rhymes* (London: Frederick Warne and Company, Ltd., 1895).

Read the transcription of the speech in the left-hand column at least once aloud.[1] Examine the speech to see how information is made clear and interesting. After you have studied the speech, read the analysis in the right-hand column.

Classifications of Nursery Rhymes

Speech	Analysis
"Hey diddle diddle, the cat and the fiddle, the cow jumped over the moon, the little dog laughed to see such sport and the dish ran away with the spoon." You recognize this as a nursery rhyme, and perhaps you always considered these nursery rhymes as types of nonsense poetry with little if any meaning. As we look at the four classifications of nursery rhymes, I think that you'll see as I did that there's more to nursery rhymes than meets the ear.	Miss Woistmann uses a common rhyme to capture our attention. After noting our certain recognition, she anticipates our reaction toward nursery rhymes. Her next sentence is an attempt both to indicate that there's more to these rhymes than we might anticipate and to forecast that there will be four classifications covered in the speech.
One of the major classifications of nursery rhymes is ditties. Ditties are fortune-tellings, little wise sayings, or little poems on love fidelity, and they are the most popular form of nursery rhyme. There are various ways of telling your fortune through ditties. One is saying, "A gift, a ghost, a friend, a foe; letter to come and a journey to go." And while you say this little ditty, this fortune-telling, you count the little white spots on your fingernails. Or you can say, "Rich man, poor man, beggarman,	She begins the body of the speech by identifying the first classification. The next sentence gives us the three subdivisions of the major classification. The commendable part of this and all sections of the speech is the use of the specific examples to illustrate the various types and subtypes. As far as real information is concerned, this main point doesn't go much beyond labeling and classifying our own knowledge. The last part is of some interest in that it shows the evolution of wording.

[1] Speech given in Fundamentals of Speech class, University of Cincinnati, 1968. Printed by permission of Susan Woistmann.

thief, doctor, lawyer, merchant chief," and count your buttons. Whichever button you end up on is the type of guy you are going to marry. Another kind of ditty is the wise saying. Just as in *Poor Richard's Almanack* by Benjamin Franklin, Mother Goose had her own little sayings. She said, "A pullet in the pen is worth a hundred in the fen," which today we say as "A bird in the hand is worth two in the bush." Love fidelity, the third kind of ditty, can be proven while plucking the petals off a daisy. "Love her, hate her, this year, next year, sometime, never." But today's usage has brought it up to "Love me, love me not, love me, love me not."

Another classification of nursery rhymes is those used as teaching aids, such as in the saying "Hickory dickory dock." This is the use of onomatopoeia, which is trying to develop a sound from the use of words. In this case, he's trying to show the ticking of a clock. London Bridge, although it has some historical background, is used for teaching children coordination, such as running around the circle raising their hands up and jumping back down. Similarly, in the ancient times, man made up rhymes in order to make things easier for him to remember, such as in the saying, "one, two, buckle my shoe; three, four, close the door." And as time went on, he eventually found out that he could use the fingers and toes to count. This is where "This little piggy went to market and this little piggy stayed home" originated.

Also, did you know that nursery rhymes have historical background? The third classification of nursery rhymes are those of historical significance. In the Middle Ages, which

Again the main point is clearly stated. She begins this section with an interesting look at a common rhyme. Once more, an excellent use of specifics to illustrate the point she is making. Although speech language should be informal it should not be imprecise. Notice that the antecedent for "he" in "he's trying to show the ticking" is unclear. You should be careful to avoid these common grammatical errors. This section of the speech illustrates how information can sometimes be communicated in such an interesting way that we aren't even aware that we have learned anything.

Again Miss Woistmann moves smoothly into the statement of the main point. As far as the quality of information is concerned, this is probably the best section of the speech. Because it is when most nursery rhymes were formed, the saying, "Jack Sprat could eat no fat, his wife could eat no lean; and so betwixt the two of them, they licked the platter clean," refers to the Catholic Church and the government of the old Roman Empire. This is when the Catholic Church was blessing tithes, and wiping the country clean. The government came in and collected the taxes; and between the two of them, the country had no wealth and no money. The Druids, in their relics of old formulas for selecting human sacrifices, used the "eeny meeny, miny, moe." And cannibalism is quite prevalent in almost all the nursery rhymes. Such as in "Jack and the Beanstalk," the big giant eater, and "Fee, Fi, Foe, Fum, I smell the blood of an Englishman. Be he alive or be he dead, I'm going to use him to make my bread." This also came up again in Shakespeare with *King Lear* and *Midsummer Night's Dream.* "Little Jack Horner" is about a man named Jack Horner, who was steward of the abbot of Glastonberry. And in 1542, he was sent by this abbot to King Henry VIII of England with a pie. And in this pie were documents which were the documents of the ownership of land around the Abby of Glastonberry, in Somersetshire. And on his way to the king, he stuck in his thumb and pulled out a document to the ownership of Meld, which he kept to himself. And until this day, over in Somersetshire, the Manor of Meld belongs to the Horner family.

The fourth classification of the nursery rhyme is the modern use, parodies and jokes, such as in "Mary had a little lamb, its fleece was white as snow," today the kids go around saying, "Mary had a little lamb and was the doctor ever surprised." Or else

seems to be the best part of the speech, it should probably be placed as the last point in the speech. Since there is an equally logical reason for placement of her last point, her violation of the placement principle may be necessary. Notice that she continues to use her examples and illustrations very well.

Of all the single examples in the speech, this is probably the best. To Miss Woistmann's credit it is given excellent placement within the main point and represents excellent proportion.

Once more we are aware of the statement of a main point. Miss Woistmann returns to classifying and labeling information that as an audience we have in our possession.

From the foregoing criticism it can be seen that the speech is

they tend to make parodies of these nursery rhymes. Such as the famous little prayer, "Now I lay me down to sleep. I pray the Lord my soul to keep. If I should die before I wake, I pray the Lord my soul to take." It was first published in 1737, so you can see the age of this prayer. But, nowadays, the children say in joke, "Now I lay me down to sleep with a bag of peanuts at my feet. If I should die before I wake, you'll know I died of a stomach ache."

very clear, extremely interesting, and informative enough to meet the criteria for expository speaking. Two possibilities for strengthening the speech are worth considering. Since the third main point is so informative, it might have been better for the speaker to limit the entire speech to this particular subject. She could have mentioned the other three classifications in the introduction, then told us why she would focus on historical significance. The advantage of such a revision would of course be that the information level of the speech would have been better. Secondly, since the bibliography accompanying the outline shows the amount of research, she could have taken better advantage of the research by including some of the scholarly methodology involved. She could have told us where the scholars uncovered their information. She could have told us which aspects of the analysis were fact and which were theory. As it is, the speech is a good one. It could have been perhaps equally as interesting and just a little more informative.

So every song, ballad, hymn, carol, tale, dance rhythm, or any cute little saying that you might come up with may contribute to the future culture of our nation. So remember, the next time you start spouting wise sayings, using rhymes as a teaching aid, referring to our history, or when you start making jokes of the traditional nursery rhymes, who knows, you might be the next Mother Goose.

This conclusion ties the speech together pretty well. The wording of the summary gives the conclusion a necessary lift.

Research Reports

14

The very first and perhaps the most often repeated advice we have given about speech preparation is that you should select a topic area that meets your interest, then you should consider an aspect of the topic that you can adapt to audience and occasion. However, in school or on the job, you will occasionally be called upon to report on a topic that is selected for you, a topic on which your knowledge and interest may be minimal. Although there is no excuse for selecting a subject outside your realm of interest when you have control over the decision, there is no need to panic when you have no choice. In fact, as a final assignment in your work on informative speaking, the research report might be the best test of what you have learned during the term. In order to clarify this assignment, a research report may be defined as a specialized type of expository speech, in which the emphasis is placed upon the status of or the progress with a problem, an organization, or a movement.

Research

Our discussion begins with the assumption that you have been *given* a contemporary subject area phrased like one of the following:

Methods of solving problems of air pollution
Modernization of police forces
The supersonic airplane
Progress in research on cures for cancer
The "new math"

The shortage of copper
Fashions as an indication of changes in morality or social revolution
Pesticides
Underground movies
Black Power
Teaching machines
Urban renewal
TV programming
International monetary problems
Using the sea around us to solve our world food problems
The shortage of silver
Weather—devices for forecasting and determining
Intercontinental TV
Pop art

After receiving such an assignment, you will begin general research. Since you may be less familiar with a subject area you are given than with one you select from your background, you must analyze prospective sources with care. If you are unsure of your ability to evaluate information in the field, you may be able to use the advice of experts. For example, you might take your bibliography to a professor in a department that works with the subject you have been given and talk with him about the quality of the sources you have found. In addition to helping you evaluate, he may even suggest some other useful material for you.

Don't take your subject to a professor and expect him to produce a bibliography and a line of development. Although most professors are willing to help you after you have shown some initiative, they are not about to do your work for you.

Suppose you were given the topic "New uses for plastics in industry." Your procedure would be to consult *Readers' Guide*, the card catalog, and other indexes first. After half an hour or so, you may have a bibliography of ten to fifteen sources. Then you could go to someone in the chemistry department for help in evaluating your list, for suggestions about different sources, or about a meaningful line of development. For less specialized topics or with topics you are somewhat familiar with already, you should be able to evaluate the material on your own.

Limiting the Topic—The Specific Purpose

With research reports perhaps more than with any other kind of speech, students get into trouble by trying to cover too much information for the time limits. To avoid this problem, you should take special care to phrase a specific purpose sentence that will limit the subject sufficiently so that you can cover it within the time allotted. Reminding yourself that you should be focusing on the status of or the progress with a problem, an organization, or a movement will help. Nevertheless, you should take a hardhearted approach to your research materials. Because you will be devoting so much time and energy to gathering a rather large amount of material, you may be somewhat reluctant to admit that some of it won't be usable in the speech. But look at it this way: Giving a good speech rests as much on what material is excluded as it does on what is included. By limiting the topic carefully and by setting aside all that does not directly relate to the purpose sentence, you can keep control of your topic. For instance, "underground movies" can be discussed for hours. If, after you have read several sources, you believe that a key feature that leads to understanding of the genre is knowing basic contrasts with commercial movies, the purpose statement "I want to inform the audience about four major contrasts between underground movies and commercial movies" will allow you to focus your attention on relevant material.

Idea Development

Good research will insure the informative quality of the content. The final special problems of a research report are how you can introduce source material into your speech and how you can make the report interesting. In presenting any speech in which you are using ideas that are not your own personal knowledge, you should attempt to work the source of your material into the context of the speech. Such efforts to include sources not only will help the audience in their evaluation of the content but also will add to your credibility as a speaker. Since a research report is supposed to reflect a depth of research, citing the various sources of information will give concrete evidence of your research. Your citation need not be a complete representation of all the bibliographical information. In most instances, the following kinds of phrasing are appropriate:

According to an article by Senator Muskie in last week's *Look* magazine . . .

In the latest Gallup poll cited in last week's issue of *Newsweek* . . .

One conservative point of view was well summed up by Barry Goldwater in his book *Conscience of a Conservative*. In the opening chapter, Goldwater wrote . . .

But in order to get a complete picture we have to look at the statistics. According to the 1968 *Statistical Abstract*, the level of production for underdeveloped countries rose from ...

In a speech before the National Association of Manufacturers given just last fall, Governor Rhodes said ...

Although you don't want to clutter your speech with bibliographical citations, you do want to make sure that you have properly reflected the sources of your key information. If you will practice these and similar short prefatory comments, you will find that they will soon come naturally.

A second special problem of a research report is to consider how you can make the speech interesting. Make sure that you give yourself at least two or three days to reflect on the speech. Since making research material interesting may require all of your creative powers, perhaps you can gain a line of development by asking what kinds of materials would interest you if you were a member of the audience. Perhaps you could try out one or two ideas on a friend or member of the family, then ask them what kinds of additional material they would find interesting. Also consider the opportunity for using visual aids. Two or three carefully prepared visual aids might make a great deal of difference in audience interest.

And finally, remember that when you are giving a report, it is up to you to read widely enough that you will have a command of the subject matter. It will take a lot of reading to enable you to duplicate the reserve knowledge of examples, illustrations, and supplementary material that you have to draw from for topics taken from your own background. In any event, the greater the amount of good material to draw from and the greater your familiarity with that material, the more likely it is that you can make your speech meaningful and interesting.

Assignment

Prepare an eight- to ten-minute report on some aspect of the topic you have been given. Outline and bibliography are required. Focus on the status of or the progress with the problem, organization, or movement. Criteria for evaluation will include (1) how well you have limited the topic, (2) how substantial is your resource material, (3) how well you have introduced bibliographical citations, and (4) how interesting you have made the development.

Outline: Research Report
(8–10 minutes)

The following is a clear and well-organized outline.

Purpose Sentence: To inform the audience about the progress of the race for supersonic aircraft, including the participants, the aircraft, and the problems involved.

Introduction

I. Imagine a typical transatlantic flight for 1971.
II. Three nations have been in a race to dominate supersonic transportation.
III. I want to talk about the participants and the problems they have encountered.

Body

I. The U.S., Russia, and England-France have been working on supersonic aircraft.
  A. England and France got together twelve years ago.
    1. They originally estimated the cost would be $450 million.
    2. Costs have soared to $1.5 billion.
    3. They gambled because they couldn't compete with the U.S.'s subsonic aircraft.
      a. They hope to gain world prestige.
      b. They hope to build their knowledge of computers and other electronic devices.
      c. They had hoped to sell them to other nations making perhaps millions of dollars.
  B. The U.S. is also in the race.
    1. Our effort is government supported.
      a. It's backing 90 percent of development costs.
      b. It's the only way the U.S. can compete.
      c. The Russians are also in the race, but not much is known about this effort.
II. The designs and capabilities of the various aircraft are quite different.
  A. The designs themselves are a contrast.
    1. The SST has a radical swing-wing design.
    2. The other two have a Delta wing.
  B. The capabilities of the SST and the Concorde are also quite a contrast.
    1. The SST will carry 350 passengers to 136 for the Concorde.
    2. The SST will travel at 2,000 miles per hour; the Concorde at 1,500 miles per hour.
    3. The SST will have a range of 4,000 miles; the Concorde, 3,500 miles.

4. The SST is 360 feet long; the Concorde is 196 feet long.
5. The SST uses titanium for better heat resistance.
6. The SST will cost about $45 million compared to $18 million for the Concorde.

C. The Concorde appeared to have the advantage, but it may not.
   1. Their range is limited to 3,500—a small margin of safety for transatlantic flight.
   2. The SST is bigger and faster.
   3. As a result, the developers of the Concorde are quite worried.

III. Critics have questioned the development of supersonic transportation.
A. They fly so high that passengers wouldn't have a chance if the plane lost pressure.
   1. You would need a space suit to survive.
   2. Originally they were planned without windows to help the problem, but it created a psychological problem.
B. The movable wings of the SST are a hazard.
   1. Any malfunction of one wing would result in the plane twisting and tearing itself apart.
   2. Also, if the wings didn't expand, the plane would have to land at 300 miles per hour.
C. Duplicate and triplicate backup systems are needed.
D. The planes are very expensive.
   1. Initial cost is very high.
   2. Jumbo jets carrying 500 passengers can cover the distance for a lot less than an SST.
E. The biggest problem of all may be the sonic boom.
   1. Boeing admits that it may be so bad that SSTs will be limited to over-water flights.
   2. This cuts the potential market in half.

Conclusion

I. I would describe the race for supersonic aircraft as boom to the boom to the bust.
A. The economic boom which is the result of continued effort for an SST.
B. The second boom is the sonic boom.
C. And the bust is what happens if it never comes to pass.

Bibliography

Clark, Evert, "Up in the Clouds with the SST," *Saturday Review* (Jan. 8, 1968), pp. 47–48, 83–85.

Ruppenthal, Karl, "Supersonic Transport: Blind Stakes in the Poker Game," *Nation* (June 19, 1967), pp. 786–789.

Ruppenthal, Karl, "Supersonic Transport: Heat, Cold, Radiation and the Boom," *Nation* (May 29, 1967), pp. 685–689.

Shannon, W. V., "Incredible SST," *Commonweal* (July 28, 1967), pp. 462–463.

"Showing off the Concorde," *Time* (Dec. 15, 1967), p. 98.

"SST Pushed by Johnson," *Business Week* (May 6, 1967), p. 176.

"Supersonic Travel: Will the Gamble Pay Off?" *U.S. News & World Report* (Sept. 11, 1967), pp. 74–75.

The following speech, transcribed in the left-hand column, contains many of the flaws of the beginner's attempt at a long speech on a topic on which he is not an expert.[1] Nevertheless, it illustrates many characteristics that are worth emulating. Read the speech at least once aloud. As you study the speech, analyze the depth of information, the citation of sources, and the interest potential of the development. What changes would you have made in order to make the speech even better? After you have read and analyzed the speech, read the criticism in the right-hand column.

The Race for Supersonic Aircraft

Speech

I would like you to imagine with me the typical transatlantic flight for the year 1971. Picture yourself in the London airport around one o'clock, just finishing your lunch. You hear your plane call, you hurry down to your plane, you board the exceptionally long and narrow superstructure. Within thirty minutes, you are traveling at 1,500 miles per hour, more than twice the speed of sound, at approximately 12 miles above earth —that's way above the clouds. The sky would be a deep purple color. You won't have any real realization of the earth below because you'll barely be able to see it. But as you settle on your trip, before you know it you're landing in New York, and as you adjust your watch for the three-and-a-quarter-hour trip, you find that when the plane comes down it will be something like noon—time for lunch again. You just ate lunch three hours before, and now it's time for lunch again.

You have just taken a trip in a supersonic air transport. But this isn't some kind of a dream—this could come about in 1971. For years, three nations have been in a kind of race

Analysis

This opening illustrates what can be done with a hypothetical narrative as an introduction to a longer speech. Because attention is a little harder to get for reports, this was an especially good opening.

Mr. Voss leads into the body of the speech quite smoothly. Although his forecast doesn't enumerate the main points, it gives a pretty good idea of what the speech will cover.

---

[1] Speech given in Fundamentals of Speech class, University of Cincinnati, 1968. Printed by permission of Thomas Voss.

to dominate supersonic transportation. Today I want to talk about the participants in the race and the problems that some of the designers and manufacturers have come across in their actual development of a supersonic plane.

There are three nations that have actually been working on supersonic aircraft: the U.S., Russia, and a combined English and French effort. England and France got together nearly twelve years ago, to consider such a project—whether the possibility would really be beneficial. An article in the December 15 issue of *Time* magazine indicates that they originally estimated that four hundred and fifty million dollars would be the cost to complete such a project, and it's since grown to one and a half billion, which is roughly fifteen dollars for every man, woman, and child in the two countries. But even if they get this thing in the air in 1971, they don't expect ever to recover their development funds. But they feel it is necessary because they will be able to accomplish or gain world prestige; by gaining knowledge in the use of computers and other areas of electronics and, of course, they also had the possibility of getting millions and millions of dollars in selling these planes to foreign countries.

Now, the United States is another competitor in this race for supersonic aircraft. Our government is supporting the industry research and backing 90 percent of the development cost with the government funds. This is the only way it is possible for the United States to compete. I can't say much about the Russian development because no one knows much about it.

Notice the effortless documentation of the material from *Time* magazine.

This is a vivid comparison.

The explanation of the England-France effort is quite clear. The explanation for the American effort tells how it is being financed, but it doesn't indicate why the project was started in the first place.

Mr. Voss neglected several available sources that would have given him information about the Russian effort. His assertion that "no one knows much" is only partly accurate.

Now to get a little more realistic view, let's examine some comparative statistics of the various aircraft reported by W. V. Shannon in an article entitled "Incredible SST" in last July's issue of *Commonweal* and Evert Clark in his *Saturday Review* article "Up in the Clouds with the SST." Here's the SST, the British-French Concorde, and the Russian TU-144. As you see, SST has a fairly radical swing-wing design. These other two, the Concorde and TU-144, have the Delta wing which is pretty common. Let's compare the capabilities of the SST and the Concorde just briefly. We pretty much consider these two because we don't know much about the Russians', but it's on about the same timetable as the Concorde—they're both supposed to be flying or in service by 1971, and it's supposed to have about the same size and features. The SSTs will carry 350 people maximum, compared to 136 for the Concorde; it will fly at 2,000 miles an hour compared to 1,500 for the Concorde; with a range of 4,000 miles compared with the Concorde's 3,500. The SST is 360 feet long, that is as big as the football field in Nippert Stadium. The tail section is five stories high. Imagine the size, in comparison to the Concorde's 196 feet. So if you put the Concorde this way you can see its relative size compared to the SST. Basically, the main difference between the two—or the three actually—is the SST uses titanium which is the main reason why it is possible to travel at a much faster speed, because the heat characteristics are a little better with titanium. The cost estimate is 45 million dollars for the SST compared with the 18 million for the British Concorde. If you look at, consider the facts, you would think that the British Concorde had

This grouping of articles is a satisfactory method of showing the source of a large amount of information.

At this point Mr. Voss showed pictures of the three planes. His statistical contrast is clear and reasonably vivid.

The comparison between the SST and a football field is a natural for clarity. But note the syntactical error in the development. In the speech, it sounds as if the tail section of the SST is being compared to the length of the Concorde. Although this kind of error is common in extemporaneous speaking, it can be avoided. Of course, overcoming any difficulties in style takes time, effort, and desire on the speaker's part.

This sentence represents good audience adaptation.

the advantage between the two, at least between the United States and theirs, but the range is a very limited 3,500 miles. There has been some question whether it is safe enough to carry across, people across the ocean. This is a pretty limiting factor here, and the United States with their 350-passenger maximum and a lot faster speed is closer to three times the speed of sound, 2,000 miles per hour. As a result, the Concorde hasn't been selling like the SST has and they're actually worried about whether even though it might be a very good plane —technically successful—it can be a commercial failure and then most of the airlines will go toward the SST.

This last sentence of the paragraph illustrates what can happen when a speaker gets ahead of himself.

In researching this topic, I came up with several articles about critics and the positions they have taken against supersonic aircraft. Two of the best are Karl Ruppenthal's two-parter in *Nation* magazine last May and June and Evert Clark's article in *Saturday Review* this January. First of all is that I'm sure if you have taken any type of flight on a jet, you know how the stewardess takes time to show you how to use your oxygen mask. It won't be necessary in a supersonic aircraft because if cabin pressure is lost for any reason you won't have too much of a chance, because the body will go in an explosion from within and body interior pressure will be so much greater it will actually explode, the blood will boil, and you'll die in a couple of seconds. According to Ruppenthal, the only hope would be if you had an astronaut's type of space suit. Can you imagine anyone wearing a space suit on an aircraft? Now the original intention of the design of SST was to be made without windows. This would do away with a lot of problems of sealing the planes, but they thought this would be too much of

Mr. Voss should have stated this last main point more precisely. Notice how Mr. Voss says, "First of all is that I'm sure if..." Always complete the idea before you begin to develop it. He should have said, "First of all is the problem of maintaining cabin pressure." As it is, the audience has to figure out what his point is. Nevertheless, the description is vivid.

Many of Mr. Voss's problems come later in the speech. Perhaps another practice period would have allowed him to get command of the flow of ideas. Remember, as speeches get longer, you must allow yourself more time for practice.

Throughout this section Mr. Voss discusses important problems. As a result, I think we have a rather complete idea of most of the important considerations in making a decision about supersonic planes.

a psychological effect on people, because with no windows, it's walking into this massive long tube, taking off, and not knowing where you are going and whether you will get back. Concerning this SST, just the mere fact of designing a plane this size, large as a football field with movable wings is one of the problems. If one of these wings would turn and the other wouldn't, you would have the plane twisting like this and tearing itself apart. Or another instance, if the plane's wings didn't expand for landing, it would be impossible to get the darn thing down. Evert Clark points out that you would have to come in at 300 miles an hour, which no pilot in his right mind would want. But we could go on and talk about manufacturing problems, the restrictions, the systems that are involved. They have duplicate, triplicate systems of hydraulic and electronic systems, all these have to be made so there wouldn't be the slightest possibility of failing. But still you have to get back to the question whether this plane will be successful. These are very expensive planes; 18 million for just the Concorde, up to 25 for the average SST is very expensive. When you consider at the same time the government is proposing a use of jumbo jets with passengers up to 500 people which will lower transatlantic fees to something about 150 dollars, whereas with the SST it would be three or four times as much to cross the Atlantic. Would people be willing to pay this just to save three hours to cross the ocean? Now, another problem is, I'm sure you're all aware, is the sonic boom. You've heard an awfully lot about it and you've also heard at least in the beginning of the SST that it wouldn't be a problem. But now, according to a report in

Throughout this section the description and explanations are vivid.

Throughout the speech Mr. Voss uses plenty of specifics to develop his points. The informational level of the report is very high. The organization of the speech is clear. Although Mr. Voss uses personal pronouns, rhetorical questions, and other kinds of audience adaptation, his style needs to be improved. Even for extemporaneous speaking he makes too many syntactical errors.

last September's *U.S. News,* even Boeing admits that sonic boom would be such a problem that they can see that the only practical use of the SST is over water—right away you're cutting the potential market in half, taking nearly 60 percent of the available routes you could use them on. So you're cutting the potential of actual supersonic transportation in half.

What does this all lead to? What is the final story of the SST going to be? Three things: the boom, to the boom, to the bust. The way I would like to explain that is the boom, the economic boom which is the resultant of this continued and pressing effort to get an SST. The second boom in my little research is the sonic boom and the rest of the problem associated with the SST. And finally the bust, what happens if this all doesn't come into being and they can't get anything worth while out of the SST and its counterparts.

The audience liked this conclusion. Mr. Voss used his imagination to summarize the main points of the speech. Because of the quality content and the clear organization this is a good report.

**Persuasive
Speaking**

Part Four

Requirements
of Persuasive
Speaking

15

In the previous chapters, our focus has been primarily on informative speechmaking. Now let us consider the second major type of speaking, persuasive. You will recall that the sole intent of informative speeches is to enhance the audience's understanding of the subject you select for your speech. In persuasive speaking, however, your concern goes further than achieving an understanding of ideas or procedures. Now you must affect audience attitudes *about* ideas or procedures. In order to understand the nature of persuasive speaking more fully, let's investigate the process of its preparation and at the same time note some of the similarities and differences between these two types of speeches. Our consideration will include an examination of purpose sentence, function of main points, function of idea development, and speech organization.

Statement of Purpose Sentence

You may choose any topic area possible for a persuasive or an informative speech. The difference in the two types of speeches is found in the wording of the purpose sentence. Whereas the informative purpose sentence indicates the boundaries of the information to be communicated, the persuasive purpose sentence, called a proposition, indicates what you want your audience to do or to believe. For example, "to explain the three major causes of juvenile delinquency," would be informative and "to prove that juveniles should be judged by a panel of their peers," would be persuasive. The informative speaker wants the audience to understand a set of facts, an interpretation, or an insight into the facts; the persuasive speaker wants to create in the members of his audience an attitude about a set of facts, then, perhaps, get them to act upon that attitude.

Despite the difference in intent, the proposition should still be a complete, meaningful, specific, declarative sentence containing only one expected response from the audience, "I want to persuade the audience to think about air pollution" would be neither meaningful nor specific. "I want to persuade the audience to support air-pollution ordinances and to support land conservation" would involve two purposes. "I want to persuade the audience that air-pollution laws should be strictly enforced" would be a clear, specific proposition.

Ordinarily, the proposition will be phrased to reinforce a belief held by an audience, to change a belief held by an audience, or to move the audience to act. "Every eligible citizen should vote" and "Everyone should love his country" are examples of propositions for speeches to reinforce beliefs. It is quite unlikely that many members of the audience would advocate hating their country. In both instances, the speaker would be trying to strengthen a prevailing attitude. "Red China should be recognized" and "Selling marijuana should be made legal" would indicate the purpose of changing the beliefs of the audience. Even though some classmates would be in favor of them, these two propositions are in opposition to current policy. "We should buy Easter Seals" and "We should eat at the Manor Restaurant" are both phrased to gain action. In these instances, the speaker wants more than intellectual agreement—he wants us to act.

Function of Main Points

A second major contrast between persuasive speaking and informative speaking lies in the function of main points. The main points of an informative speech elaborate, explain, or clarify the purpose sentence. The main points of a persuasive speech supply the justification for the desired belief or action. When someone says, "You ought to watch the special on TV tonight," you would probably ask "Why?" You would want some justification for watching. The statements that answer *why* a proposition is justified are called *reasons*. If the reasons given to justify your watching a particular television show satisfied you, you would probably watch—if they didn't, you wouldn't. In these examples, analyze the statement of the reasons and the relationship between the reasons and the proposition.

Purpose: To persuade the audience that they should read labels on products carefully before they use them. (Why?)

I. Taking time to read labels saves time in the long run.

II. Taking time to read labels may save money.

III. Taking time to read labels prevents errors.

Purpose: To persuade the audience that Oscar Robertson is the best player in the National Basketball Association. (Why?)

I. He is always one of the leading scorers in the league.

II. He is an outstanding playmaker.

III. He is an excellent defender.

Purpose: To persuade the audience that the federal government should guarantee a minimum annual cash income to all its citizens. (Why?)

I. A minimum cash income would eliminate the present poverty conditions that breed social unrest.

II. A minimum cash income would eliminate the need for all the overlapping state and federal welfare agencies.

III. A minimum cash income would go directly to the people in need.

The Function of Idea Development

In an informative speech, idea development clarifies or elaborates the main points. In a persuasive speech the idea development (examples, quotations, and the like) helps to establish the climate of persuasion that affects audience attitudes. It is up to you to decide whether you will use amplifying materials primarily to reason with your audience, to motivate your audience, or to demonstrate your credibility.

Reasoning with an Audience

When you reason with an audience, you build your persuasion by a logical appeal that adapts to a rational process leading to a decision. What kind of process is judged rational? Suppose you decide to buy a necktie or a scarf. In preparation for the purchase, you might decide how much you wanted to pay, what color you needed, and what kind of material would go best with your other clothes. If you then went to a store and looked for and bought the tie or scarf that best met the criteria you had set up, you would be using a rational process for the decision.

What is characteristic of the rational process? For the most part it is knowing why you made a decision in a particular way. How do you build speeches based on rational or logical appeal? By giving your audience clear reasons for the suggested belief or action and by developing each reason with proof. By reasoning with an audience, you satisfy their *why* questions on a conscious level. The major components and types of reasoning and how reasoning can be tested will be discussed in Chapter 16.

Motivating an Audience

Another way to use your persuasive materials is to motivate an audience. When you motivate an audience, you base your persuasion on emotional appeals to that audience, emotional appeals that complement the rational process for decision making. Suppose you used the following outline for the main ideas of your speech:

Purpose Sentence: I want to persuade the audience to eat at the Manor Restaurant.
  I. The food is good.
 II. The prices are low.
III. The atmosphere is pleasant.

Although each of the above reasons contributes to a rational process for making a decision about where to eat, the persuasiveness of the speech can be enhanced by stating the reasons in a more compelling manner in the speech and by wording the development so that the emotional appeal of the content is emphasized. For instance, consider the first reason stated. If in your speech you said, "You should eat at the Manor Restaurant because the food is good," the reason would be clear, but hardly impelling. If you said, "You should eat at the Manor Restaurant because their carefully prepared food always tastes delicious," the statement would be more impelling. If during the development, you painted such vivid word pictures of the thick juicy steaks, the aromatic savory sauces, and crisp fresh salads that the audience could almost *taste* the food, you would be motivating them to follow your advice.

Although motivation should accompany and not supplant reasoning, the realization that some persuaders attempt to influence our decisions on the basis of motivation alone leads us into an analysis of when the use of motivation by a persuader is unethical. The use of motivation is unethical when it is meant to take the place of the rational process and when it is misleading or untrue. Suppose you were trying to sell toothpaste. Suppose that the toothpaste you were selling (1) cleaned teeth quite well, (2) helped fight tooth decay, perhaps even better than most, and (3) tasted good. Because a rationally conceived

decision about what kind of toothpaste to buy would involve consideration of cleaning effects, decay-fighting power, and taste, in using these
three reasons you could try to motivate your audience, as long as
your motivation was related to one or more of those reasons. Suppose,
however, in planning your sales campaign, you determined to use any
appeal that would help sell the product. Suppose, then, you told the
audience that the toothpaste would increase their sex appeal, regardless of whether you could prove that it did. In this circumstance, the
use of motivation would be unethical on at least two counts: first, because it would be trying to substitute an appeal to the sex drive for a
rational process of decision making; second, because the implication
that the toothpaste would increase sex appeal would be misleading
and probably untrue.

We are not talking about what kind of persuasion is successful.
Unfortunately, unethical persuasion has proved so successful that
many of our highest paid advertising agencies persist in unethical use
of motivation. Unless we want a society in which anything goes as
long as it sells, we must recognize and penalize unethical behavior. One
way to combat unethical persuasion is to have an audience that understands such means of persuasion. An important benefit of this section
is to prepare you to be a critical member of an audience, as well as to
help you use ethical persuasion more effectively.

As an ethical persuasive speaker your goal is to use motivation to
get an audience to respond to rationally conceived ideas. The means
of motivation will be discussed further in Chapter 18.

Demonstrating Speaker Credibility

If you will analyze your experience, you will find that your belief
or trust in some people is so great that you may accept their ideas
solely because of that respect. Actually, such a dependence is necessary
at times when you are unable to obtain all the information needed to
make a decision. Furthermore, even with the presence of suitable information, you might not have the know-how, experience, or frame of
reference needed to allow you to take greatest advantage of that particular knowledge. Speaker credibility relates to the confidence that an
audience has in the speaker. Audiences are more receptive to ideas of
speakers who earn their respect.

Let's go back to our illustration of the tie or scarf. Suppose you
want a tie or scarf within a certain price range that will go with the
new outfit you are wearing. You may rely on the sales clerk to suggest
whether a particular tie or scarf complements the outfit. You may even
let him select one for you. You trust some sales personnel almost
instinctively; others you wouldn't trust under any circumstances.

What qualities in some people earn your trust or respect? Ordinarily, speaker credibility is a product of good judgment, good sense, good will, dress, voice, manner, confidence, apparent knowledge, and interest in the audience. Obviously, some of this credibility has an emotional base. You may make a judgment about a speaker before he says a word. Since appearances can deceive, an opinion made before the person even talks can't be logical.

Credibility, however, may have a logical base. You may reason that a person's previous record entitles him to or denies him the benefit of the doubt in the future. A decision made favoring the hiring of an applicant who has a record of punctuality, cooperativeness, and completing assignments satisfactorily over an applicant who has a history of tardiness, hostility toward coworkers, and failure is a logical one.

Credibility is not something that you can gain overnight or turn off or on at your whim. Nevertheless, you can avoid damaging your credibility and perhaps even strengthen it somewhat during a speech or series of speeches. You will probably see the cumulative effect of credibility during this term. As your class proceeds from speech to speech, some individuals will grow in stature in your mind and others will diminish. Being ready to speak on time, approaching the assignment with a positive attitude, showing complete preparation for each speech, giving thoughtful evaluation of other's speeches and demonstrating sound thinking—all of these contribute to classroom credibility. Some people earn the right to speak and to be heard. Having once earned that right, they command the confidence of their listeners. Others never earn the right and nothing they do will have a very real, lasting effect on their audience. Think about how you are representing yourself to your audience. What kind of a person are you projecting to the class? Credibility can be an important means of persuasion.

Speech Organization

As stated in Chapter 4, speech organization consists of determining the main points of the body first, then developing an introduction and a conclusion. For persuasive speeches, each of these processes provides some contrast with informative speech development.

Organizing the Body of the Persuasive Speech

The body of a persuasive speech is composed of reasons and their support. Once you have determined which reasons will be presented in the speech, you can decide the placement of the reasons and the approximate amount of time you will spend developing each. As you consider the relationships among your reasons, you may well discover certain similarities in the nature or goals of the reasons. Just as most informative speeches may be organized following a time, space, or topical order, persuasive speeches may be organized to correspond with recognizable patterns. Depending upon the nature of your topic, the nature of your audience, and your personal preference, you may find that you can utilize one of the following typical arrangements for your reasons.

The Problem-Solution Method   If you are attempting to prove to the audience that a new kind of procedure is needed to remedy some major problem, the problem-solution method will provide you with the framework for clarifying the nature of the problem that needs to be solved and for illustrating why the new proposal is the best measure for accomplishing the purpose. When you follow the problem-solution method, your speech will always have three main points: (1) that there is a problem that requires a change in attitude or action, (2) that the proposal you have to offer will solve the problem, and (3) that your proposal is the best solution to the problem. For the proposition, "I want to persuade the audience that the federal government should guarantee a minimum annual cash income to all its citizens," you could state three reasons:

I. A high percentage of our citizens are living in a state of abject poverty.
II. A guaranteed cash income would eliminate poverty.
III. A guaranteed cash income would be the best way to solve the problem.

Comparative Advantages Method   In your proposed speech, you may not be trying to solve a grave problem as much as you are suggesting a superior alternative course of action. Under such circumstances, your concern is with superiority of your proposal over any others. Let's say that you want to persuade your audience to take their dry cleaning to a particular establishment. Since people are already taking their clothes to some dry cleaner, the problem of how the class should take care of their cleaning is already being solved. You are trying to persuade them that a particular cleaner has advantages over any of the places where they may already take their clothes. Your speech then is built with the advantages of your proposal over any other proposal. The advantages then become the main points of your outline.

Purpose: I want to persuade the audience to take their clothes to Ace Dry Cleaners.
I. Ace always does that little bit extra for no additional charge.
II. Ace gives students a 10 percent discount.

Criteria-Satisfaction Method   In some situations, particularly with hostile audiences, you may find it to your advantage to establish audience agreement—a yes-response—before you attempt to present the proposition and reasons. Although reasons are still the basis for the persuasion, the preliminary statement of criteria is essential to the method. If your proposition were "I want to persuade the audience to vote for Jones," you might organize your speech to show the criteria and how Jones meets them.

    I. You want a man who meets certain criteria.
        A. He must be wise.
        B. He must have a plan of action.
        C. He must be fearless.
    II. Jones meets these criteria.
        A. Jones is wise.
        B. Jones has a plan of action.
        C. Jones is fearless.

The Negative Method   Sometimes the only way of establishing one course of action is by proving that the alternatives won't work. What you are doing is proving a course of action with negative reasons. Of course, this system will work only when the audience must select one of the alternatives. Again, if your proposition were, "I want to persuade the audience to vote for Jones," you might organize your speech by evaluation of his opponents.

    I. Smith does not have the proper qualifications.
    II. Brown does not have the proper qualifications.
    III. Martin does not have the proper qualifications.
    IV. Jones does have the proper qualifications.

In evaluating these methods of organization (and of course these do not exhaust the possibilities) remember that regardless of the way you organize the speech, the main points are still reasons.

Introductions and Conclusions

Although the introductions of both persuasive and informative speeches should get the attention of the audience focused on the particular topic, the persuasive opening may be considerably longer than the informative introduction. When your audience is uninformed about the proposition, you must spend more time in orienting them. Furthermore, audience opposition may force you to approach the subject indirectly, which also will take more time. Whereas the introduction for an informative speech is seldom more than 5 or 10 percent of total content, the introduction for a persuasive speech may take 25 percent or more of the content.

As mentioned in Chapter 4, the conclusion for a persuasive speech is often a direct appeal for action. Moreover, since you need to conclude in a way that will leave the speech on a high note, a narrative, an example, or an anecdote that illustrates the essence of the persuasive message may well provide an excellent supplement to either an appeal or a summary.

The assignments in the next three chapters will give you an opportunity to work with various persuasive procedures. The first two, speeches of reasons and speeches of refutation (often referred to as argumentative speeches), will allow you to focus on the logical requirements of persuasive speaking. The final assignment, speeches of motivation, introduces the means and methods of heightening the response to persuasive messages.

Speeches
of Reasons

16

Since beginning speakers need to understand the logical requirements of their propositions, a speech of reasons assignment offers an
excellent opportunity for gaining a mastery of the logical basis for
persuasive speaking. In preparing the speech of reasons, you should
select reasons carefully and test the logic of your idea development.

Selecting Reasons

In the last chapter we defined reasons as complete-sentence justifications for a proposition. Now we want to concern ourselves with
establishing a number of reasons in support of a proposition and selecting the two, three, or four that have the greatest possibility of
achieving audience acceptance.

How do you determine reasons? As with the main points for any
kind of speech, reasons may either be discovered or invented. If you
are trying to discover reasons, look for the reasons that writers suggest in their particular works. If, in an article on capital punishment,
an author uses statistics to indicate that capital punishment does not
seem to deter potential criminals, the statement "capital punishment
is not a deterrent to crime" should be written down and considered as
one of the possible reasons to be used in your speech. If, in that or a
different article, you read that rich people are less likely to be executed
than poor people and that white people are less likely to be executed
than people from minority groups, then "capital punishment is not

just" would be another reason you would want to note. A reading of four or five articles or parts of books would probably yield several reasons to choose from.

But you are not limited to reasons discovered from your readings. Especially for domestic, campus, and other familiar areas, your observations or your experience itself may well suggest one or more reasons that are worth considering. Suppose you wanted to persuade the audience to eat at a particular restaurant. From your experience in eating at the restaurant, you may have noted that the waitresses always take your order with a smile, that the waitresses are always willing to do a little extra to make your meal a special occasion, that the atmosphere is particularly enjoyable, that the prices are reasonable, that the tables are arranged in such a way that you have some elbow room, and that the food is always served piping hot. These are reasons for eating at that restaurant, and each should be considered as potential support for the proposition.

After you have a list of five or more reasons, you can select the best ones on the basis of which are most adaptable to your audience. You may discard some reasons on your list because you do not have and cannot get material. From those that are left, you can determine which will probably have the greatest effect on your specific audience. For most speeches, you need at least two and probably not more than four of the best, most applicable reasons.

Testing the Logic of Your Development

Since a speech of reasons is an exercise in logical development, you must assure yourself that the speech development is sound.

Testing the Logic of Structure

The logic of structure of a speech is tested by use of the speech outline. Thus, in slightly abbreviated form, an outline on the direct election of the President might look like this:

Proposition: I want to persuade the audience that the United States should determine the President by direct election.

Introduction

I. In 1968, we barely avoided the electoral catastrophe of selecting the President in the House of Representatives.

II. The time to reform the electoral system is now.

III. Direct election of the President offers the best alternative to the electoral college.

Body

I. Direct election of the President is fair.
   A. It follows the one-man, one-vote policy laid down by the Supreme Court.
   B. It allows every vote to count equally, regardless of where it is cast.
   C. It eliminates the possibility of the election of a candidate who receives a lesser number of popular votes.
II. Direct election of the President is certain.
   A. The identity of the new President would be public knowledge once the votes were counted.
   B. The election of the President would not be subject to political maneuvers.
III. Direct election of the President is a popular plan.
   A. A recent Gallup poll showed that the majority of people favor direct election.
   B. Many political leaders have voiced their approval of this plan.

Conclusion

I. The time to anticipate possible catastrophe is now.

II. Support direct election of the President.

With such an outline, you can test the clarity of the proposition, the clarity of the reasons, and the support for each of the reasons. If you have an outline that looks like this abbreviated one, you are reasonably certain to have a speech of reasons that *sounds* logical.

Although the outline illustrates idea relationships, it does not describe the reasoning process nor does it test the logic. If you are familiar with formal logic, you know tests that you can apply to your thinking. If you have not taken formal logic, however, you may still plot your arguments in a way that will allow you to describe the reasoning you have done and test the logic of the arguments used. The suggested framework is based upon the Toulmin model of argumentation.[1]

Testing the Logic of Argument

A workable test is based upon the assumption that any argument is reducible to three basic requirements. These requirements are called

[1] See Stephen Toulmin, *The Uses of Argument* (Cambridge, England: Cambridge University Press, 1958).

the *data*, the *conclusion*, and the *warrant*. An understanding of these words will enable you to construct and analyze the simplest or the most complex arguments. "Data" means the evidence, assumption, or assertion that provides the basis for a conclusion; "conclusion" means the end product of a specific argument; "warrant" is the description of the reasoning process, the justification for the conclusion. The warrant, which denotes the substantive relationship between data and conclusion is the key term of this model, the one that provides the essential test, and the only one of the essentials that is not included in the structural outlines.

To illustrate the three essentials, let's put a simple argument into its layout form. Suppose that the temperature today reads 38°, the wind is blowing, and a hard rain is falling. As you come into the classroom, you might say to your neighbor, "It's a crummy day, isn't it?" Using (D) for data, stated or observed; (C) for conclusion; (W) for warrant; and an arrow to show the direction of an argument, the argument could be laid out schematically:

(D) Temperature 38°
    Wind blowing   ⟶   (C) It's a crummy day.
    Rain falling

    (W) (Low temperature, wind, and rain are three
         major characteristics of a crummy day.)

How did we get from (D) to (C)? The warrant, written in parentheses because it is implied in the argument and not actually stated, describes the thinking process. Thus, the statement, "low temperature, wind, and rain are three major characteristics of a 'crummy' day," bridges the gap between (D) and (C).

The tests we apply to this argument are twofold. First we test the data. For a logical conclusion to follow, the data must be sufficient in quantity and quality. If either no data or insufficient data are presented, you must supply more; if the data are inaccurate, biased, or from a questionable source, the conclusion will be suspect. If you are satisfied that "temperature 38°," "wind blowing," and "rain falling" are accurate, you can examine the logic of the descriptive warrant. The warrant is tested by casting it as a "Yes or No" question: "Is it true that low temperature, wind, and rain are the major characteristics of a 'crummy' day?" If the answer is Yes, the reasoning is sound; if the answer is No, the reasoning process is fallacious.

Now let's apply our testing procedure to the speech on direct election of the President. In schematic form, the speech in its entirety would look like this:

(D) Direct election is fair.
(D) Direct election is certain.   ⟶   (C) The United States should
(D) Direct election is popular.   determine the President
                                             by direct election.

(W) (Fairness, certainty, and popularity are the
three major criteria for determining how a
President should be elected.)

To test this warrant, we ask, Is it true that fairness, certainty, and popularity are the criteria for selecting a method of election? If experience, observation, and source material indicate that these three are of fundamental importance, the speech is logical. If, on the other hand, source material indicates that some other criterion is more important, or that two or three others are of equal importance, then the warrant does not meet the test of logic and the argument should be reconsidered.

Assuming that this warrant does meet the test of logic, we can be assured that the over-all structure of the speech is logical. But what of the individual units that make up the speech? Each of the three items of data listed above is in itself a conclusion of an argument that must be tested. Let's make a schematic examination of the first of those statements: "Direct election is fair":

(D) Direct election follows the one-
man, one-vote policy.
(D) Direct election allows every
vote to count equally.   ⟶   (C) Direct election is fair.
(D) Direct election eliminates the
possibility of the election of a
candidate who receives a lesser
number of popular votes.

(W) (Fairness of election procedure requires that
all votes must count equally and that the majority rules.)

First, we should test the data. Since we are working with an abbreviated outline (probably only half as detailed as an outline you would be working with), for purposes of this analysis, we will assume our data are representative and accurate. Next, we would test the warrant by asking, Is it true that election method fairness requires that all votes must count equally and that majority rules? If we find from experience, observation, and source material that election system fairness does require these, then the argument is logical. But if election fairness is determined by criteria apart from those included as data, the warrant is faulty and the argument would need to be revised.

Analyzing the argument schematically in the data, conclusion, warrant framework does not insure the infallibility of the logic. But if you take the time to write the arguments out in this manner and ask whether the warrant is supported by research, the chances of discovering illogical arguments are increased considerably.

Although warrants could be phrased in many ways for any given unit of argument and literally hundreds of variations are possible in the kinds of arguments, most arguments will fall into one of the five major categories. Since these categories do supply so many warrants, you should familiarize yourself with them. The tests following the warrants indicate under what circumstances the warrants are reasonable.

Generalization

A generalization warrant says that what is true in some instances is true in all instances. Generalization warrants are the basis for polls, predictions about how some individual or some team will perform, and numerous other common kinds of situations. The following illustrates the kind of generalization you might make about a course you are taking.

(D) Tom studied and got an A.
    Jack studied and got an A.   ⟶   (C) Anyone who studied will
    Bill studied and got an A.   get an A.

(W) (What is true in representative instances will
       be true in all instances.)

A generalization warrant may be tested by these questions:

Were enough instances cited?

Were the instances typical?

Were the instances representative?

Causation

In causation, a special kind of generalization, we assume that one single circumstance always produces a predictable effect or set of effects. The following illustration exemplifies a causative argument:

(D) The temperature has dropped to 10°. } ⟶ (C) My car won't start in the morning.

(W) (Whenever the temperature drops below 20°, the coldness causes the battery to be so weak that my car won't start.)

A causation warrant may be tested by these questions:

Are the data alone important enough to bring about the particular conclusion?

Do some other data that accompany the data cited really cause the effect?

If we eliminate the data, would we eliminate the effect?

Analogy

Analogy is another special kind of generalization. In reasoning by analogy, you are attempting to show that similar circumstances produce similar conclusions. A warrant in the form of an analogy would be stated, "What is true or will work in one set of circumstances is true or will work in another comparable set of circumstances." Perhaps you have used this form of reasoning in situations like this:

(D) Joe was accepted as a member last year. } ⟶ (C) I'll be accepted this year.

(W) (Since Joe had certain qualifications and was accepted, I will be accepted because I have the same [or similar] qualifications.)

An analogy warrant may be tested by these questions:

Are the subjects capable of being compared?

Are the subjects being compared really similar in all important ways?

Are any of the ways that the subjects are dissimilar important?

Definition

A definition is a kind of verbal generalization. A definition warrant is usually stated, "when a situation has all the characteristics that are usually associated with a term, then we can use that term to describe the product of those characteristics." The warrants on pages 159 and 160 are both slight variations of the definition warrant. The following is a typical example of a definition warrant that may be familiar to you:

(D) He takes charge.
     He uses good judgment.
     His goals are in the best
     interests of the group. $\longrightarrow$ (C) He is a leader.

      (W) (Taking charge, showing good judgment, and considering the best interests of the group are the characteristics most often associated with leadership.)

A definition warrant may be tested by these questions:

Are the characteristics mentioned the most important ones in determining the definition?

Is an important aspect of the definition omitted in the statement of the characteristics?

Are those characteristics best described by some other term?

Deduction

With all the warrants so far, you have been examining one item or a series of items and drawing a generalized conclusion about those or similar items. In using deduction, you examine a classification and make some judgment about one member of that classification. A deductive warrant is usually stated, "what is true about a classification of circumstances will be true about a member of that classification." On the first day of a new course you might have used the following argument:

(D) Professors who read lecture
     notes are boring lecturers.   (C) Professor X will be a
     Professor X is reading his   boring lecturer.
     notes.

      (W) (What is true about a classification [professors who read lecture notes are boring lecturers] will be true about a member of the classification.)

A deduction warrant may be tested by these questions:

Does the generalization being used as the data approach certainty?
Is the subject being judged really a member of the classification?

The above are some of the common warrants. As you are testing your arguments, you may find that the description you use to explain your reasoning does not fall into one of these classifications. Nevertheless, by describing the reasoning verbally, you can determine some of the necessary tests that will help you judge the soundness of your logic.

Assignment

Prepare a three- to five-minute speech of reasons. Outline required. Criteria for evaluation will include the clarity of the proposition, the clarity and quality of the reasons, the quality of the data used to support the reasons, and the logic of the units of argument presented.

Outline: Speech of Reasons
(3–5 minutes)

Because this is the first complete persuasive speech outline and will as a result stand as a model for persuasive speech outlining, it will be analyzed in detail.

Outline	Analysis
Purpose: To persuade the audience that they should purchase insurance while they are young.	The purpose sentence for a persuasive speech is a complete, declarative sentence that indicates specifically what you want your audience to believe or to do.

Introduction

I. Insurance in my mind was always a form of savings for older people.	As with the informative speech outline, the material included in the introduction should allow you to gain attention and lead into the body of the speech.
II. There are four reasons for young people to buy life insurance.	

Body

I. Buying insurance while you are young provides a financial savings and gain.	Main point *I* is a clear reason. If you ask, "Why should people buy insurance while they're young?" the reason "because it provides financial savings and gain" answers the question.

A. Between the ages of 21 and 25, the rates per thousand are low.
   1. Age 25—about $16 per thousand.
   2. Age 35—about $23 per thousand.
   3. Age 45—about $33 per thousand.
B. In addition to lower rates the dividends are higher.
   1. Dividends left to accumulate between ages 25 and 65 amount to $777 per thousand.
   2. Dividends left to accumulate between ages 35 and 65 amount to $432 per thousand.
   3. Dividends left to accumulate between ages 45 and 65 amount to $250 per thousand.

The logic of main point *I* is described as follows:

Data: Between 21 and 25, rates per thousand are lower than they would be at older ages.

Between 21 and 25, dividends per thousand are higher than at older ages.

Conclusion: Buying insurance while you are young provides a financial savings and gain.

Warrant: (By definition, paying lower rates means making a financial saving and accumulating higher dividends means making a financial gain.)

II. Buying insurance while you are young provides a systematic, compulsory savings.
   A. Each month, quarter, or year a reminder is sent to you of your premium's being due.
      1. This service is not provided by a bank, building and loan, or the stock market.
   B. Once money is invested it is saved.
      1. There is no put and take with insurance.

Main point *II* is a clear reason. If you ask, "Why should people buy insurance while they are young?" the reason, "because it provides a systematic, compulsory savings" answers the question. Technically, this point includes two separate but related reasons: systematic and compulsory. Ordinarily it is better to limit each main point to one idea. Since they do overlap, handling them together in this case is acceptable.

The logic of main point *II* is described as follows:

Data: Periodic reminders of premiums due are sent to you.

Money invested in insurance cannot be withdrawn.

Conclusion: Buying insurance provides a systematic, compulsory savings.

Warrant: (By definition, if payments are made at fixed intervals, they are systematic; and if payments must be made and cannot be withdrawn, they are compulsory.)

III. Buying insurance while you are young enables you to have an insurability clause put into the contract.

Main point *III* is a clear reason. If you ask, "Why should people buy insurance while they are young?" the reason "because it enables you to have an insurabil-

A. This means that from the age of 21 to 40 you can reinvest the same amount up to $15,000 every three years at the standard rate for your age.

B. By this I mean that your premium doesn't go up due to medical reasons or a job considered dangerous provided you are in good health and in a safe job at age 25.

ity clause put into the contract" answers the question.

The logic of main point *III* is described as follows:

Data: From age 21 to 40 you can reinvest the same amount every three years at the standard rate for your age.

Premiums do not go up due to medical reasons if you are in good health.

Conclusion: Buying insurance while young enables you to have an insurability clause put into the contract.

Warrant: ?
In this case, there doesn't seem to be a clear relationship between the data and the conclusion. The data explain what an insurability clause is. The explanation is important to the speech. But in order for the conclusion stated to follow, the data must include proof that an insurability rider can be put in "while you are young." This part of the outline needs some repair.

IV. Buying insurance while you are young enables you to protect your personal financial value.
   A. Your background and future are monetarily valuable.
   B. Your family is dependent on this value for their support.
      1. At age 25 your value may be $400,000.
      2. If you die uninsured at the age of 27, your family is unprotected with a loss of $380,000.
      3. Insurance provides the money if you die.

Main point *IV* is a clear reason. If you ask, "Why should people buy insurance while they are young?" the reason "because it protects your personal financial value" answers the question.

The logic of main point *IV* is described as follows:

Data: You have a lifetime of earning power.

Your family is dependent upon your potential life's earnings.

Conclusion: Buying insurance enables you to protect your potential earnings.

Warrant: (If an insurance plan provides the same money that you would have made if you had worked, then by definition the insurance plan protects your financial value.)

Conclusion

I. You should buy insurance while you are young because it provides a financial savings; it provides a

This conclusion, a summary, is satisfactory for a speech of reasons.

systematic, compulsory savings; it enables you to attach an insurability rider; and it protects your financial value.

Now let's describe and test the logic of the entire outline:

Data: Insurance while young provides financial savings.

Insurance provides systematic, compulsory saving.

Insurance while young enables you to attach an insurability rider.

Insurance while young enables you to protect your financial value.

Conclusion: You should buy insurance while you are young.

Warrant: (Financial saving, compulsory saving, having an insurability rider, and financial protection are major criteria for determining whether and when you should buy insurance.)

Because these criteria are for the most part the key criteria, the outline is logical.

As you analyze the following speech of reasons in the left-hand column, judge whether each of the reasons is clearly stated in the speech and whether the developmental material supports the reasons clearly, completely, and interestingly.[2] After you have made your analysis, study the analysis in the right-hand column.

Buying Insurance While You Are Young

Speech

I'm sure you're all familiar with the value of insurance for older people. However, the more I learned about it the more I realized it's wise to buy it while you're young. And what I'd like to do this morning is give you four reasons why we should invest in life insurance while we're young. It's a financial saving; it's a method of compulsory saving; you can have

Analysis

Miss Horan begins with a sentence that establishes a point of audience agreement from which she can begin her argument. The next sentence shows that the speaker approached the topic with an open mind and suggests that the audience should do likewise. Since the speech of reasons calls for direct presentation, her preview of major reasons is appropriate.

[2] Speech given in Fundamentals of Speech class, University of Cincinnati, 1968. Printed by permission of Elaine Horan.

an insurability rider put into your contract; and it is wise to secure your own personal financial value.

First, the financial saving. When you are young, the rates are lowest. For instance, at age twenty-one, insurance is about 16 dollars per thousand. Purchased at age thirty-five, it's 23 per thousand, and at the age of forty-five, it's 33 per thousand. This is an indication that while you're young your rates are lowest. In addition to saving money while buying while you're young, you also gain a higher dividend. For instance, if your money is invested in insurance, and it remains from the age of twenty-five to sixty-five, your dividend is 727 dollars per thousand. At the ages of between thirty-five to sixty-five, the dividend is 432 dollars per thousand and if it's left to remain between forty-five and sixty-five, your dividend is about 250 dollars per thousand. So you see there is an increase of about 500 dollars if your money is left to remain from between the ages of twenty-five to fifty-five rather than forty-five to sixty-four. This is all done by the process called compound interest.

Since it is usually not a good idea to state main points as labels, her first sentence would be better stated, "First, buying insurance now, while you're young, means a financial saving to you." The data showing costs per thousand provide the necessary specifics. Incidentally, the statement of those statistics would be improved by using the verb "costs" rather than "is." Active verbs are preferable to "is," "are," "was," and "were." Her developmental material indicates that the financial saving will come in the areas of "costs of insurance" and "increased dividends." The reason is a good one; the support is clear and logical.

Compound interest leads me into the second reason why it's wise to buy life insurance at a young age, that is, it is a method of compulsory savings. After each month, or quarter, or each year, your life insurance company will send to you a reminder that your premium is due. This is a service not rendered by a bank, a building and loan or mutual fund. In addition, when you invest in life insurance, your money remains there; it cannot be withdrawn such as in a bank account, where you might be tempted to withdraw it for various reasons. Instead, it remains until your policy is redeemed and compounds interest

Miss Horan uses a good transition to lead her to her well-stated second reason. Her whole idea grows from the assumption that we want to save money, but that most plans do not provide the necessary motivation. Notice that she does not say that insurance savings would be greater than bank savings. By staying with the subject of motivation she adds strength to her argument. The subpoints which show that we are obligated to pay premiums at regular intervals and that we can't withdraw the money are clear and logical.

for you. Of course it's not wise to invest all your money in life insurance because you do want some money available to purchase a house or car. Nevertheless, it is good to put your money in a safe place where you cannot touch it. There's no put and take in life insurance.

The third reason why you should invest in life insurance at a young age is rather complicated but a very rigid reason. That is, you can have an insurability rider put into your policy contract. Now, an insurability rider allows you to purchase the same amount of insurance every three years until the age of forty, based on standard rates for your age. And, you ask, what does this mean? Well, it means that if you are in good health, between the ages of twenty-one and twenty-five and you have a safe secure job, your rates are at the standard rates. However, if you should contract an ulcer, or accept a dangerous job such as piloting an aircraft or even a spacecraft, the premiums are going to go up, unless you have this insurability rider. So with an insurability rider it means you pay only the standard rate for a person of your age every three years between the ages of twenty-five and forty and you may purchase the same amount of life insurance up to 15,000 during this period.

Although we know *when* Miss Horan begins her third reason, her statement of the reason is unclear. What is a "rigid" reason? Could she have simplified the entire point by saying, "By purchasing insurance now, we can guarantee our opportunity to buy more insurance later at standard rates"? Although her approach is somewhat clarified by the developmental material, she may have lost a few less interested listeners. Moreover, better audience adaptation in her examples of jobs or conditions would have increased audience interest.

The fourth reason why it is wise to invest in life insurance at a young age is to secure your own personal financial value. Now, this means that your parents, or yourself, have invested a lot of money in your education and in the attainment of a certain social status. With your background you are capable and have the potential of securing a high paying job which increases your own per-

The fourth reason is clearly stated and logically developed. Even though Miss Horan improves her direct audience adaptation in this section, she misses an excellent opportunity for direct adaptation. Instead of saying "Now, take, for example, a man twenty-five," she could have said, "Now, take, for example, one of the fellows in this room. Let's say that after he graduates he gets a job paying..." You should relate to your audi-

sonal value. Now, take, for example, a man twenty-five. Upon graduation from college, he receives a job paying 10,000 a year. Assuming that he maintains this at the same salary, his own personal financial value is worth 400,000 dollars, which will be used to support his family. Now, in case this man should die at the age of twenty-seven, the family not only loses him, but his potential earnings of 380,000. For this reason, a man must protect his own personal financial value in order to secure the support for his family. A woman too has a personal financial value. As the housekeeper and mother she has certain duties. However, upon her death a maid or housekeeper must be brought in to assist and assume these duties for her. For this reason, a woman, too, has her own personal financial value, which must be protected.

So what I have tried to do this morning is to give to you four reasons to buy life insurance while you're young. First, there is a financial savings, second, it is a method of compulsory saving, third, you can have an insurability rider put into your contract, and, fourth, it is wise to secure your own personal financial value.

ence wherever and whenever possible.

Her final examples about women aren't as vivid as her examples about men.

The conclusion, a summary, meets the requirements of a speech of reasons. Although summaries are always acceptable, they are usually better when they are coupled with an appeal, an example, or an anecdote that will leave the audience with a little more vivid impression of the specific purpose.

This is a good example of a speech of reasons. The proposition is clearly stated, three of the four reasons are clearly presented, and each reason is clearly supported. The speech would have been improved with the addition of sources for some of the statistics, better examples to illustrate some points, and more direct audience adaptation.

Speeches
of Refutation

17

For every assignment suggested in this textbook so far, you have been concerned with preparing a speech, delivering it to the audience, and then retiring to your seat to listen to either another speech or an evaluation of your speech. Although your professor may provide question or discussion periods for some speeches, he probably has not asked you to defend or attack any position taken. A useful assignment in a persuasive speaking unit is one that provides an opportunity for direct confrontation of ideas, a speech of refutation. In order to make the best use of your potential in social, legislative, vocational, and other decision-making bodies you must develop some confidence in your abilities to reply.

Specifically, refutation means disproving, denying, or invalidating an idea that was presented. A speech of refutation assignment gives an experience with confrontation without all the trappings of formal debate. Such an assignment has at least three parts: a speech advocating a debatable proposition, a speech by an opponent refuting the advocate's speech, and a second speech by the advocate refuting the opponent's speech. The speech of reasons discussed in Chapter 16 provides the framework for the advocate's first speech. Our discussion that follows is concerned with how the opponent can refute that speech and how the advocate can refute the speech of the opponent. We will focus on what can be refuted and how refutation is prepared and presented.

What Can Be Refuted

Refutation, like all other aspects of speechmaking, can and should be handled systematically. A speech of refutation begins with anticipation of what the opponent will say. If you research your opponent's side of the proposition as carefully as you research your own, you will seldom be surprised by his arguments. The second step of refutation is to take careful notes on your opponent's speech. The key words, phrases, and ideas should be recorded accurately and as nearly in his actual words as possible. You don't want to run the risk of being accused of distorting what your opponent really said. Divide your note paper in half vertically and outline your opponent's speech in the left-hand column. The right-hand column will be used for noting your line of refutation on each of the particular points.

At this stage you will have anticipated your opponent's preparation and you will have a reasonably accurate account of all that was said. Now, how are you going to reply to his speech? You will present refutation based upon the quantity of the data, the quality of the data, and the reasoning from the data.

Quantity of Data

Human beings are notorious for asserting opinions. "It always rains on my birthday," is an assertion, a statement with no visible support. Assertions are not necessarily false. It's just that from an assertion alone, an audience has no way of testing the validity of the reasoning. A speaker is obligated to substantiate his statements. If he asserts with no substantiation, no data, you have the opportunity to refute his argument on that basis alone.

Likewise, you can refute an argument if you think that the total data were insufficient. For instance, if a person says, "Food prices are terrible, the price of a dozen eggs has gone up ten cents in the last week," you could question whether the price of eggs is indicative of other products. Perhaps last week eggs were on sale at ten cents below normal prices. Perhaps other food products have actually gone down in price. A single item of data is seldom enough to support a major conclusion.

Attacking quantity of data is the easiest form of refutation. Although students who understand argumentative speaking should not make the mistakes of asserting or using too few data, you may still find the opportunity to refute a speech on that basis.

Quality of Data

A better method of refutation is to attack the quality of the data presented. Quality refers to the substance of the data. Cicero, the great Roman speaker and writer, said, "In my own case when I am collecting arguments ... I make it my practice not so much to count them as to weigh them." [1] Data are weighed by judging source, recency, and relevancy.

Source of the Data   On a topic of the President's role in determining foreign policy, a statement by a political scientist who has studied executive power would be worth far more than several opinions from athletes, musicians, or politicians who have not studied the subject. Nevertheless, even a qualified source may be biased. For instance, an economist with a conservative view of economic trends might not be expected to give an objective analysis of a new liberal theory. If data come from a poor source, an unreliable source, or a biased source, no reliable conclusion can be drawn, and you should refute the argument on the basis of the dubious quality of those data.

Recency of the Data   In our age as never before, products, ideas and other data become obsolete almost as soon as they are produced. You should be very much aware of *when* the particular data were true and *when* they were stated to be true. Five-year-old data may not be true today. In scientific or technological circles, two-year-old data may be obsolete. Furthermore, an article in last month's *Time* may still be using five-year-old data. If all the data used to establish the claim are "old," attack the argument on that ground.

Relevancy of the Data   You may find that the data are true and come from a desirable source but have little to do with the point being presented. This question of relevancy may well lead you into the reasoning process itself.

Reasoning from the Data

What makes argumentative speaking so exciting is the opportunity for exercising the intellect. Even after individuals have learned to use data to support conclusions and to test the quality of those data, they find that reasoning can still be faulty. Reasoning, the process we use to get from data to conclusion is the source of the greatest number of errors in argumentative speaking. A line of argument on a recent intercollegiate debate proposition illustrates how faulty reasoning can come from useful data. The speaker was trying to prove that "20 percent of all Americans cannot obtain adequate food and shelter." He said, "The federal government has set the threshold of poverty for a family of

---

[1] Cicero, *De Oratore*, Vol. II, trans. by E. W. Sutton and H. Rackham (Cambridge, Massachusetts: Harvard University Press, 1959), p. 435.

four at $3,100." This statement was well documented. He continued by saying, "By definition, then, 20 percent of all American citizens are living in poverty." This is sound reasoning from the data. But when he said, "So that proves that 20 percent of all Americans cannot obtain adequate food and shelter"; he was making a conclusion that could not be drawn from the data presented. Nothing in the argument showed that an income of less than $3,100 meant a family could not obtain adequate food and shelter. More relevant data would be needed in order to draw this conclusion.

To prepare yourself to judge the reasoning, go back to the explanation of warrants in the last chapter. For practice, get in the habit of framing warrants for all the arguments you hear. As you listen to your opponent, write your wording of the warrants for all the arguments presented by him in the right-hand column of your note sheet. Remember, it is unlikely that your opponent will state his warrant. It's up to you to record a warrant and test its logic. Although attacking the reasoning process is difficult, it is by far the best method of refutation. Quantity of data can be increased; quality of data can be upgraded; faulty reasoning cannot be readily repaired.

How to Refute

Since this assignment is an exercise in direct refutation, your goal is to examine what your opponent has said, then to deal with each part in a clear direct manner. Although you don't have as long to consider exactly what you are going to say, your refutation must be organized nearly as well as your planned informative and persuasive speaking assignments. If you will think of refutation in terms of units of argument, each of which is organized by following four definite steps, you will learn to prepare and to present refutation effectively:

1. State the argument you are going to refute clearly and concisely. (Or in the case of the advocate, state the argument you are going to rebuild.)

2. State what you will prove; you must tell the audience how you plan to proceed so that they will be able to follow your thinking.

3. Present the proof completely with documentation.

4. Draw a conclusion; don't rely upon the audience to draw the proper conclusion for you. And never go on to another argument before you have drawn your conclusion.

In order to illustrate the process of refutation, let's examine both a small portion of a typical note outline sheet (based upon Miss

Horan's speech of reasons presented in Chapter 16) and a short unit of refutation directed to one of her arguments.

Outline	Comments
(Including one point of advocate's speech)	(Thoughts recorded by the opponent as he listens to advocate's speech)
II. Buying insurance provides a systematic, compulsory savings.	True, but are these necessarily beneficial?
A. Each month you get a notice. (Banks, etc., don't provide service.)	True, but what if you miss a payment?
B. Once money is invested, it is saved. (You can't get it out at your discretion.)	True, but what if you need money? You can borrow, but you have to pay interest on your own money! Cash settlement results in loss of money and benefits.

In the following abbreviated statement, notice how the four steps of refutation (stating the argument, stating what you will prove, presenting proof, and drawing a conclusion) are incorporated. For purposes of analysis, each of the four steps is enumerated:

(1) Miss Horan has said that buying insurance provides a systematic, compulsory savings. (2) Her assumption is that "systematic, compulsory savings" is a *benefit* of buying insurance while you are young. But I believe that just the opposite is true—I believe that there are at least two serious disadvantages resulting from this. (3) First, the system is *so* compulsory that if you miss a payment you stand to lose your entire savings and all benefits. Most insurance contracts include a clause giving you a thirty-day grace period, after which the policy is canceled...(evidence). Second, if you need money desperately, you have to take a loan on your policy. The end result of such a loan is that you have to pay interest in order to borrow your own money...(evidence). (4) From this analysis, I think you can see that the "systematic, compulsory saving" is more a disadvantage than an advantage for young people who are trying to save money.

Assignment

Working with a classmate, select a debatable proposition and clear the wording with your professor. Phrase the proposition so that the first speaker is in favor of the proposal. Advocate's first speech—four minutes; opponent's speech—five minutes; advocate's second speech—two minutes. Criteria for evaluation will include soundness of argument and skill in refutation.

Outline: Speech of Refutation
(advocate's first speech)

Purpose Sentence: I want to persuade the audience that a voluntary army should replace the Selective Service System.

Introduction

I. A voluntary army should replace the Selective Service System.

Body

I. A voluntary army would end the injustices of conscription.
   A. Controversies over deferments and equity would be eliminated.
      1. *Time* magazine states that volunteer army appeals to those who see the injustice of the draft.
   B. Selective Service boards, local boards that contribute to this inequity, would be eliminated.
II. A voluntary army would allow the individual to determine his own destiny.
   A. Abolition of conscription would allow young men to decide whether they wanted to serve.
   B. Selective Service compels the individual to give up his private life.
III. A voluntary army would make a highly professionalized army possible.
   A. It would attract and maintain the skilled manpower we need.
   B. Unskilled combat soldiers could be replaced by the skilled specialists.
      1. At end of World War II combat soldiers accounted for 23.6 percent of enlisted personnel.
      2. In 1962 the figure was 14.5 percent.
      3. In the future it will be even less.

Conclusion

I. A voluntary army should be adopted because it would end the injustices of conscription, it would allow young men to decide for themselves what they wanted to do, and it would make a highly professional army possible.

The following section includes Miss McClure's four-minute speech advocating a voluntary army, Mr. Steltenkamp's four-minute speech refuting Miss McClure's speech, and Miss McClure's two-minute speech refuting Mr. Steltenkamp's speech.[2] As you study the speeches, pay special attention to the key arguments and how they are refuted. After you have analyzed the three speeches, read the analysis in the right-hand column.

---

[2] Speeches given in Argumentation and Debate class at the University of Cincinnati, 1969. Printed by permission of Kathy McClure and Gerald Steltenkamp.

Miss McClure's Speech in Favor of a
Voluntary Army

Speech	Analysis
This morning we're going to talk about the proposition "Resolved: that a voluntary army should replace the Selective Service System."	"This morning we're going to talk about" is not a good introduction. Even for a speech of refutation assignment, the opening words should capture the interest of the audience. The first reason, "ending injustice of conscription," is clearly stated. These quotations could be introduced more interestingly and could be related to the main reason and to each other a little better. Miss McClure has presented enough data to establish the reason.

A voluntary army would, number one, end the injustices of conscription. Controversies over deferments and equity would thus be eliminated. An essay which appeared in the January 10, 1969, issue of *Time* magazine states that "the idea of a voluntary army appeals to all those who have become increasingly aware that the draft weighs unfairly upon the poor and the black, the drop-out and the kid who does not get to college." John Medrison, who is former research associate for the Institute for Policy Studies, in an article which appeared in *Current History,* August, 1968, points out that the problem of equity exists because the armed forces do not need all the men between the ages of eighteen and twenty-five who make up the draft pool. The Selective Service policy of autonomy for local boards increases the inequity of the draft. There are no national deferment standards. A man deferred in one jurisdiction may be drafted in another. An editorial entitled, "Should There Be a Draft" appearing in the March 20, 1967 issue of *The Nation,* stated: "The surest way for a young man sound in mind and in limb to avoid going to war is to stay in school." Automatically then, the poor, and especially Negroes, who cannot aspire to higher education, do a disproportionate part of the fighting and dying. A voluntary army would, number one, end the injustices of conscription.

Although this repetition of the first reason may not be necessary for the short speech, it does emphasize the structure.

A voluntary army would, number two, allow young men to decide for themselves what they wanted to do. An article entitled "The Pros and Cons of a Voluntary Army," appeared in *Current History*, August, 1968. It stated that the abolition of conscription would give young men greater personal freedom. It would allow them to decide whether they wanted to serve. The rhetoric of a free society, which allows men to make their own decisions, would become a reality. Dr. John M. Stromley, Jr., who is a professor of ethics and religion at St. Paul's School of Theology in Kansas City, states "For the most part, conscription means postponing or interrupting boys' plans for a job or for marriage or college, and an abrupt severance of the home and family relationship that under normal conditions are only gradually relinquished in our society. It compels the individual to give up his private life to train and to perform acts which in other contexts would be recognized as morally wrong and demeaning."

This second reason is also clearly stated. Notice how Miss McClure documents each source clearly and completely. For debate speeches, it's usually a good idea to establish the quality of the data. Yet, a more artistic statement of the documentation would create a little more audience interest.

Here the movement from point to point is very abrupt. Some kind of transition is needed.

A voluntary army would, number three, make a highly professionalized army possible. It would attract and maintain the skilled manpower which we need. Proponents of a voluntary force feel it would help resolve the armed forces' present inability to attract and retain the skilled manpower. The advances in military technology since the end of World War II have changed the armed forces' manpower needs. The development of ballistic missiles, nuclear submarines, and electronic computers has meant the replacement of the unskilled specialist. It would also place emphasis on technical skill. At the end of World War II, combat soldiers accounted for 23.6 percent of enlisted personnel.

Miss McClure continues to state her main points clearly and concisely. Under this reason, she has included the necessary data. Notice, however, that she needs to show idea relationships a little better.

Although Miss McClure shows that a highly skilled force is desirable, her data do not indicate whether a voluntary army plan would be able to provide such a force.

In this section, the statistics are left hanging. We need to see *how* these figures support the third reason.

In 1962, the figure was 14.5 percent. During the same period, the ratio of electronic specialists increased from 6 to 13.8 percent and the ratio of technicians and mechanics rose from 28 to 32 percent.

In summary, a voluntary army should be adopted because number one, it ends the injustices of conscription; number two, it would allow young men to decide for themselves what they wanted to do; and number three, it would make a highly professionalized army possible.

This summary statement provides a satisfactory conclusion.

Mr. Steltenkamp's Speech Opposing a Voluntary Army

Speech

Well, first of all, I must say that I'm highly impressed with the amount of research my opponent has done. But, so far as the proposition is concerned, I don't think we have to do away completely with conscription. I think the problem is in the way it operates and not in the system itself.

Now, in saying that a volunteer army would end the injustices of conscription, my opponent mentioned that the Negroes of today do a disproportionate share of the amount of fighting and dying. Yet, I think a volunteer army, unless our society is completely revamped, will still have a large proportion of Negroes in it. Labor leader Gus Tyler, who has written extensively on problems of minority groups, has said, "A volunteer army would be low income and ultimately, and overwhelmingly, Negro." One of the benefits, supposedly, that a volunteer army would bring is that it would raise the wage level to that of a policeman. In other words, Negroes would be attracted into this

Analysis

Mr. Steltenkamp begins his speech with a personal reference. Even though he is going to try to refute Miss McClure's ideas, he wants to gain a little good will from the audience. He continues his introduction by giving his over-all point of view toward the topic.

Although this is not a complete statement of his opponent's first reason, it's good enough for us to see what he will be attacking. Notice that he follows the statement of the opponent's argument with the statement of his position on this issue. His entire refutation is centered on the reasoning behind the argument. He shows that the change would not yield a change in the composition of the army.

field because they would be able to get three square meals a day and have some sort of status.

As far as ending the draft is concerned, I think that this is inconceivable in our time. The volunteer army was tried in some way between 1947 and 1948 when the selective system didn't operate at all. In other words, hardly any men were drafted at all. And it was shown that, during this time, manpower needs were not met. Five years ago, the Department of Defense did a study concerning a volunteer army and proved to the department's satisfaction that it would not work. As far as the foreign policy implications go, America has a leading role in the world; and whether we like it or not, America is the peace keeper. Hanson W. Baldwin, who is a military editor for the *New York Times*, has stated, "The elimination of the draft would have international, political, and psychological implications that would be adverse to the image of a strong and determined America." As far as the draft is concerned, such men as George Marshall, Harry Truman, and Dwight Eisenhower have all favored the Selective Service Act.

> This second unit of refutation attacking the underlying assumptions of Miss McClure's case would be strengthened by showing its relationship to her case better. He might have said: "Miss McClure has given us three reasons for adopting a voluntary army. Although she hasn't said so, her argument implies that a voluntary army would be workable. I don't think it would." Then, he could continue his refutation as stated.

Now, my opponent has said that having a volunteer army would allow young men to decide for themselves their choice in life and would give them more personal freedom. I'd just like a little show of hands from the men in the audience how many men here would volunteer to go into the army. Well, this points out one of the problems of a volunteer army. It's obvious that since no man in this room raised his hand that a voluntary army isn't going to get in the kind of men that my opponent says will make it a highly professionalized and skilled army.

> Mr. Steltenkamp's clear statement of the argument he will refute exemplifies accepted method. Although his in-class survey provides for audience adaptation, it doesn't prove anything. Whether the men of the class would volunteer to go into the army right then has nothing to do with the total argument. It *sounds* good on the surface, but it is fallacious.

I'd just like to sum up by saying that, right at this time now, a voluntary army is not feasible because of the great needs that the United States has in the world today as far as keeping the peace. The draft should be reorganized, but it doesn't have to be necessarily done away with. I feel that by destroying some of the inequalities in our draft, we'll be able to better meet the challenges that the world offers us today.

Rather than asserting again that the draft should be reorganized, Mr. Steltenkamp should have re-stated what he had refuted.

Miss McClure's Second Speech

Speech

First, my opponent brought up the point that a voluntary army would naturally have more Negroes and low-income people in it. President Nixon, for one, has thrown this argu-ment aside and said that the money which is appealing to a black man is just as appealing to a white man. And if you pay enough you'll get men who want to serve in the armed forces.

The study that was done by the De-partment of Defense five years ago, which my opponent mentioned, was simply not valid. Walter, Oig, Alt-man, and Fetcher—these are all peo-ple who worked in the Department of Defense on the study of the draft —feel that a voluntary army force is possible. Their conclusions result at least in part from the material gath-ered from the Department of Defense —material which was not released. In the first place, the questions asked sixteen -to-nineteen -year -olds were not specific enough. It was as-sumed when these questions were asked that the respondents knew that the salary for the first year en-listee was less than $100 per month and the minimum amount that vet-

Analysis

Although Miss McClure states the argument to be refuted clearly, her single testimonial from Presi-dent Nixon doesn't really refute the argument made by Mr. Stel-tenkamp.

Here Miss McClure has the mak-ings of a very good refutation of Mr. Steltenkamp's attack on work-ability. She examines the same study used by her opponent and shows why the results were ques-tionable. Had she followed the four steps of refutation more care-fully, her unit of refutation would be clarified considerably.

erans receive for schooling is $1,200 a year. Nothing was explained to these people before they asked them the questions. These assumptions are open to question.

When my opponent mentioned that since the United States is the world's peace keeper, we would need more people to go to these remote parts of the world and take care of our friends. Yet, after Vietnam, the possibility might be a little lower that the United States will engage in this kind of activity.

This unit of refutation is more speculation then logical argument. Although we may hope she's right, her material does not really refute the point.

So because a volunteer army would end the injustices of conscription, allow the young man to decide his own future, and make a highly professionalized army possible, I think we should support it.

Refutation is the most difficult kind of speaking. These examples point out common mistakes as well as effective methods of refutation. Although you, too, will find it difficult to prepare and present spur-of-the-moment refutation clearly and concisely, if you will study the suggested procedure and practice with care, you will be able to improve your ability to refute considerably.

Speeches
of Motivation

18

Motivation is the incentive or inducement that moves one to action. Although motivation can and often does result from logical reasons, the term usually refers to the way ideas are adapted to the audience to bring about the desired response. Motivation often provides the persuasion in a persuasive speech. Because of the importance and power of motivation, let's review the two principles that are fundamental to a sound, ethical basis for its use.

First, you have an ethical responsibility to advocate propositions that you believe are in the audience's best interests. You should speak against capital punishment only because you believe that it is wrong, not because it is the first topic you ran across; you should speak in favor of serving beer on campus because it serves some constructive purpose, not because all students are bound to be for it; you should speak favoring a pass-fail system because you believe it will help the educational system, not because you want to knock the university. Persuasive speaking is not for self-gratification, it's for the purpose of bringing about a situation or condition that would better the lives of the audience as "citizens" of a student body, a community, a state, a nation, or the world.

Second, regardless of what kind of emotional climate surrounds your topic, you must have a logical framework to support your proposition. Although your speech may not be a "one, two, three" statement and development of reasons, it should be logically conceived and logically based. You are not meeting the requirements of ethical persuasive speaking unless you meet these tests.

In this assignment your goal is not only to work within the framework of logical development but also to provide the kind of motivation that will bring about action. Motivation would not be possible or necessary if man were a truly logical being. But since man is human, he needs to be moved emotionally as well as convinced logically.

Preparing a speech designed to motivate an audience requires at least two kinds of analysis and adaptation: (1) an analysis of the attitude of the audience toward the proposition in order to determine the over-all method of procedure and (2) an analysis of the specific kinds of motivation to see which could best be used to advance your proposition for that particular audience.

Audience Attitude

Obviously, much of your success will depend on the kind of audience you face for the particular speech. A persuasive speech cannot be prepared in isolation. It must be prepared with the attitudes and knowledge of the audience in mind. To determine how you will motivate your audience, you must have an accurate appraisal of whether or not they favor the proposition and to what degree they favor it. Through a sample of attitude, an insight into audience behavior, or a good guess, you can place your audience in one of the following classifications: *no opinion*—either no information or no interest; *in favor*—already holding a particular belief; *opposed*—holding an opposite point of view. Although these classifications may overlap, since you will have neither the time nor the opportunity to present a line of development that would adapt to all possible attitudes within the audience, you should assess the prevailing attitude and knowledge and work from there.

No Opinion

With some topics, your audience will have no opinion. Often this lack of opinion results from a lack of knowledge on the subject. Suppose you wanted to persuade the class "that elementary schools should explore the feasibility of ungraded primary schools." Unless your class is composed of prospective elementary teachers, only a few will know what an ungraded primary school is. Even those who know the term may not have enough knowledge to formulate an opinion. In this instance, yours will be a problem of instruction before you can hope to create a favorable attitude. Since they lack preconceived biases, you can usually approach the uninformed audience directly. If you can show enough advantages to meet their requirements, you have a good chance of persuading them. Despite this advantage, you may have a burden of explanation that must precede argumentation. If you have only five minutes to speak and you can't even define the program in that length of time, you will have a very difficult time creating any attitudes.

A lack of audience opinion may also result from apathy. When apathy is the problem but knowledge does exist, you can spend your entire time in motivation. Although an apathetic audience is difficult to motivate, you will have nearly the entire speech time to create interest and commitment. An apathetic audience presents a challenge and an opportunity for the persuasive speaker. Since the challenge is getting the audience to act, an organization based on comparative advantages may allow you to place emphasis where it is needed.

In Favor

In your analysis, you may find that the audience is already favorably disposed toward the proposition. Although this sounds like an ideal situation, it carries with it many hazards. When an audience is already in favor, they are seldom interested in a rehash of familiar material and reasons. Because of an ill-considered approach, a favorable audience can become hostile or apathetic to you as a speaker—a result as undesirable as negative commitment. If your campus is typical, a common complaint is the lack of on-campus parking. As a result, the subject matter of a speech in favor of increased parking space would already be accepted. In situations of this kind, the best line of argument is to develop a specific course of action satisfying the felt need. A speech on the need for an underground garage or a high-rise parking garage on a present site or a new system of determining priority would build upon the existing audience attitude. The presentation of a well-thought-out specific solution increases the potential for action. In summary, when you believe your audience is on your side, don't just echo their beliefs. Try to crystallize their attitudes, recommit them to their direction of thought, and bring the group to some meaningful action that will help to solve or alleviate the problem.

Opposed

With many of the kinds of propositions that call for a change in existing attitudes and procedures, your audience attitude may range from slightly negative to thoroughly hostile. These two degrees of negative attitude require a slightly different handling. For instance, with the proposition "The United States is spending too little on the race for space," most people will have an opinion. Since this is a debatable proposition, about half the audience will probably be at least slightly negative. Yet, the other half may even be slightly favorable to strongly favorable. Usually, the best way to proceed is with the generalization that the audience can be persuaded if you can give good reasons and if you can motivate them. A straightforward, logically sound speech may convince those who are only slightly negative and will not alienate those in favor. A problem-solution method provides a usable framework for these conditions.

However, suppose the topic were "The federal government should guarantee a minimum annual income to all its citizens." With this proposition, there is an excellent chance that the majority of the audience would be negative to hostile. Hostile audiences can seldom be persuaded with one speech. In fact, a hostile audience may well turn itself off with the statement of the problem. To get this kind of an audience even to listen calls for a great deal of motivation. Give an interesting speech and leave a favorable impression of yourself. A criteria-satisfaction approach provides a usable framework for a hostile audience. If you have done a good job, you will be able to plant the seeds of persuasion. The next week, the next month, or even the next year, one or more of that audience might well come to your way of thinking—but don't expect too much to happen during the speech.

Kinds of Motivation

No matter how well selected your purpose or how clearly organized your ideas may be, you can't hope to improve your chances of persuasion until you learn how to deal with human nature. With all of us, something that goes beyond logical reasons brings us to act. Why did you put on the shirt or blouse you are wearing today? Why are you going out with a particular boy or girl this weekend? Why did you select that particular meat or vegetable for lunch today? Many of these and similar decisions are based upon some inner drive that must be satisfied. "When I wear my red sweater the whole world looks brighter" and "When I'm in my Corvette I feel as if I own the world" are typical comments you hear every day. Some of the motives that heighten or perhaps occasionally replace logical assessment are pleasure, wealth, responsibility, justice, health, conformity, and sex. You will need to look for ways of using these motives to advance your proposition.

Pleasure

An old saying goes, "People do those things that they want to do." Those common excuses "I was going to go see the movie, but I didn't have time" or "I was going to read that book first chance I got" really mean that the people did not want to do these things very badly. After all is said and done, people do things that give them pleasure. Pleasure is sometimes a result of something being easy. If you are able to shoot a basketball through the basket a higher percentage of times than most others, you probably enjoy the experience. At other times, pleasure is a result of accomplishing something that is difficult. You may get more pleasure from solving a difficult crossword puzzle than in solving an easy one. Getting an *A* in a class you regard as difficult may give you more pleasure than getting an *A* in a class that you regard as easy. Now, let's see how this knowledge of human nature can be used in a speech. Your classmates will tend to respond favorably when they see that your proposition will give them pleasure. What is it about your proposition that will yield pleasure for your audience? How can you show a pleasurable experience in going to a movie, in giving to the Easter Seals campaign, in fighting air pollution? With some topics you can make pleasure the major line of motivation. For other topics, appealing to pleasure might not be appropriate.

Wealth

Monetary consideration is another strong motivater. People are concerned about making money, saving it, losing it, or finding it. Sometimes the value of a product or an idea is enhanced by emphasizing its cost. Cadillacs and mink coats are excellent examples of prestige items that are bought because they are expensive. Making large amounts of money motivates many people. Some will write a book, bet on a horse, or buy a stock if they think they can make a fortune. Saving money is a major motivater for individuals and groups who want the best buy for the least cost. People will change apartments or dorms if the rent is lower; they will shop at a different store if they can save money. Since wealth is such an important motivation, you should examine your proposition to see whether it will save money, make money, or give the impression of wealth. If you have the opportunity, at least a portion of the speech could be directed to this motive.

Responsibility

People like to believe that they have earned the right to bear certain responsibilities. For children, the goal of adult responsibilities is a major motivater. In an occupation, being given new responsibilities is a source of pride. Moreover, people see and accept certain responsibilities because they are members of a fraternity, a university, a nation: we buy savings bonds out of responsibility; we study candidates for office out of responsibility. Can you relate your proposition to the audience's sense of responsibility, duty, or loyalty? Is our concern for the problem you are considering a matter of responsibility? As students belonging to the university or as members of a community, do we have some responsibility for the problem area? How can you present that responsibility to your audience?

Justice

Americans have been characterized as a people with a strong sense of fair play. We like to think that certain things should be done because they are right, because they are just. All around us we hear people saying, "It isn't right for a professor to give a student a lower grade because he doesn't like him," "It isn't right for a judge to make the punishment greater for one individual than another," "It isn't right for people to make money by exploiting the poor," "It isn't right for the possession of marijuana to carry a greater penalty than second degree murder." Because most people have this almost innate sense of justice, you have the opportunity to appeal to this sense in your speeches. But for justice to be meaningful, it must be stated in specific, concrete terms. Audience agreement on the abstract term "justice" won't help to move them. You must get them thinking about specifics. Is there anything about your proposition that will appeal to the audience's sense of justice? If so, what? How can you make it apparent to your audience?

Health

Perhaps one of our most important motivations should be health. Although many people do not respond to health as a motive on a conscious level as much as they probably should, it is still the basis for many actions. Perhaps health is a motivater as long as achieving health does not cause us undue pain or hardship. We endure preventive shots, blood tests, and the like, but the thought of pain or hardship often causes us to discount the health motive. Although people put other motives before health, health considerations have stopped some people from smoking, they have slowed down some drivers, and they have motivated some people to exercise. Is there something about your proposition that will affect the health of the audience? If so, what? How can a person improve his health by following your suggestion? Can he improve his health without being hurt or uncomfortable?

Conformity

Although many young people like to deny it, conformity is a major motivater. People often respond in a given way because a friend, a neighbor, an acquaintance, or a person in the same age bracket has so responded. At other times, people can be motivated by opposing conformity. Some will be more likely to do something if they can be the first one to do it or if it makes them distinctive. Nevertheless, most people feel more comfortable when they are members of a crowd. The old saying "There's strength in numbers" certainly applies. Is there something about your proposition that will appeal to either conformity or to nonconformity? What ? How can it be developed?

Sex

No discussion of motives would be complete without some mention of sex. As you know, advertisers are very much aware of its power. It is hard for us to find a commercial on television that doesn't have some sexual orientation. Because television appeals to sex are largely unethical, you should not use them as examples. Nevertheless, appeals to sex would be useful and appropriate in speeches on exercising, dieting, grooming, and other topics where sexual attractiveness might be a legitimate goal. In contrast to these, for speeches on air pollution, capital punishment, student government, and grading system, appeals to sex are inappropriate. Is there some aspect of your topic that has a legitimate relationship to sex? If so, how can you appeal to that motive?

Although we haven't exhausted the supply of motives, in this coverage of pleasure, wealth, responsibility, justice, health, conformity, and sex, we have considered the majority of the most applicable motives. Through these motives, you can appeal to a variety of emotions.

Three Special Devices of Persuaders

Before leaving motivation, let's consider three special devices, yes-response, common ground, and suggestion, that are used by persuasive speakers to condition an audience response. Like most means of persuasion, they apply equally well to ethical and unethical persuasion. You should learn to use them ethically and to recognize their unethical use by other persuaders.

Yes-Response A favorable climate for persuasion is built upon audience agreement. Psychologists have found that when an audience gets in the habit of saying Yes, they are likely to continue to say Yes. If you can phrase questions that establish areas of agreement early in your speech, the audience will be more likely to listen to you and perhaps to agree with you later. In contrast, if you create areas of disagreement earlier, you may not be able to get agreement later. For instance, an insurance salesman might phrase the following questions: "You want your family to be able to meet their needs, don't you? You want to be able to provide for them under all circumstances, don't you? You want your family to have the basic needs, don't you? Then of course you want to have an insurance program that meets all these criteria, don't you?" With this set of yes-responses, the potential client is led to a yes-response he might not have made earlier; that is, he may well say Yes to the suggestion that he buy an insurance policy.

Common Ground   This motivational device is based on an establishment of the same type of response pattern as the yes-response, but the initiation of the response pattern follows a somewhat different route. Essentially, the over-all response sought is: "We agree, or have common ground, on so many variously important subjects; it is, therefore, not proper that we should have disagreement in a single area so insignificant when compared to the vast area of our agreement." The politician might say to his constituents:

> You know, I was born just a quarter-mile west of this very spot. And I went to school over there at Central High. You remember Mrs. Wilson, the history teacher? She sure gave me a rough time, too. But then we had plenty of good times—the dances, the picnics.... You got to know me and my ideas pretty well, and then you sent me down to the capital to represent you—a job I've been doing for you for thirteen years. Perhaps your son or daughter is now going to old Central High just like my boy is. And we know that the old schoolhouse just isn't big enough or modern enough for today's kind of education. Now, about that school appropriations bill that some of you have been asking me about...

Suggestion   Suggestion involves planting an idea in the mind of the listener, rather than saying it directly. Much of the presentation of sex in commercials is by suggestion. If a handsome, virile young man or a beautiful, well-built young lady is seen driving an automobile, the suggestion is that the automobile is associated with sex appeal. In almost all instances of this kind, the use of suggestion is really unethical because it is misleading. The advertisers say indirectly something that the Federal Communications Commission could prosecute them for saying directly. Unfortunately, we as consumers accept the blatant use of suggestion because we enjoy the sexual association even when we know it is untrue.

As an ethical speaker, however, you will find your use of suggestion limited. One prevalent use of suggestion in speechmaking is the use of directive. Such expressions as "I think we will all agree," "As we all know," and "Now we come to a most important consideration" are forms of suggestion that will help you to direct audience thinking. Another use of suggestion is to associate the name of a prominent individual to add prestige to a proposal. Of course, ethical use of this method is limited to those individuals who have given their backing to that particular proposal. In contrast to saying that a proposal is favored by notable men, you can say that Senator X, who received an award for his work on air-pollution control, favors the proposal to curb air pollution. This kind of use helps the audience to make the association between the proposal and responsible public officials. A third way to use suggestion is by phrasing ideas in specific, vivid language. Audiences are drawn to favor proposals that are phrased in memorable language. Winston Churchill's use of "iron curtain" in a speech at Fulton, Missouri, suggested an attitude about Russian ideology that has permeated western thinking for more than twenty years. Because the subtle, less obvious statement of an idea may be more easily accepted by an audience, suggestion is an aid to persuasive speaking.

Assignment

Prepare a four- to seven-minute persuasive speech. Outline required. In addition to clarity of purpose and soundness of reasons, criteria for evaluation will include how well you are able to motivate your audience. Appeal to at least two of the following motives: pleasure, wealth, responsibility, justice, health, conformity, and sex.

Because of the complexity of persuasion, two speeches reflecting somewhat different approaches are included to illustrate speeches of motivation.

Outline: Speech of Motivation
(4–7 minutes)

Notice the similarity in structure between the following outline and the one used to illustrate a speech of reasons. Use of motivation in a speech affects idea development; it should seldom, if ever, affect structure.

Purpose: I want to persuade the audience to buy private label brands at their supermarkets.

Introduction

I. Would you like to save money on your next food shopping list?
II. By buying private label brands you can lower your grocery cost, have a high-quality product, and help the economy.

Body

I. You can lower your grocery costs.
  A. Let's compare prices for thirteen selected common items.
    1. In each case, the Kroger brand is lower than the national brand.
    2. You'd save 47½ cents in one week—$24.70 a year—on those items alone.
  B. How can private companies afford to give you these low prices?
    1. They eliminate the middleman.
    2. They don't have to research or introduce new products.
      a. Instead of a Green Giant niblet corn commercial, you'll see "Let's go Krogering."
II. You get good quality with the private brands.
  A. Quality is specified by the U.S. Department of Agriculture.
    1. Let's use corn as an example.
      a. It's tested for tenderness, for liquid, cut, and defects.
  B. Some of the suppliers for private labels are national brands.
    1. Del Monte is a national supplier for canned and bottled goods.
    2. Birdseye does frozen package work for private companies.
  C. The small company can send back a shipment that doesn't meet specifications.
  D. Small companies often test their various supplier's brands with the consumer.
    1. If they don't rank high, they try to improve them.
III. Buying private label items also helps the economy.
  A. We need more companies in a competitive society to keep the prices down.
  B. The lower price of the private brand keeps a check on prices of national labels.
  C. Private companies also hire many students for part-time jobs.

Conclusion

I. If you want high quality at a low price, and to give a boost to the economy, buy the private brand.

Read the following speech recorded in the left-hand column at least once aloud and analyze the use of motivation.[1] What motives is she appealing to? What are her methods for incorporating motivation? After you have analyzed the speech, read the analysis in the right-hand column.

[1] A speech given in Fundamentals of Speech class, University of Cincinnati, 1968. Printed by permission of Jan Scudder.

Buy Private Label Brands

Speech	Analysis

If you like to save money, raise up your hand—or perhaps you are one who likes to have the finest quality food products on your table at home that you can buy. I'm going to tell you how you can have a low cost for your grocery bill, how you can have a high-quality product on the table and give our economic system a kick to boot. When you do your shopping you can buy private label brands, not national brands, but private label brands.

Although this opening emphasis on wealth as motivation is well considered, Miss Scudder would have been wiser to begin with a rhetorical question such as, "Would you like to save money the next time you do your food shopping?" Even though most people like to save money, they may not want to raise their hand after only the first sentence of a speech. If you want your audience to participate actively, you must give them time to warm up to you. From the way Miss Scudder begins, it appears that she will be presenting a straightforward speech of reasons. But remember, using motivation doesn't necessarily mean that the logical speech approach should be abandoned.

First of all, on the matter of cost, I would like to show you a chart of items sold in the Kroger store where I work. I composed it myself. These are thirteen items which any lady or man who comes to the store might buy at a given time. You can see orange juice for a one-and-one-half-pint container and a Minute Maid national brand would be a quarter, the Kroger price is 20 cents. The frozen potatoes are 29 cents if they were Ore-Ida, which is a national brand, 25 cents if they're the Kroger brand. And on down the line of such items as ketchup, cake mixes, canned vegetables, canned fruits, and not even counting things such as bread, on which you might get as much as a 12 cents difference in price. If you just count up the differences on these items on the list above, the difference is 47½ cents—that's 47½ cents you will save in *one week*. If you would continue to buy these items, over a year you would save $24.70. Now re-

A better opening sentence for this section might have been, "Now, I said you can save money buying private brands—let's see how much." Since Miss Scudder supplemented her remarks with a visual aid here, the verbal development is very selective and less complete than it would have been had she not shown a visual aid. Here is where Miss Scudder begins to use motivation purposefully. Although the amount of savings isn't spectacular, her method for showing them is good. Notice she tries several different ways to impress the idea of specific amounts on the audience. For a comparison, turn back to Miss Horan's speech of reasons. In this speech, Miss Scudder's method is more impressive.

member that's a $24.70 saving on these items alone. By buying private label brands exclusively, your saving could go as high as fifty dollars to one hundred dollars a year. Now, to you and me this would mean that we would have our student union fee paid for an entire year, to your mother it would mean a trip to the hairdresser every other week, to you fellows it would mean at least six months gasoline for your car. Now, this is a lot of money you can save in a year's time without making a single sacrifice in time or quality of products.

How can private labeled companies afford to give you these low prices? Well, some of the reasons are they have the elimination of a middleman or a broker in the private label company. That most of these private labels are put on the market by such companies as Kroger, Colonial Food, A&P, Parkview, things like this, where they put their items directly in their own store. Where a company like Lipton or Del Monte has to send a broker to these companies and has to pay them to get them to put these on their shelves.

This is a well-placed question. Since we're bound to be a little skeptical about private brands, she gives us a logical explanation for the lower prices.

In addition, the small company does not have to worry about being a researcher and introducing new products. They are, in the words of Mr. Laycamp, who is the director of quality control at the Kroger company, "they are using the policy of follow the winner." Now, follow the winner means that they don't have to put out the money for the research, they get ahold of the product after it is on the market and see what makes it good, what makes it a seller. An example of this is the Green Giant brand a couple of years ago came out with pouch cookery Now, you'll pay from 35 to 49 cents for any kind of vegetable in the

Remember, we said that when an audience is uninformed, the speaker must give information. In this part of the speech, the specific information serves a persuasive goal. Her example here is an excellent one. It is specific, it meets the tests of logic, and it works on the monetary saving motive.

pouch cookery line, from Green Giant. The Kroger brand also has come out with the pouch cookery item. You'll only pay a quarter for anything that you buy. Now you realize that this can be a quarter savings on a *single item* and the weight and all the quality that is in the product is exactly the same.

"Now you realize . . ." is an excellent statement reinforcing the appeal to wealth motive that pervades this entire section.

Now, the third reason why the cost is less for a private label brand is that they advertise the family name and not the individual product. On television, you'll see a big commercial about Green Giant's niblet corn or Heinz ketchup and they spend a lot of money for this. But the only kind of commercial which you're going to see for a private label is a commercial that advertises the whole store, like "let's go Krogering." You know, something like this. So this, then, also is a check on the quality of the product, because if you get ahold of a bad Kroger product, you're going to feel like all their products are bad. So they have to watch their quality.

Miss Scudder continues giving us specific examples that bolster her point.

And this leads us into my second major point, quality. Now, all of the products that are put out by the national people and by the private owner, their minimum quality is specified by the United States Department of Agricultural specifications. Now, some of the reasons why a private company will have the same quality products as our national brands: many of the suppliers of the private company are national brands themself. Del Monte, for instance, is a national supplier for many of the small companies, for canned goods and for ketchup and things of this sort that are in bottles. Also, Birdseye does a lot of the frozen packing work for them. And the small company has the option of sending back a shipload that does

Her transition into this second major reason is good, but her statement of the reason is only a label. After the first sentence, she might say: "By purchasing private label foods, you can have the same high quality as with higher priced products." This emphasis on quality is also a well-considered line of motivation. Thus, by implication, buying private label products will insure your getting the best.

Here Miss Scudder includes some very important information that helps to dispel possible prejudice against private labels. In addition, she builds credibility for private brands based upon responsibility. She shows that the private companies believe in their responsibility to provide high-quality products.

not meet with their specifications. So, in many cases, the private label product is exactly the same as the national label product. Now these small companies have what they call quality audits, where they will buy all different kinds of private label and national label things and they will have housewives test the products and report back to the company which item they like the best. And if their private labeled items are not highly rated, the companies look into it and see what can make the product better for you. Occasionally the testers or a paying customer complains about a certain product. Because of the way the cans are marked, the private company can also tell where this can came from, the producer who produced it, the factory it came from, and the shipment that it came from at this factory. If there are more than three or four complaints on one carload of goods, they are all sent back. So you can see that this quality is checked very closely.

Then I'd like for you also to consider that we have a competitive society and in this competitive society we need more companies to keep the prices lower down. The private label companies are able to give a lower price, and this is a check on the national level company so that they cannot have a monopoly over price. Also the private label companies hire many college students for part-time jobs working at stores or unloading trucks at their docks.

So you can see if you want a high-quality product at a low price and to give our economic system a little kick, you should buy private brands.

Here we see that Miss Scudder was running short of time. Her third reason is barely stated. What can you do when two reasons take longer than you had planned? Because of the importance of positioning and proposition, it is probably better to drop a reason that you won't have time to develop than it is to try to squeeze it in.

In Miss Scudder's speech we see at least two classifications of motivation. First, by selecting the two most important criteria for buying a product (quality and cost), she provides a logical motivation. Second, she appeals to both monetary gain and responsibility. This speech shows how mo-

tivation can assist a speech of reasons. The next speech shows a
much more emotional use of motivation.

**Outline: Speech of Motivation
(5–7 minutes)**

Purpose: I want to persuade the audience to write letters to congressmen
to help save Biafra.

Introduction

I. What would you do if the Hong Kong flu became fatal?
    A. What if there were no doctors or food was at a premium?
II. This is the problem facing the people of Biafra.
    A. They aren't facing Hong Kong flu—they are facing starvation.
III. You can take action by writing your congressman.

Body

I. Biafra, fighting for its independence, is on the brink of disaster.
    A. On May 30, 1967, Biafra, the eastern region of Nigeria, declared
       its independence.
       1. Its voice in government had diminished.
       2. Its cries for medical supplies and food were unheeded.
    B. Since then, conditions have worsened.
       1. In early summer, 300 people were dying daily.
       2. Today the figure reaches 6,000.
    C. Senator Edward Kennedy said that he can't believe that our gov-
       ernment stands paralyzed.
II. If Biafra gave up the fight, it would lead to her extinction.
    A. Colonel Ojukwu said that such inaction would lead to self-extinc-
       tion. Genocide would result.
       1. Genocide is the deliberate and systematic destruction of a racial
         or cultural group.
       2. Genocide was a threat twenty-eight years ago when Hitler tried to
         destroy the Jews.
    B. The U.S. came to the aid of the Jews then.
       1. How can they avoid today's war?
       2. We're fighting in Vietnam, but Biafra has ten times the number
         of casualties.
III. We need action now.
    A. Our plan has been to airlift goods into Biafra.
       1. The plan has failed.
    B. Another four-part plan was offered by Senator Kennedy.
       1. Have the General Assembly accept the international obligation.
       2. Have the Secretary General personally intervene.

3. Have the U.N. take over implementation of a relief program.

4. Have member governments contribute logistical support.

C. These are just two plans.

1. Write to your senators.

2. Writing to congressmen got strong gun legislation for us.

Conclusion

I. Quotation from Committee to Keep Biafra Alive.

II. The world stood still while six million Jews were massacred. Are you now?

Read the following speech transcribed in the left-hand column aloud. Analyze it to see how Mr. Frankel uses motivation to affect the emotions of his audience.[2] After you have studied the speech, read the analysis in the right-hand column.

We Must Save Biafra

Speech

WUBE on its broadcast said that in mid-January the Hong Kong flu will reach epidemic proportions. Now, supposing Hong Kong flu became fatal, and let's say it reached epidemic proportions that killed six thousand per day. What would you do? Go to a doctor? Let's say there were none. Food? It's at a premium. There is no relief in sight. What would you do? This is the problem that is facing the people of Biafra today. They aren't facing the Hong Kong flu but they're facing what is known as the kwashiorkor, which is protein deficiency. They need our help, they need your help. How? By writing to your congressmen and senators and asking that they take positive action in aiding Biafra.

Before I tell you about the conditions today, let me tell you why Biafra is fighting for its independence.

Analysis

Mr. Frankel's introduction builds an emotional framework for his analysis. He believes that in order to get us to support a movement to save Biafra, he must involve us emotionally. He begins by alluding to the predicted Hong Kong flu epidemic (he is working for a common ground). In the winter of 1968–1969, the Cincinnati campus, like most other places, was wondering just how bad the epidemic would be. It isn't until after Mr. Frankel builds a hypothetical situation in which he gets us to feel a sense of panic that he alludes to Biafra. Nevertheless, he probably should have held the action he wanted us to take until later.

In this section, Mr. Frankel's reason may be stated, "We should support Biafra because it is on

---

[2] Speech given in Fundamentals of Speech class, University of Cincinnati, 1968. Printed by permission of Richard Frankel.

On May 30, 1967, the eastern region of Nigeria declared its independence, when its voice in government diminished from a proportional one to absolutely nothing. Its pleas for aid, as people needed food and other medical supplies diminished to nothing, they were left unheeded, unanswered. Is there any doubt why Biafra declared its independence? Conditions today have gravitated tremendously. To give you an example, in early summer, only—and I use this word relatively—only three hundred people were dying a day. Today that figure has now approached six thousand. In six minutes, a population equal to the size of this class will die, in five days, a population equal to the size of the entire enrollment of U.C. will die. Senator Edward Kennedy, in his first speech after his brother's assassination, in the Senate said, "I cannot believe that our government and the international community stands paralyzed in the face of this recriminating stalemate. As though the parties of the conflict were debating a centuries-old political argument."

Now, the question that always comes up is, "Wouldn't it be more humanitarian for the Biafrans just to give up? Lay down their arms and let Nigeria, the government, come in and offer them food and aid?" Well, on October 7, 1968, the *Cincinnati Enquirer* had an AP release which had an interview with the head of state of Biafra, Colonel Ojukwu. And in it he said, and I quote, "The crime of genocide has not only been threatened but fulfilled. The only reason any of us are alive today is because we have our rifles. Otherwise the massacre would be complete. It would be suicidal for us to lay down our arms at this stage." Genocide as defined in *Webster's New Collegiate*

the brink of disaster." We get this reason from the context without it's ever being stated. Although allowing reasons to emerge indirectly is risky, when it is well done, it is very effective. He continues to cast this information in emotional language.

Here he means something different from "gravitated." Since motivation is increased when content is stated in a way that allows us to feel as well as to understand, Mr. Frankel's method of showing the number of deaths is impressive. We see and we feel the plight of Biafra.

Mr. Frankel anticipates our logical question, "Why don't the Biafrans give up?" He demonstrates the answer by giving us the consequences of such an action.

Dictionary is "the deliberate and systematic destruction of a racial, cultural or political group." Genocide was a threat twenty-eight years ago in Europe when Hitler came to power and massacred approximately six million Jews. However, at that time, a country that was dedicated to the protection of the individual's freedom abandoned its role of isolationism to save or try and stop this massacre. How can they avoid today's war? Today we claim to be fighting in Vietnam under the same principles, but how can you avoid a war that has ten times as many casualties as does the Vietnamese war? Ten times.

Now, I used in the beginning of my speech, the term "positive action." I used this because there are many roles available to the United States in aiding Biafra. One plan is just airlifting goods into Biafra. But this is impractical in the international politics for the United States to do this alone. Another plan was suggested by Senator Kennedy in the speech that I had previous reference to. In it he outlined four main points. And I'd like to give these points to you now. One, the general assembly passed a resolution accepting international humanitarian obligation. Two, the Secretary General personally intervene to bring a mercy agreement. Three, the U.N. take over the implementation of relief program with the Red Cross and other private agencies. Four, member governments contribute to the United Nations effort, including the logistical support to mount an airlift into the area of need. This plan is more logical than the other one. And yet there's been no action, but it has been endorsed by various Senate

He shows us that the effect would be genocide. To dramatize the tragedy of genocide, he alludes to World War II. To dramatize the relevance of the Biafran plight, he alludes to Vietnam. These and similar efforts gain our sympathy and prepare us to respond to the action he will suggest.

Here and in other places in the speech Mr. Frankel uses repetition for emphasis.

At this stage, our logical question would be "What can we do?" Mr. Frankel tries to show that we have the power to act, and that any action, however small, is still important.

Mr. Frankel loses a little of his effectiveness by offering a general rather than a specific course of action for us to follow.

leaders including the majority of the House, the majority of the Senate, and our own Frank Lausche.

Now, these are just two possible plans. But we need your support. We need you to send letters to your congressmen and your senators. If you think that your one letter doesn't mean anything, then look at the strong gun legislation that was passed by Congress this year. Something to think about.

Ordinarily calling upon the audience to write their congressmen is a weak form of action. In order to heighten the effectiveness of his proposal, Mr. Frankel shows where a letter campaign worked in helping to bring about congressional action. The implication is that if letters helped get gun control legislation, they can also help get aid to Biafra.

In conclusion let me read you a quote from a leaflet that's distributed by the Committee to Keep Biafra Alive. "Today Nigeria is engaged in the genocide of eight million Biafrans, calling it an internal problem and a political solution. The Nigerian army which rapes, pillages, and burns everything in its path is supported by Russian Migs that are flown by Egyptian pilots, who are training for their next war with Israel." The world stood still while six million Jews were massacred. Are you now?

The conclusion shows how a good quotation can help a persuasive appeal.

Mr. Frankel's speech is built upon appeals to justice and to responsibility. He tells us that we have a responsibility to deal with injustice on an international level. Working with a fairly loose, but still logical structure, Mr. Frankel presents an emotionally powerful speech of motivation.

**Small-Group
Communication**

Part Five

Group Discussion

19

The characteristic American response to problem solving is "Let's form a committee." Despite the many jokes about committees and the often justified impatience with them, the committee system and the group discussion it encourages can and should be an effective way of dealing with common problems. For our purposes, discussion will be defined as a systematic form of speech in which two or more persons meet face to face and interact orally to arrive at a common goal. The goal may be to solve a problem, it may be to gain understanding of a topic, it may be for the entertainment of the participants, and in some situations it may be for therapeutic purposes. In addition to competence in the use of fundamental speech principles, effective group discussion requires knowledge of the forms, the methods for preparation, and guidelines for participation in interacting discussion.

The Forms of Discussion

Practically speaking, group discussions are either public or private. Since these two basic forms influence goals and procedures, let's examine each to show their characteristics and some of their advantages and disadvantages as well.

Public Discussion

In a public discussion, the group is discussing for the information or enjoyment of a listening audience as much as they are for the satisfaction of the participating members. Two prevalent forms of public discussion are the symposium and the co-acting panel.

Symposium   A symposium is a discussion in which a limited number of participants (usually three to five) present individual speeches of approximately the same length dealing with the same subject area to an audience. After the planned speeches, the participants in the symposium may discuss their reactions with each other or respond to questions from the listening audience. Although the symposium is a common form of public discussion, participation in one is often a dull and frustrating experience. Despite the potential for interaction, a symposium is usually characterized by long, sometimes unrelated individual speeches. Moreover, the part designated for questions is often shortened or deleted because "our time is about up." Discussion implies interaction—a symposium often omits this vital aspect. If the participants make their prepared speeches short enough so that at least half of the available time can be spent on real interaction, a symposium can be interesting and stimulating. Because a good symposium is so much more difficult than it appears, it is usually better to encourage participants to engage in a panel discussion.

Panel Discussion   A panel discussion is one in which the participants, usually from four to eight, discuss a topic spontaneously, under the direction of a leader and following a planned agenda. After the formal discussion, the audience is often encouraged to question the participants. So the discussion can be seen and heard by the audience, the group is seated in a semicircle, with the chairman in the middle, where he can get a good view of the audience and the panelists. Since the discussion is for an audience, the panelists need to be sure that they meet the requirements of public speaking. Because a panel discussion encourages spontaneity and interaction, it can be very stimulating for both a listening audience and the participants themselves.

Private Discussion

Although your classroom assignment may be in the form of a panel, the majority of discussions that you participate in will be private. Private discussions are ones in which the participants meet to solve a problem or exchange ideas on a particular topic without the presence of an onlooking or participating audience. Committees convened for the purpose of formulating a recommendation to be submitted to the larger legislative body, to another committee, or to the various individuals or agencies authorized to consider such recommendations engage in private discussion. Likewise, individuals who meet informally for the purpose of sharing ideas on topics of mutual interest engage in private discussion. Private discussions are most productive when they are conducted in an atmosphere where all members of the group have equal prominence. The best seating arrangement is a full circle, so that each person can see and talk with everyone else. Sometimes, as a stimulant for study groups, a "resource" person sits in with the group to suggest ideas and to add needed information. Because of the proximity of the participants in private discussion, the group need not be so concerned with public speaking. Furthermore, since no audience is present, the group can adjust its time to meet the needs of the topic. If the question cannot be resolved in one sitting, the group can meet later.

Lately, a "new" kind of private discussion, the T-group, has attracted the attention of business and industry. This sensitivity training can be very valuable for gaining insight into self and fellowman. Since it relates more to psychotherapy than to public speaking, sensitivity training will not be discussed in this chapter.

Preparation for Interacting Discussion

For either public or private discussion, preparation requires a systematic procedure for determining topics, selecting main points, amplifying ideas, and outlining the development.

Topics for Discussion

Although topics for discussion may be drawn from any subject area, they should be (1) of interest to the group, (2) controversial, (3) capable of being discussed within the time available, and (4) written in question form. Participant's interest is a primary test of topic for all forms of speechmaking, including group discussion. Discussion, however, also requires that the topic should be controversial. If all discussants have about the same point of view or if the subject matter leaves little room for interpretation, there is really very little need for discussion. "How to make a book" may be a satisfactory topic for an informative speech; for a discussion, however, the topic would generate very little collective reaction. On the other hand, the topic "Should *Catcher in the Rye* be included on the required reading list for tenth-grade English?" would leave room for various viewpoints. Even if a topic is interesting and controversial, it should not be considered for discussion unless it can be discussed within the time available. In an informal social discussion, there is value in coping with a problem regardless of whether consensus can be reached. For most group discussions, however, the resolution of the topic is the reason for meeting, and until or unless a satisfactory conclusion is reached, the discussion is for nought. If the topic is so broad that discussion can only begin to scratch the surface, then a more limited aspect should be considered.

Finally, a discussion topic should be stated in question form. Questions elicit response. Since the goal of discussion is to stimulate group thinking, the topic itself and all of the subheadings are phrased as questions. In phrasing the question, make sure it considers only one subject, that it is impartial, and that the words used can be defined objectively. "Should the United States cut back the space program and the war on poverty?" considers two different questions; "Should the United States recognize those wretched Red Chinese?" would be neither impartial nor definable.

As you consider various phrasings, you will discover that changes in wording affect the kind of response you are seeking. In order to test whether your wording correlates with your intentions, you should understand the implications of questions of fact, questions of value, and questions of policy.

Questions of Fact   Such questions consider the truth or falsity of an assertion. Implied in the question is the theoretical possibility of measuring the truth of the answer on an objective scale. For instance, "What is the temperature today?" is a question of fact because the temperature can be recorded and read. "Is Jones guilty of murder?" is also a question of fact. Jones either committed the crime or he did not; and, on a theoretical level, whether he did or did not is verifiable. "What would Russia's reaction be to an American invasion of Cuba?" is also a question of fact. In this case, however, the question considers a future fact which would not be verifiable until and unless we did invade Cuba. Although questions of fact like the one on the temperature are poor for group discussion because they can be answered so easily with so little room for discussion, many questions of fact make for excellent discussions. Each of the following is a discussable question of fact:

What are the goals of the "new left"?

What can be done to stop cheating in college classes?

Does the "pass-fail" system help to relieve the pressures of college life?

Questions of Value   These questions consider relative goodness or badness. They are characterized by the inclusion of some evaluative

word like "good," "better," "best," "effective," or "worthy." The purpose of the question of value is to compare a subject with one or more
members of the same class. For instance, "Who is the *best* basketball
player in the National Basketball Association?" would be a question
of value. Although we can set up criteria for "best" and measure our
choice against those criteria, there is no way of verifying our findings
—the answer is still a matter of judgment. Because questions of value
encourage us to consider the relative importance of values, they often
lead to spirited discussions. Each of the following is a discussable
question of value:

Was Eisenhower (Kennedy, Truman, or whoever) an effective
President?

What is the best way of studying for an essay exam?

Is the British style of debate better than the American style?

Questions of Policy   Such questions judge whether a future action
should be taken. The question is phrased to arrive at a solution or to
test a tentative solution to a problem or a felt need. "What should the
United States do to lower the crime rate?" seeks a solution that would
best solve the problem of the rise in crime. "Should Ohio abolish
capital punishment?" provides a tentative solution to the problem of
how criminals should be punished in the state of Ohio. The inclusion
of the word "should" in all questions of policy makes them the easiest
to recognize and the easiest to phrase of all discussion questions.
Because most discussion groups are convened for the purpose of
determining what action should be taken, questions of policy are the
most prevalent type of discussion question. Each of the following is
a discussable question of policy:

Should the United States recognize Red China?

What should the downtown merchants do to meet the competition
of suburban stores?

Should *X* University abandon its system of required courses?

What should *X* University do to relieve its parking problem?

In addition to knowing the kind of question, you should also be
aware of whether the discussion question is general or specific.
Specific discussion questions include a single fact, a single value, or
a single course of action to be discussed; general questions include the
entire subject area. Specific questions are answered Yes or No; general
questions are answered with a sentence. Let's contrast three sets of
questions:

How will Russia respond if the United States invades Cuba? (General question of fact.)

Will Russia declare war on the United States if the U.S. invades Cuba? (Specific question of fact.)

Which Presidents of the United States were effective Presidents? (General question of value.)

Was Truman an effective President? (Specific question of value.)

What should Cincinnati do to lower the crime rate? (General question of policy.)

Should Cincinnati hire more policemen in order to lower the crime rate in Cincinnati? (Specific question of policy.)

Because a specific question contains one item to be evaluated, the outlining procedure is less complicated and the resulting discussion is often much shorter, a desirable goal for groups with short time limits. Yet, because they tend to polarize opinion, specific questions often result in less objective discussions. Since with "Yes and No" questions there is little room for a middle ground and compromise, there is a much greater possibility that debate will result. When discussants begin to debate, the discussion process usually breaks down. Because general questions are open ended, allowing for differing points of view, they are characterized by a more cooperative procedure. Unless your time is severely restricted or unless the group is convened expressly to discuss a specific question, general questions are preferable for group discussion.

Main Points of Discussion

When we talked about informative speaking, we said that the main points are the complete-sentence statements that best developed the purpose sentence; when we talked about persuasive speaking, we said that the main points are complete-sentence justifications that answered the question "why" placed after the proposition. In discussion, main points are the key questions that must be answered in order to answer the topic question. Instead of explaining or proving the purpose sentence, in discussion the main points stimulate inquiry. To help you in determining the selection of main point questions, each of the three kinds of discussion questions suggests a line of development consistent with that type of question. Once you understand the lines of development, with a little practice you can phrase a short list of key questions for almost any discussion topic question.

Questions of Fact   Remember that with a question of fact, you are determining the truth or falsity of a statement. As a result, the major

questions will deal with definition and classification. The definitions
of key words lead to the classification. Sometimes the task is to discover the characteristics of the classification; sometimes the task is to
select a choice from among various classifications. Consider the following examples:

What are the goals of the Republican Party?
   What are goals? (Definition)
   What is the Republican Party? (Definition)
   What is one goal? What is another? Another? (Establishing classi-
   fications that meet definitions)

Is Jones guilty of murdering Smith?
   How is "murder" defined? (Definition)
   Did Jones cause the death of Smith?
   Can the cause of death be classified as murder?

Questions of Value   Questions of value deal with relative goodness
or relative badness. Whenever we judge comparative value, we need
standards of judgment from which to work. Since a standard is
discovered by establishing criteria for judgment, analysis then depends upon definitions of key terms, statement of the criteria for
evaluation, and then a measuring of the object against those criteria.
Consider the following examples:

Was Eisenhower an effective President?
   What are the criteria for determining the effectiveness of the
   President?
   How did Eisenhower's decisions, actions, policies, and the like
   conform to these criteria?
   Did he meet the criteria well enough to be called effective?

What is the best method of curbing cheating in the classroom?
   What are the criteria for determining a good method?
   What are the available methods?
   Which of these available methods best meets the criteria?

Questions of Policy   Because by their nature questions of policy deal
with courses of action, they involve two necessary aspects: (1) the
presence of a problem that needs to be solved and (2) a solution that
meets the problem better than any other. For our analysis of a question
of policy, we can draw from a modification of John Dewey's problem-
solving method: becoming aware of the problem, defining the problem,
discovering the possible solutions, and deciding upon the best solution. Consider the following examples:

What should be done to lower the crime rate in the U.S.?
  What is the problem?
    What are the symptoms of the problem?
    What are the causes of the problem?
  What criteria should be used to test the solutions?
  What are some of the possible solutions?
  What is the best solution?
    How do each of the solutions meet the criteria?
    Which solution best meets the criteria?

Should Ohio abolish capital punishment?
  What is the problem that capital punishment is supposed to be solving?
    What are symptoms of that problem?
    What are the causes of the problem?
  What criteria should be used to test the effectiveness of capital punishment?
  Does capital punishment solve the problem?
  Does capital punishment meet the criteria established?

These two examples further illustrate the difference between specific and general questions. Notice that although the discussion group considers the same kind of questions, the presence of the specific course of action abbreviates the analysis. Regardless of whether the question is one of fact, value, or policy, the group must still consider all the questions that are fundamental to the resolution of the topic question. With questions that are specific, however, the subordinate questions will also be more specific.

This entire section illustrates another of the major contrasts between group discussion and the informal social discussion. In a social discussion no order is expected and no order is necessary, because you aren't trying to come to a conclusion that meets the needs of the entire group. In group discussion, since you have a set goal, you must seek that goal in the most logical manner. The suggested methods of analysis discussed above give you a *modus operandi* to consider. Analysis is a key to the planning of a discussion. The areas deemed necessary for the resolution of the topic question will eventually serve as the main points in discussion itself.

Content and Idea Development in Discussion

Just as in informative and persuasive speaking, the content for discussion comes from personal experience, observation, and resource material. The combined pool of material eventually provides the basis for conclusions. Since valid conclusions can be chosen only from sound data, you should find the best material possible. Because the "information" in an informal social discussion is often little more than opinion, social discussions seldom yield more than enjoyable conversation. In group discussion, however, every member of the group is obligated to present the best material he can.

The Discussion Outline

A basic assumption of this textbook is that outlining is the best way of testing the soundness of speech preparation. For discussion as well as for public speaking, a sound outline is prerequisite to sound speaking. In contrast with public speaking, however, in discussion there are two kinds of outlines possible: the group outline and the individual discussant's outline. The group outline consists of the main-point questions that need to be answered in order to resolve the topic question. Although these outlines may be as brief as those used to illustrate the process of analysis, sometimes the discussion outline includes a more complete listing of all the subordinate questions that might be covered. How such a preliminary outline is obtained varies from group to group. If there is an appointed leader, he may assume the obligation to prepare the group outline. For rather simple questions that can be answered without research (for example, "What should be the arrangements for the annual picnic?"), the leader may give copies of the outline to the group at the beginning of the discussion. When the topic is more complex, requiring research, the leader will usually get the preliminary outline into the hands of the discussants well before discussion time. When no leader has been designated or when that leader does not wish or deem it advisable to write out an outline, the group usually meets to work out such preliminary considerations. If time is available, it is usually better if the entire group has an opportunity to share in the writing of the group outline.

The individual outline differs in purpose and scope. It corresponds to the outline prepared for any regular speech. For a simple question (for example, the annual picnic), the discussants would probably not need individual outlines. They could cope with the problems at the time of the discussion. For a question such as "Should the United States recognize Red China?" however, the individual would probably want to get some of his reading and thinking down on paper. In addition, he would want to key the material he had to various parts of the outline so that during the discussion he would know what material was relevant. The following are examples of the group outline or agenda and a portion of an individual outline for the same discussion question:

Group Agenda

Discussion Question: What should be the criteria used by the United States in determining which countries receive economic aid?

   I. What are the present criteria for economic aid?
      How is it determined?
      What aspects are emphasized?
  II. What problems have resulted from the present policy?
      Are there economic problems?
      Are there social problems?
      Are there political problems?
 III. What are alternative criteria?
  IV. Which of these alternative criteria should be incorporated?
      Which will help solve the problems?
      Which are feasible?

Individual Outline

   I. What are the present criteria for giving economic aid?
      A. Military criteria.
         1. Securing military bases for economic aid.
         2. Gaining mutual defense treaties for economic aid.
      B. Preventing spread of communism.
         1. The Marshall Plan provided food, fuel, and machinery to rebuild war torn countries after WWII.
         2. The Point Four Program provides technical, industrial, and scientific know-how to underdeveloped and backward areas of the world.
      C. Goodwill.
         1. Gifts without specific purpose.
      D. Humanitarian reasons.
         1. Aid to people of the world in disaster areas caused by floods, earthquakes, disease, etc.
  II. What problems have resulted from present criteria?
      A. Endless bidding between ourselves and Russia to gain favor with other countries.
      B. The loss of prestige in some areas where American capital controls a large portion of another country's industry—example, South America.
      C. Waste.
         1. In the types of programs.
         2. In the administration of the program at home and abroad.

Participation in Interacting Discussion

Participation in group discussion involves two separate kinds of activities, content contribution and leadership. Ordinarily we think of an appointed or elected individual acting as leader and all others in the group acting as content contributors. Although that's the way it's often done, it doesn't have to be that way. A group can be so organized that everyone shares the burden of leadership. Thus, a group can have leadership whether it has a designated leader or not. In order to decide whether your group should vest leadership responsibilities in one person or not, you must understand the advantages and disadvantages of each kind of situation.

When someone is appointed or elected leader, the group looks to him for leadership. If he is a good leader, the group will benefit. Each participant can concentrate on considering the issues being raised, confident that the leader will guide the group justly. Disadvantages are related to inadequacy of the leader: when that person is unsure, the group may ramble about aimlessly; when the leader dominates, participants don't feel free to contribute spontaneously and the discussion follows a path predetermined by the leader; when the leader is unskilled, the group can become frustrated and short-tempered. Good leadership is a necessity. When the appointed leader can't provide it, the group suffers.

When the group is leaderless, everyone has the right and the obligation to show leadership. Ordinarily, leadership will emerge from one, two, or perhaps three members of the group. Since no one has been given the mantle of leadership, everyone is on equal footing, and the discussion can be more spontaneous. Disadvantages are seen in a group where either no one assumes leadership or where a few compete for leadership. In such situations, the discussion becomes "leadershipless." Depending upon the qualities of the participants, a leaderless discussion can arrive at truly group decisions or it can be a rambling, meaningless collage of fact and opinion. If you have only one round of discussion, I would suggest trying the method that the group would have most confidence in to begin with.

Regardless, however, of whether there is a clear division between leader and content contributors, good discussions must illustrate certain characteristics.

Discussants Should
Have Equal Opportunity to Speak

Conclusions are valid only when they represent the thinking of the entire group. Yet, in discussions some people are more likely or more willing to express themselves than others. For instance, if a typical eight-man discussion group is left to its own devices, two or three may tend to speak as much as the other five or six together; furthermore, one or two members may contribute little if anything. At the beginning of a discussion, at least, you must operate under the assumption that every member of the group has something to contribute. To insure opportunity for equal participation, those who tend to dominate must be held somewhat in check, and those who are content to observe must be brought into the discussion more.

Accomplishing this ideal balance is a real test of leadership. If an ordinarily reluctant talker is embarrassed by another member of the group, he may become even more reluctant to participate. Likewise, if a talkative yet valuable member of the group is constantly restrained, he may lose his value.

Let's first consider the handling of the shy or reluctant speaker. Often, apparently reluctant speakers want to talk but can't get the floor. As leader you may solve this problem by clearing the road for that speaker when he gives visual and verbal clues of his desire to speak; he may come up on the edge of his seat, he may look as if he wants to talk, or he may even start to say something. Because the reluctant speaker in this posture may often relinquish his opportunity if another more aggressive person competes to be heard, you can help considerably with a comment such as "Just a second, Jim, I think Mary has something she wants to say here." Of course, the moment that Mary is sitting back in her chair with a somewhat vacant look is not the time for such a statement. A second method of drawing out the reluctant speaker is to phrase a question that is sure to elicit some answer and then perhaps some discussion. The most appropriate kind of question is one requiring an opinion rather than a fact. For instance, "Joe, what do you think of the validity of this approach to combatting crime?" is much better than "Joe, do you have anything to say here?" Not only is it specific, but also it requires more than a Yes or No answer. Furthermore, such an opinion question will not embarrass Joe if he has no factual material to contribute. Tactful handling of the shy or reluctant speaker can pay big dividends. You may get some information that could not have been brought out in any other way; moreover, when the shy person contributes a few times, it builds up his confidence, which in turn makes it easier for him to respond later when he has more to say. Of course, there are times when one or more members do not have anything worth saying, because they just are not prepared. If it becomes apparent that this is the reason why a person is not contributing, it is best for you to leave him alone.

As a leader you must also use tact with the overzealous speaker. Remember, the talkative person may be talkative because he has done his homework—he may have more information than any other member of the group. If you "turn him off" the group may suffer immensely. After he has finished talking, try statements such as: "Tom, that's a very valuable bit of material, let's see whether we can get some reactions from the other members of the group on this issue." Notice that a statement of this kind does not stop him; it suggests that he should hold off for a while. A difficult kind of participant to deal with is the one who must be heard regardless of whether he has anything to say or not. If subtle reminders are ineffective with this individual, you can forget about hurting his feelings; he probably doesn't have any. You may have to say, "Bob, I know you want to talk, but you're just not giving anyone else a chance. Would you wait until we've gotten everyone else's views on this point?" Of course the person who may be the most difficult to control is the leader himself. Leaders often have a tendency to engage in little dialogues with each member of the group. They sometimes exercise so much control that participants feel that they can talk only in response to the leader.

There are three common patterns of group discussion (see illustration, in which the lines represent the flow of discussion among the eight participants). Discussion *A* represents a leader-dominated group. The lack of interaction often leads to a rigid, formal, and usually poor discussion. Discussion *B* represents a more spontaneous group. Since three people dominate and a few aren't heard, however, conclusions will not represent group thinking. Discussion *C* represents something closer to the ideal pattern. It illustrates a great deal of spontaneity, a total group representation, and theoretically at least the greatest possibility for reliable conclusions.

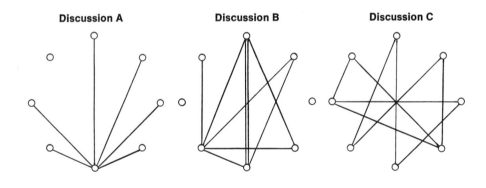

Discussion A   **Discussion B**   **Discussion C**

Discussants Should Contribute Responsibly

As we noted earlier, one of the greatest differences between a group discussion and an informal social discussion is in the quality of the developmental material included. Responsible discussion is characterized by documented factual material, careful analysis of every item of information, and sound conclusions and evaluations about and from the factual material. Let's examine each of these characteristics. Since you need documented factual material, your preparation should be extensive. The more material you have sampled, the better knowledge you will have of the subject and the more valuable your contributions will be. As a guideline to quantity of resource material, you should have access to considerably more than you could get into the discussion. It is not uncommon for discussants to be familiar with eight or ten sources. Since, of course, you can't predict all of the ideas that will be covered in the discussion or when you will be speaking, you can't prepare your actual contributions ahead of time. Nevertheless, you should be familiar enough with the material that you can find any item you need when you need it. Usually, you will bring your sources with you to the discussion. If you are disallowed the use of the actual sources by your professor, then make note cards containing all the material you are likely to need for the discussion.

A second characteristic of responsible contribution—careful analysis of every item of information—is shown by raising questions about and probing into contributions of others. Your obligation does not end with the reading into the record of items of information. Once an item of data has been submitted, it is the obligation of the membership to determine whether the item is accurate, typical, consistent, and otherwise valid. Suppose that in a discussion on reducing crime, a person mentioned that, according to *U.S. News & World Report*, crime had risen 33 percent in the past five years, the group should not leave this statement until they have explored it fully. What was the specific source of the data? On what were the data based? What years are being referred to? Is this consistent with other material? Is any counter material available? Now, the purpose of these questions is not to debate the data, but to test them. If these data are partly true, questionable, or relevant only to certain kinds of crime, a different conclusion or set of conclusions would be appropriate.

Sound conclusions about and from the factual material, a third characteristic of responsible contribution, refers to the real goal of the discussion itself. Discussants must pool information to provide a basis for conclusions about the topic question. Students sometimes blame the sterility of their discussion on the need to present information responsibly. Yet sterility is a result of poor discussants, not the format. You can still offer opinions, but unlike social sessions in which opinions substitute for data, in discussion, your opinions are based upon the previously tested materials.

Discussion Is Characterized by Objectivity

Discussion is a method of group inquiry. Unlike the debater who seeks to impose his opinions and who desires agreement, acquiescence, or approval, using only the data that will prove his point, discussants seek to ask questions, to share ideas, and to work together toward mutually satisfactory answers utilizing all the data at their disposal. Let's focus on two recommendations for insuring objectivity of approach. First, report data, don't associate yourself with it. If you reported that crime has risen 33 percent in the past five years, don't feel that because you presented the data that you must defend it. An excellent way of presenting data with a degree of disassociation is illustrated by the following: "According to *U.S. News & World Report*, crime has risen 33 percent in the past five years. That seems like a startling statistic. I wonder whether anyone else found either any substantiating or any contradictory data?" Presenting data in this way tells the group that you want discussion of the data and that, whether it is substantiated or disproven, you have no personal relationship with it. Contrast that disassociative approach with the following statement: "I think crime is going up at a fantastic rate. Why, I found that crime has gone up 33 percent in the past five years, and we just can't put up with that kind of thing." This speaker is taking a position with his data. Since anyone who questions the data or the conclusions is going to have to contend with the speaker, there's a good chance that the discussion that follows will not be the most objective.

A second recommendation for insuring objectivity is to solicit all viewpoints on every major issue. Suppose you were discussing the question "Was Eisenhower an effective President?" Suppose that after extensive reading you believed that Eisenhower was not. If in the discussion you spoke only to support your position and you took issue with every bit of contrary material, you would not be responding objectively. Although there is nothing wrong with formulating tentative opinions based upon your research, in the discussion you should present material objectively whether it supports or opposes your tentative claims. If the group draws a conclusion that corresponds to your tentative conclusion, fine. At least all views have had the opportunity to be presented. If the group draws the opposite conclusion, you are not put in a defensive position. By being objective, you may find that during the discussion your views will change many times. Remember, if the best answer to the topic question could be found without discussion, the discussion wouldn't be necessary.

Discussion Is
Characterized by Numerous Summaries

Many discussion groups talk for thirty minutes, only to have the leader say, "All right, now that we have discussed, what is your opinion?" at which time each discussant in turn tells what he thought before the discussion started. A discussion group should move in an orderly manner toward intermediate conclusions represented by summary statements seeking group consensus. For instance, on the topic question, "Was Eisenhower an effective President?" the group would have to reach consensus on each of the following questions:

> What is one criterion of effectiveness? (Draw intermediate conclusion, ask whether group agrees)
> What is another criterion of effectiveness? (Draw conclusion)
> What is a third? (Draw conclusion)
> Any others? (Draw conclusion)
> Did Eisenhower meet the first criterion? (Draw conclusion)
> Did he meet the second? (Draw conclusion)
> Did he meet others? (Draw conclusion)
> Did Eisenhower meet enough of the criteria to be labeled an effective President? (Final conclusion)

This group might draw six, eight, or even ten conclusions before it is able to arrive at the answer to the topic question. A group cannot arrive at the tenth and final conclusion until each of the subordinate questions is answered.

It is up to you as a leader to point up these conclusions by summarizing what has been said and seeking consensus on a conclusion. You must always be conscious of when the group has really arrived at some decision. If left to its own devices, a group will discuss a point for a while, then move on to another before a conclusion is drawn. You must sense when enough has been said to reach a consensus. Then you must phrase the conclusion, subject it to testing, and move on to another area. You should become familiar with phrases that can be used during the discussion:

> "I think most of us are stating the same points. Are we really in agreement that..." (State conclusion)
>
> "We've been discussing this for a while and I think I sense an agreement. Let me state it, and then we'll see whether it does summarize group feeling." (State conclusion)
>
> "Now we're getting on to another area. Let's make sure that we are really agreed on the point we've just finished." (State conclusion)
>
> "Are we ready to summarize our feelings on this point?" (State conclusion)

Discussions Should Have an Apparent Organization

Whether the group is to be functioning with a leader or not, someone must be responsible for presenting the panel, stating the question, presenting the agenda, getting the discussion started, and ultimately, concluding the discussion. The following illustrates a typical opening for a public discussion on foreign aid:

> Each year the topic of foreign aid is debated vigorously in Congress. From those and similar debates, it seems obvious that most Americans favor some kind of assistance to selected foreign nations. The question that seems to focus on the key issue of foreign aid and the question we are going to discuss tonight is "What should be the criteria used by the United States in determining which countries receive economic aid?" Discussing with me this evening are, from my right to my left, Barbara Mason, Jim Green, Phyllis Merrit, Steve Conway, Art Vlasik, and I'm Harry Stevens. In order to cover the topic, we've decided to ask what are the present criteria for economic aid, what problems have resulted from present policy, what are alternative criteria, and which of these alternative criteria, if any, should be incorporated. Let's begin with our first question, What are the present criteria for determining economic aid?

If the designated leader opened the discussion, he will ask questions, elicit response from all members, help to maintain objectivity, summarize where needed. If the group is leaderless, each member will shoulder a portion of the leadership responsibility. At the end of the discussion, after the group has reached consensus on the discussion question, the leader, or designate, thanks the panel and the audience for their participation.

Group Assignment

Participants select a question of fact, value, or policy for a 20- to 40-minute panel discussion. Determine method of leadership, establish an agenda, and prepare an individual outline. Criteria for evaluation of the discussion will include quality of participation, quality of leadership, and ability to arrive at group decisions.

Analyze the following portion of a classroom discussion.[1] Notice the contrast between the first part in which discussion is very stilted and the second part which exemplifies many of the characteristics noted above.

Discussion	Analysis
Loder: What are the present criteria for economic aid?	Mr. Loder begins this section by asking the question listed on the agenda.

[1] A portion of a discussion presented in Fundamentals of Speech class, University of Cincinnati, 1969. Printed by permission of the participants.

Brown: According to Robert Kennedy, the criteria which the U.S. has used in the past and I quote: "Full stomachs may not save a democracy, but empty ones can seal its doom." I think that during the last eight or even ten years this sums up about what we've been doing. I would cite Public Law number 430, the Agriculture and Trade Redevelopment and Assistance Act, as an example. Under this act which was passed in 1965, underdeveloped countries such as Egypt, India, Pakistan, to cite a few, can receive food from the U.S. government at about one eighth of its wholesale market value.

Loder: Do you have anything to add to this, Mrs. Wynne?

Notice that here and throughout this section Mr. Loder asks these stilted, "Yes or No" questions that don't stimulate very much discussion. At this point, a better observation and follow-up question would have been "Mr. Brown says that a major criterion for determining foreign aid is the country's ability to support itself. How much data do we have to support this position?"

Wynne: Yes, we also offer assistance under our foreign aid program, both directly and through international organizations, to those less developed countries that show a determination to master their own resources toward self-development.

Loder: Mr. Baker, what do you have to say about this?

Baker: Well, I think military reasons are probably one of our major reasons governing our economic aid, and I mean by this securing military bases, in exchange for economic aid. Mutual defense treaties—again a lot of them are connected with our economic aid program. And I think many of our military bases are more or less on the you-scratch-my-back-and-I'll-scratch-yours.

Notice that even though each individual presents interesting and important information there is no real discussion of that information.

Loder: Miss Leigh, do you have anything to add?

Leigh: Only that economic aid has been given for many reasons.

This example shows that phrasing of the question can yield a rather uncomfortable response.

Loder: Then I assume that economic aid is given on the criteria of making friends with foreign countries both

Mr. Loder needs to test his assumption. He could ask "Is the group agreed that our major criterion for giving aid has been to

at the economic level and the military. Let's go on to the second problem here. What problems have resulted from our present policy of economic aid?

Baker: I think one of the major problems is that we are embarked on a program of endless bidding between ourselves and Russia to gain favors with other countries. It seems like the smaller countries are in an enviable position where they can sit there and see which big power offers them the most before they make up their mind which way they are going.

Wynne: And I also think that with our aid to other countries many times instead of giving assistance, we become the doers. Instead of letting the people of the country develop and work with us, we actually go in and take over. And they have no say in what should be done or what should be developed. As a result, I think we create chaos in countries.

Loder: In other words, what we're saying here is, because we are advancing economic aid, we want to manage the economic aid that we are giving to other countries. And this creates problems of ill will and ill feelings.

Baker: I think this is evident in South America, where a lot of American capital has been spent; and, for a great part, we control the industries of these countries. And we've seen where some of the South American countries have gone so far as to take over the industries.

Brown: As far as the aid to South America and the no-strings-attached type of gift, it has seemed that in the past, whenever U.S. money has gone with no strings attached, graft has gone with it. For example, in

make economic and military aid?" Actually the group was not ready to draw a conclusion yet. It needed to explore the data in more detail.

The responses to this second question are more representative of effective discussion.

Notice that instead of the leader breaking in and asking whether anyone has anything to add, Miss Wynne carries the point being made a little further.

Here Mr. Loder exemplifies excellent leadership. Notice how he summarizes the point, getting at the essence of what Miss Wynne had to say.

Because of the way the idea was summarized, Mr. Baker has had a chance to reflect on the point and now is able to offer additional data.

Here Mr. Brown picks up the South America allusion and carries it further. In each of these last four contributions, we can sense the discussants thinking *with* each other.

Vietnam, in 1967, there was 578 and four tenths million dollars given to Vietnam for their reconstruction and their rural program. It has been estimated by our own government and our representatives in Saigon, that only about one eighth to one ninth of this huge sum ever reached the people. The rest of it has been doled out between the elite of the country. I think that that has been our big problem, not only managing the smaller dependent countries, but we tend to make the rich richer.

Baker: I think we could summarize that and say that it is a waste in the administration both at home and abroad in the foreign countries themselves that is a big problem.

Now Mr. Baker distills much of the last contribution down to the one word "waste." Although he is not the designated leader, this summary exemplifies leadership. Notice, this second part of the discussion incorporates interaction, good data, some good reasoning, and more effective leadership. Conclusions drawn from this section of the discussion will be truly group decisions.

Appendix

Four
Contemporary
Speeches

Appendix

The following speeches, all delivered in 1968, illustrate how four men in responsible positions met their challenge of effective speaking. The first two are basically informative; the latter two are persuasive. In order to get the greatest value from your analysis, examine each of the speeches in terms of the questions asked on page 7 of this textbook.

Interpol: History and Mission

A speech by James Hendrick,[1] Special Assistant of the Treasury— for law enforcement—and Vice President of Interpol, delivered to the 631st graduating class of the Treasury Law Enforcement School, November 22, 1968.

The other night I saw the beginning of a movie replayed on the TV. Scene: A mountain high up in the Alps. Down the steep slope speeds a skier, performing his traverses and parallel turns with unusual verve and grace. One heard in the distance a crack, as if a small branch of a tree had been broken. Then suddenly the skier fell. How could so expert a man be so clumsy? But no—it was not a fall, something had hit him. He was lying inert. Now the camera zooms back up the mountains. We see a heavy-jowled man in military uniform caressing his telescopic sight rifle. "One more Interpol agent dead!" he growls in a thick foreign accent. "Decadent capitalistic stooges! My country will get rid of them all!"

[1] Reprinted from *Vital Speeches*, Vol. 35 (March 1, 1969), pp. 306–308, by permission of *Vital Speeches*.

So starts the movie and so go the impressions of many people in regard to this extraordinary organization, the International Criminal Police Organization, familiarly known as Interpol (a name which, by the way, has been registered as a trademark by the Organization in the United States and a number of other member countries).

Actually the movie gave a completely false impression of what Interpol is about. Interpol deals with law enforcement when it involves crossing international borders—a robber, a counterfeiter, a rapist, or what have you, who after committing his crime flees from one country to another. But Interpol never involves itself in political, military, religious or racial matters. These activities are forbidden by its constitution.

Interpol concerns itself only with normal, every-day crime, and it is pledged to action always in conformity with the Universal Declaration of Human Rights, whose twentieth anniversary we have recently celebrated. It is concerned with apprehension of criminals, exchange of information, identification, arrest, extradition. In addition, it also works in the field of crime prevention. It puts out literature on counterfeits, automobile thefts, and any number of other subjects designed to facilitate the law enforcement officer in his task of dissuading potential criminals from breaking the law before they actually do so. It also holds symposiums on these and other subjects.

There is such a symposium going on right now on technical methods of tracking down criminals. Treasury's Dr. Mayard Pro, from the Alcohol and Tobacco Tax Laboratory, is in Paris at this moment advising other member country experts of the extraordinary progress made by the United States in neutron activation. This technique makes possible conviction of a safecracker by proving that dust on the floor by the safe in question is the same as that on his trouser knees, gathered there when he knelt to do his work. And by proving further that such dust could not have come from any other place in the world.

A word about the Organization's history.

The idea of Interpol arose in 1914 when a number of police officers, magistrates and lawyers met in Monaco to lay the foundations for international police cooperation. Here was established an International Criminal Police Congress. A few months later World War I broke out and the plan was shelved.

In 1923 the International Criminal Police Congress met again, this time in Vienna. Delegates from some 20 countries approved creation of an International Criminal Police Commission. Its headquarters was established in Vienna and a satisfactory start made with operations limited to Europe. But again hostilities brought a stop to the activity with the advent of World War II.

In 1946 high ranking enforcement officers met in Brussels to breathe new life into the temporarily discontinued Commission. At this meeting the Organization's constitution was revised and headquarters set up in Paris. This time there were only 19 member countries represented, but in contrast to the past they came from all parts of the world.

By 1956 the membership had increased to 55 countries. A meeting was held in Vienna; here significant regulatory changes were agreed to which have remained for the most part unchanged.

Since grown to more than 100 members, from Algeria to Zambia, Interpol is directed by a General Assembly, meeting once a year to discuss matters of crime and of organization.

The 1968 Assembly recently held in Iran took up, among other substantive matters: Recent developments in juvenile delinquency, disaster victim identification, international currency counterfeiting, forged bills of lading, police planning, international drug traffic, and protection of works of art.

Among organizational subjects considered, in addition to budget, elections and appointments, was a United States plan, which was unanimously approved, for better auditing procedures.

Held each year in a different country (the last Washington meeting was in 1960), the Assembly provides an unrivaled opportunity for top echelon enforcement officers throughout the world to exchange views and to become well acquainted so that when problems arise involving two countries the officer in each will know just whom he is dealing with.

General Assembly resolutions are passed which often carry great weight in the international enforcement community and with the public at large.

The year before, for example, a strong resolution on the dangers of marihuana was drafted by then United States Commissioner of Narcotics Henry L. Giordano. Passed at a time when public debate raged over the question whether marihuana was not safer for one's daughter than drinking a cocktail, the resolution, which expressed law enforcement men's unanimous opposition to this permissive idea, did much to bring sanity to popular understanding of the subject.

Handling problems which must be treated in greater detail or greater depth than may be possible in the General Assembly is an Executive Committee presently formed of three members each from Africa, the Americas, Asia and Europe, together with a President, at this time a European. Ordinarily the Committee meets twice a year. The newly elected President, Mr. Paul Dickopf, is the head of the German Federal Criminal Police Office. I had the opportunity recently to visit Mr. Dickopf's headquarters in Wiesbaden and can attest to the efficiency and sympathetic intelligence with which Mr. Dickopf's operation is conducted.

While the governing policies of Interpol are established by the General Assembly and the Executive Committee, the day-to-day operations are handled by an Executive Secretariat. This consists of a Secretary General together with officers who exercise various functions, including the operation of a worldwide communications system dealing with international police work (126,000 cables in 1967), a central record of international criminals (1,000,000 cards, 40,000 criminals), a research center, a section dealing with reports to General Assemblies, major international organizations and scientific bodies, and one which produces an International Criminal Police Review. Many documents are published by the Secretariat dealing with criminals who have left home base, recidivists, or those most sought after, and dealing with the subject of international crime. In addition, a publication on counterfeit currency is widely circulated to banks and financial institutions, surely the most helpful publication of its kind that exists today.

The headquarters of the Organization was recently moved from an ancient building in Paris to a relatively small American-style office building in the environs of Paris at St. Cloud. Any of you who have been to Paris will know how rare indeed are new buildings in that beautiful city. The Interpol building is an extraordinary exception—extraordinary not only because it is new but also because the architecture, completely modern, nonetheless fits in with the surrounding countryside in a manner entirely pleasing to the eye.

One feature of the new building which is of interest to visitors is the Crime Museum on the ground floor. Here are typical exhibits of smugglers' tricks—the false bottomed suitcase, the hollow heel of a shoe; and of ordinary and extraordinary weapons, jimmys and tools of all sorts used in robberies, hold-ups and murders.

Most impressive of all from our standpoint is a beautifully carved Colt single-action revolver which was given to Interpol a year ago by Mr. Samuel Pryor, one of our General Assembly delegates. The revolver had been owned by one of America's great criminals, "Carbine" Williams. The adjective "great" is used advisedly.

While serving a 20-year term in prison for—and this is ironic—the killing of one of our Treasury agents during the Prohibition era, Williams had the imagination, energy and courage to draw up plans for an unusual rifle adopting the hitherto unknown principle of a floating chamber. Pardoned after his plans became known to a sympathetic warden, Williams explained the working of the weapon to the United States Army Chief of Ordnance, and this became the M-1 carbine used throughout World War II by our armed forces. Though he would accept no compensation for this extremely significant invention, he later worked up for commercial firms many new developments in the art. Independently wealthy as a result, Williams today is a leading and respected citizen of North Carolina.

From the financial standpoint Interpol represents something to which all international organizations, and indeed all domestic corporations and all house-holders, aspire, most of them in vain.

It has a modest budget which it does not exceed.

Moreover, its new building was completed on schedule and cost less than the amount budgeted.

Due credit for these accomplishments must be given to the extremely efficient and effective Secretary General, Jean Népote.

The over-all budget for the coming year is some 2.3 million Swiss francs, roughly $530,000. The United States share of this is $28,500 or approximately 5.4 percent. We, together with other developed countries such as the United Kingdom, France, Germany and Italy, pay a larger share than do the developing countries. Nonetheless the United States percentage for Interpol is almost the lowest percentage figure for its contribution to any international organization. We pay 30 percent or over of the dues for the United Nations, FAO, ICAO, UNESCO and WHO. For many inter-American organizations our contribution is over 60 percent.

A considerable number of the employees of the Organization are borrowed from the French police force, with the Organization paying only a relatively small amount for the work they do. The over-all annual expense for 102 employees, including those loaned from the French police, is 1,142,500 Swiss francs, which works out at an average of some 11,000 Swiss francs or approximately $2,500 per employee. No one can say that this is not an economically run organization!

The recipients of the day-to-day inquiries and releases put out by the Organization, and the transmitters of information back to the Organization or to other members, are the National Central Bureaus. Each country has one. They function in conjunction with the Executive Secretariat as a permanent and truly worldwide network of international cooperation. The United States National Central Bureau, established in 1958, when our Congress voted adherence to Interpol, is in the Office of the Secretary of the Treasury.

On a recent trip to London, I was able to talk with the Scotland Yard men who form the United Kingdom National Central Bureau. They were delighted that only a few days before my arrival they asked our office in Washington if arrangements could be made for a particular United States citizen to come to London to testify as a witness in a case which was unexpectedly being called for trial within only two days' time. To their delight, our telegraphed reply advised that the potential witness would be on a plane going to London that very night, and the reply went out within two hours.

I would like to conclude by giving a few examples of what Interpol actually accomplishes in specific cases. Of necessity, names and certain details have been fictionalized because certain aspects of the cases are still pending.

A hoodlum named "Mickey the Mite" Mannheimer had been observed on the scene of a killing in the Bronx with a smoking revolver in his hand. Before the police could arrest him he got away, but not before he had been identified by Joey Angulo, a known and trusted informant in narcotic cases.

Weeks had elapsed with no sign of Mickey the Mite. The only lead police could develop was a Bronx girl named Gretchen who lived in the apartment above Mickey. Mickey and Gretchen had been known to have been what is called "very good friends"—although this had not interfered with Gretchen's carrying on her profession which was the world's oldest.

Gretchen was German and her parents lived in the old country. Acting on a hunch, the Assistant District Attorney in charge of the investigation called our Treasury man. We sent a cable at once to Paul

Dickopf, head of the Bundeskriminalamt (Federal Criminal Police Office) in Wiesbaden. Dickopf's men started asking questions in Hamburg where it was believed the parents could be found. It didn't take long. Mickey the Mite was found with the parents. He is now back in New York. He is awaiting trial on a charge of first degree murder.

Another case: Three months ago a rather thin man with aquiline nose and heavy eyeglasses walked into the main American office of Banco di Roma e Ferrara. He presented a draft drawn on its Rome office for $60,000 together with a letter from a senior officer of the Bank of America and a passport purporting to establish that his name was Giovanni Semplice of 4001 Deep Valley Avenue. Relying on the letter and the passport the draft was cashed. The next day the same man repeated the performance at the Farmers and Mechanics Bank— another $60,000. Later on the same day, he tried it out on the Citizens First National Union Bank, again with success. In due course the banks discovered the Rome office had no funds on deposit to support the drafts and the Bank of America officer's letter was a forgery. Fingerprints were lifted from one of the papers presented, but FBI latent print files were negative on them. Once more our Treasury man was called on. Over to the Interpol Bureau in Rome went the prints and a description; back came the identification and not long after Semplice (whose name turned out to be Durante, well known to the Caribinieri with a criminal record long as his arm) was apprehended in Ferrara. The man is now awaiting trial.

One more: For eight years the police in Los Angeles had been on the lookout for a man known to them under the names of Johnson, Henderson, Smithson, Jackson, and Williamson. The name always varied, except for a "son" at the end. The reason the police wanted this man was always the same. In each case, a personalized form letter was widely circulated through the mails to persons in the retirement age bracket offering each lucky recipient an exclusive franchise for the sale of Coty perfumes within a large and carefully designated territory for a mere $6,000, only $100 down. It was surprising how many innocents accepted and surprising how Mr. ——son could never be found after the checks had been sent and cashed.

Notice of the fraud was sent to us by the Los Angeles police and we gave a description to Interpol Paris which in turn circularized it to the member countries. Scotland Yard reported a Wrightson recently had hurriedly departed from Manchester after a franchise offer. This news also was circularized to the Interpol membership. Two months later, the New Zealand police noted an advertisement in a small local paper inviting inquiries on a franchise for Ivor Johnson bicycles. It was signed by a Mr. Bankson. The New Zealand police had read the Interpol notices. Mr. Bankson was traced. He is now safe behind bars in Wellington. He would rather be there than in Los Angeles but who knows whether he'll always be able to stay away.

Soon we are going to see introduction of the new jumbo-sized planes, carrying over double the number of passengers, and at reduced rates. More and more the criminal elements will use them. More and more crime will become international. In seeking to control it, the enforcement officer must use every legal weapon in his arsenal. Among these weapons few if any can be more useful than ICPO-Interpol.

A Changing World: Communicate, Learn, and Understand

A speech by H. I. Romnes,[2] *Chairman of the Board, American Telephone and Telegraph Company, delivered to the New York Chamber of Commerce, January 4, 1968.*

I am very pleased to be here. First let me congratulate the Chamber on this upcoming 200th anniversary. It is an honor to have a part in your bicentennial observance and I unhesitatingly predict great things in the years ahead—in fact I will say the centuries ahead.

I would also like to express appreciation for the title assigned to my remarks. I couldn't have done better if I had picked one out myself. "Communications in a Changing World"—that is a fine big umbrella to move around under. It really gives a man a sense of freedom and I am going to take advantage of it.

One thing that makes the umbrella big is the very word "communications." It is a word that has different meanings and implications.

There is the simple meaning of the message transmitted and delivered, whether by hand, by semaphore, by voice through a megaphone or speaking tube or over a wire or radio beam.

Then there is the further meaning of communications as an art that uses science-based technology in ever more sophisticated ways so that people the world over—and now also machines—can send and receive information of all kinds almost instantaneously.

A third meaning, of course, broad and fundamental, goes beyond technology to the question, "How much can we human beings say to each other, in whatever ways, that may truly be regarded as exchange of knowledge and understanding?"

For any speaker on communications, I dare say, it would be convenient if these various aspects of the subject could be separated into discrete compartments and talked about one by one. However, that is not the case. The fact is that modes of communicating do have an influence on what is communicated. Reading a scenario is not the same thing as going to the movies. The student who can listen to language tapes may have an edge over one who cannot. And as someone has said—very discerningly, it seems to me—television gives us the ability not merely to look at people, but sometimes to see through them.

That is one way in which modern communications contribute to

[2] Reprinted from *Vital Speeches*, Vol. 34 (February 1, 1968), pp. 242–245, by permission of *Vital Speeches*.

the process of change—by influencing the very manner in which we apprehend the life around us. Also, of course, it is essentially the great growth of *knowledge* in modern times that makes conditions of living change so fast and it is through communication systems of various kinds that we spread the knowledge around. All in all, therefore, modern arts of communication play a fundamental part in the whole process of change and I am sure they will continue to do so.

So what about the future? Well, we have all heard many predictions about the future technical capacities of communications systems, up to and including personal color TV sets that we can wear on our wrists and radios that will engage us in interstellar conversation across light-years of space. However, I have no wish to make this a blue-sky talk and would prefer to stay with a few practical probabilities—which, by the way, from my point of view are still quite exciting.

I think for example that Picturephone service will be in very considerable use within less than ten years. By this I mean person-to-person connections over a switched network and similar connections between people and computers, with the output of the computers shown visually on the Picturephone screen.

What makes this prospect seem realistic? A number of things. We believe the market is there if we can make the price right. And new technology is helping us in this respect. In the new Picturephone, for example, we make extensive use of these new, tiny "integrated circuits" you have been hearing about. They help us give the instrument a capability we couldn't otherwise achieve except at prohibitive cost.

Another very important basic fact is that technical advances have been bringing down the costs of interconnecting circuits and we have some prospects ahead that look especially promising for several purposes including Picturephone service.

Bear in mind that to send a Picturephone picture we have to use a communication channel about 300 times as wide, electrically, as the ordinary voice channel in use today. That is, the kind of pathway we need could otherwise handle 300 conversations at the same time.

Now, however, we are developing so-called digital systems that convert *all* forms of information—speech, data, or pictures—into streams of pulses. These systems already have important practical applications in our network and will have many more. But specifically with regard to the Picturephone, it looks as though this digital method will enable us to do a fine job using the equivalent of less than 100 voice channels instead of 300. And in the long run I am sure we shall find other ways to economize.

Another interesting subject to me is overseas telephone service. This is growing about 25 percent a year and at that rate doubles in three years and triples in five. Aside from the mere increase in volume, the social implications of growth and change in global communications can hardly be overestimated. The combination of computers and communications, already so important in our domestic economy, will surely, in the years ahead, have similar influence worldwide. Management can better organize and control operations regardless of distance.

Product markets can be broadened. Growth of international business will be encouraged.

Of course political considerations, nationalistic attitudes, and so on, can stand in the way of this. And there is no special reason to expect that better communications systems by themselves will make good neighbors. Erasing the mileage doesn't always erase hostility. It may sometimes even promote it. "Proximity," it has been said, "is one of the natural conditions of enmity." That is the pessimistic view.

On the other hand, there are those who argue forcefully that in the long run, constant communication in the small affairs of every day can do more for international amity than all the negotiations of diplomats. I have to say I do not know. I simply point out here that the way communications technology and capabilities are marching will give us ample opportunity in the next decade to try for the answers we want.

To turn from global to local affairs, it has been suggested that one of the effects of our developing ability to communicate anything we want, in whatever fashion—verbally, pictorially, or in fast-moving data—will be to solve the traffic problems of modern cities. How so? Well, according to this dream of the future you won't have to go to the office. You won't have to go to the store. You can join the business conference by turning a few dials and presto! there will be the images of your associates all around you. You can shop by way of your Picturephone and when you see something you want, order it by pushing a few Touch-Tone buttons. Also, of course, your newspapers and magazines will peel out of a handy facsimile machine in the wall beside your armchair.

Now, I do believe conferences will be held by television—in fact once in a while they are right now. And there is nothing technically in the way of home facsimile machines and Picturephone shopping. But I suspect that things of this kind are best regarded as potential developments that will find their place on the basis of whatever intrinsic values experience may determine, rather than as miraculous solutions to traffic problems. Besides, we don't know yet whether people will *want* to be stay-at-homes surrounded by TV screens in the walls. I've heard it said that most people need the real presence of other human beings at least part of the time. I know I do. I even like to go to the office and lots of other places too, even though sometimes I get caught in traffic.

I don't mean to be facetious. And I would strongly assert my belief that the revolution in communications will profoundly affect us in the next decade, to name no longer a period. Television has already done so and children who have watched TV screens from the age of three will react to their use in education, I imagine, as the most natural thing in the world. This and other new communications tools and methods for imparting knowledge and aiding the learning process seem bound to be more and more widely employed. Just how is of course for educators, not businessmen, to determine, but that one way or another they *will* be used I see no reason to doubt.

Again, I would expect that as a matter of necessity, the sheer growth of information, and the need for collecting, storing, and retrieving it in an orderly and expeditious way when needed, will produce demands for communications beyond anything we have imagined in the past.

Already electronic techniques for accumulating and processing and retrieving information play an essential role in government.

In colleges and universities, access to expanding computer capacity over communications lines is more and more important to research in all the sciences.

In public health, much diagnostic and other medical information is already stored in, and can be quickly retrieved from, the National Library of Medicine.

For weather forecasting and ultimately weather modification, a data processing center now being developed in Colorado will be fed data from all points of the compass.

Within a decade, it has been said, computer techniques and computer languages will be basic subjects in the colleges and probably also in the high schools. For this too we in communications must be prepared.

Our abilities will be further challenged when data processing facilities become able to read natural language directly. This will make it possible to computerize libraries and science reference systems in a comprehensive manner.

These examples support a conviction that the needs for communications services, large as they are today, will be of a new order of magnitude tomorrow. We might say that the requirements that will be placed on our economy will make heavy demands on all available human talents. To expand and distribute our resources effectively we shall have to make the best use of all our technology and this will require, I feel confident, expanding, dependable, and ever more versatile communications.

Now I indicated a certain skepticism, a moment ago, about communications solving the traffic problem by letting us all stay at home. I did so not because I think this is out of the question, or ridiculous, or anything of the sort, but rather because it seems to me that if we develop fixed ideas along any line, in advance of experience, we shall miss the really important point.

This is that expanding capabilities continuously increase the options, the choices, available to the users of communications. Step by step the range of opportunity to make conscious choices grows.

Thus, in the past, the growth of the telephone network has given each of us a wider range of opportunity to talk with whom we will, regardless of where the individuals concerned may happen to be. And reductions in cost, and in price, have amplified this same effect.

Again, in recent years, the growing variety of instrumentalities and services available have further expanded the choices that lie open to users of communications in business as well as in social life. Moreover these choices are not merely a matter of selecting what particular style of service is most pleasing to one's personal taste. A more important consideration to a business, for example, may be the choices that expanding, more versatile communications open up as to how the business will be organized. Or the choice to be made may even be the fundamental one of what business to engage in.

I do not want to make this a sales talk so I shall not pursue this line of comment in further detail. But it does seem to me that this concept of ever-widening choice is basic to an intelligent view of communications in a changing world—to refer again to the title assigned to these remarks. Certainly it is always in the minds of those of us who help to provide communications service. It is one of our prime motivators.

Today of course there is a very wide distribution of communications skills and know-how and a great deal of competition. This too widens the user's range of choice. But apart from this, there is also an increasing variety of services—notably in data communications—that are made possible through the joint efforts of the common carrier companies and many others. Today in fact the common carrier network is wide open to attachment of all kinds of equipment—I dare say far more than anyone would have guessed even ten years ago. The only safeguard we urge is that we be allowed to provide suitable interfaces or buffer devices, so that the various types of attached equipment will not put something *into* the network that could adversely affect or interfere with the service other customers are getting.

Now, I said in starting this talk that I appreciated the size of the umbrella you gave me and planned to take advantage of it. This I shall do now in a few concluding comments that belong, perhaps, in the area of communications in its fundamental sense—the ability to convey and receive understanding.

It is possible, as we all know, to talk and talk and communicate nothing, to hear and hear and get no understanding .And some would say that it is one of the ironies of modern life that with all the apparatus we have for communicating, true communication in some respects seems more difficult today than ever. If young people, as some of them say, can't trust anybody over thirty—and if we old characters will not try to learn what is in young people's minds—this makes communication hard to bring about. Also, many of us today feel a sense of profound unease because we wonder if what is going on in government is really being communicated to us. I am sure too that we in corporate business continue to be regarded by great numbers of people with similar suspicion. In fact, the words "credibility gap" write themselves across a wide, wide spectrum of human relationships.

Including, I emphasize now, the relationships between white and Negro people and between business and the poor. Of course I do not speak of these relationships as separate and distinct. They are commingled. And as a businessman I am convinced that there is only one way for us in the business community to communicate effectively our intense desire to help solve the critical problems that clearly exist and will have profound influence on all efforts and hopes for the future. In fewest words, to communicate we must act.

About a month ago Ben Gilmer, president of our company, made a talk on this subject out in Denver. He said it so well that with your permission and his I am just going to borrow.

The social problems we now face, he said, the special problems of the cities, the need for better education—these demand understanding, yes, they demand goodwill, yes, but above and beyond these they demand action. And we are coming to the acute realization that the action required must involve all elements in the community. It cannot be pushed over onto government departments. It cannot be shifted from one section of the body politic to another.

Today there is a growing momentum of effort in business to help organize and execute programs that *will* aid effectively in meeting these problems. And it is absolutely necessary that we make this effort a success, for there is no question that the growth and vitality of private enterprise depend on the soundness and health of developing urban life.

So far as the Bell System is concerned, we have been making a studious effort to appraise what we are best fitted to do and prepare ourselves accordingly. For example, we don't see our experience and abilities as fitting us to take a frontline part in helping to deal with, say, transportation problems. However, we do think we can make a significant contribution in the specific areas of education and employment and that is what we expect, intend, and are determined to do.

I am well aware that much is required for success. Effective action depends on achieving a real sense of common purpose among the people of our business—or of any business that sets out to reach important social goals. We must bring about wide understanding of what the problems are. Employees must know what the ills of the core city portend. They must know the acuteness of the problems of the poor. They must sense the dangers that neglect will aggravate. They must increase their understanding of the Negro—his history, his environment, his attitudes, his potential. In short, we must communicate, learn, and understand among ourselves if we are to communicate with the community through significant, creative social action.

Is this self interest as well as social awareness? Yes—I think it is both and I am convinced, so far as the Bell System is concerned, that we must use all practical and possible means to alert our people to a fundamental proposition. This is that the very life of the business, and the nature of the road ahead for all employees and their families, depends on our success, and the country's success, in dealing with the social problems before us, or more accurately, the problem that is upon us, as it surely is.

Today we are still only at the beginning of the learning, the organizing, and the action required. We hope to demonstrate evidence of progress in the next several months. The challenge as a whole, I realize, is far more than a matter of communication. But the need for communication runs all through it and I can't help feeling that in a talk on communications in a changing world this vital question deserves all the emphasis I can give it. Perhaps the best way I can conclude is simply to say that in whatever context you may see the main issue, I think it needs attention and action on the part of all business and I hope you think so too.

Thank you.

The Corporate Deaf Ear: Consumerism

A speech by E. B. Weiss,[3] *Vice President and Director of Special Merchandising Services, Doyle Dane Bernbach, Inc., delivered to the 73rd Congress of American Industry, sponsored by the National Association of Manufacturers, New York, December 5, 1968.*

It is downright depressing to note that after six years of consumerism, a Sears Roebuck executive recently stated: "Let the customer take the hindmost," is the credo of the furniture industry.

It is also depressing—and a *warning* not to be ignored—to note that consumer product rating services are responsible for the sale of 15 to 35 percent of major appliance-home entertainment products.

Would consumer product rating services be necessary if the public concluded that manufacturers and retailers were functioning in the public interest?

Obviously, rating services are needed when even the *Federal* grades on foods, when available, can not be relied on as honestly descriptive. You may buy a food product labeled "U.S. Grade A," thinking that this is the best quality. But often it is only the medium grade. A housewife who observes apples packed as "U.S. No. 1" is not likely to know that this really is a lower grade, and that there are two higher grades called "U.S. Fancy" and "U.S. Extra Fancy." Similarly, if you buy cheddar cheese labeled "Grade A," you really are getting the lower of the two grades usually sold in stores. The higher one is "Grade AA."

The open season on consumers must be abolished. That is *precisely* what Consumerism aims to accomplish. Industry blocks that objective at the peril of the free enterprise system.

Business listens to the *lunatic* fringe of our society—crank letters, *just a few,* have led to the cancellation of more than several television sponsorships. Business doesn't listen to the *intelligent* members of our society!

And that is *precisely* why Government is becoming the *confidant* of the shopping public.

The public is unquestionably developing the habit of addressing its individual complaints and inquiries concerning products and services to Washington, to State offices, and even to local administrators.

---

[3] Reprinted from *Vital Speeches*, Vol. 35 (January 15, 1969), pp. 205–207, by permission of *Vital Speeches*.

Politicians are offering individuals a wailing wall, if you will. The business community has erected a wall of indifference.

Business just does *not* listen to the public—and especially to individuals.

Or, if the business community listens, it listens with one ear that has only marginal hearing capabilities.

This corporate deaf ear is the direct cause of Consumerism.

Moreover, even as consumer protection legislation multiplied, industry *still* turned a deaf ear to the new demands of a new society. It is shocking to realize that *not one piece* of consumer legislation has been *initiated* by business management.

It is even more shocking to note that *every one* of the consumer laws was fought—*usually bitterly*—by business.

The food industry fought truth-in-packaging for five years.

Truth-in-credit legislation was opposed by the credit industry for seven years.

The meat packagers' initial posture was one of confrontation; reluctant collaboration came only toward the end of the debate.

Clearly, industry has been unwilling to accept the philosophy that what is good for the *public* is good for *business*. Industry *still* has not organized systematic and continuing analysis of the additional consumer laws and regulations that are inevitable so as to have an appropriate program ready in advance.

After six years of tuning up, Government at all levels is clearly moving toward additional consumerism legislation, regulation *and organization*, including eventually a Cabinet post.

But industry's attitude tends to remain a mixture of confrontation, lamentation, pious posturing.

Yet, A. N. McFarlane, Board Chairman of Corn Products Co., recently said: "It would be a grave error to view consumerism only as a threat. Consumerism is an expression of public thinking which we attack or disregard only at great peril...."

Thomas J. Watson, IBM Board Chairman, said: "In our kind of society, there are times when government *has* to step in and help people with some of their more difficult problems. If we businessmen insist that free enterprise permits us to be *indifferent* to those things on which people put high value, then the people will quite naturally assume that free enterprise has too much freedom."

Consumer exploitation has been replacing *labor* exploitation as the real problem of our times. *We would not permit the things to be done to people as workers that we allow to be done to them as shoppers!*

A more intelligent society—especially its younger generation—insists this *must* change.

Industry argues that the market is self-policing because the shopper is sovereign.

To the more sophisticated public of today, the consumer is king concept is *pure poppycock!*

The fact is that technology is spawning such a torrent of new and improved products—and marketing spawns such complicated packages and deals—and advertising is so *uninformative* and so riddled with half truths—that it is difficult even for the *trade,* as well as consumers, to keep reasonably well posted.

The consumer cannot be chemist, mechanic, electrician, nutritionist. Nor can he be a lawyer trained to read the small type in warranties. Nor an expert on product hazards.

Then marketing makes a walking computer necessary by offering fractionated-ounce packages, trading stamps, the subtleties of cents-off deals, and other complications.

Actually, the shopper is expected to choose wisely under circumstances that baffle *professional buyers.*

Most of us are simply too busy, or too tired, or too harassed to take a computer, a slide rule, and an M.I.T. graduate to market.

Just as a rational *voting* procedure is necessary to a free *political* system, so a rational *shopping* system is necessary to a *free market.*

Just *how much* protection does the shopper need?

That is a question about which reasonable people differ; but the *need* for offering *much more* consumer protection than is presently available is beyond dispute.

Businessmen contend that *self-regulation* should be exhausted before resorting to legislative remedies. Beyond dispute, our economic system fares better when regulation of industry takes place *voluntarily.*

But let's face it—business has compiled a *poor record* of self-regulation—even in areas where its self-interest is obvious.

One reason is that there is a tendency in business to use the words "legal" and "honest" interchangeably. The common tendency is to ask, "Is it *legal?*" If the answer is affirmative, business assumes it has demonstrated its responsibility to society.

But an increasingly sophisticated society, particularly the younger segments who are tomorrow's big markets, are now saying: "That is not a modern concept of social responsibility."

They are even saying that the business community has a *legal,* as well as a moral obligation to protect the user *against his own carelessness!* And recent court decisions are upholding this concept.

During the decade of the 1970s, industry will come under *more* criticism, and *more intelligent* criticism, than ever before. A more aware young generation makes this inescapable.

This is *precisely* why business must go beyond its traditional role of opposition to social change.

I believe it is correct to say that the N.A.M. fought every major social measure of the last 30 years.

Industry must now *anticipate* social change. This may require programs involving broader dimensions of social responsibility, and I believe the N.A.M. is now moving in this direction.

As part of its new social awareness, the N.A.M. may want to consider the following steps:

1. Develop an organizational structure and procedures that will ensure more prompt and more enlightened consideration of social issues.

2. Arrange a program for keeping members abreast of their responsibilities *and their opportunities* under consumerism.

3. Collaborate with Congress (as well as State legislatures and local
civic authorities) in new consumerism legislation and regulations.

4. Organize a panel consisting of representatives of the public and
develop a sophisticated program for that panel. The several programs of this type recently introduced have tended to be mere
public relations gestures.

As for corporate management, consumerism may necessitate the
following steps:

1. A restructured organizational chart that will ensure more consideration of ethical issues affecting the public.

2. A top management policy statement defining the corporation's
responsibilities under consumerism that will be more policy than
piety, more firm commitment than loose gesture.

3. Directives that spell out the functioning of each department
under consumerism, along with yardsticks for measuring perfor-
mance in accomplishing those objectives.

4. Give the legal department, in particular, a new philosophy appropriate to the new age of consumerism. Traditional legalism and
the new wave of consumerism mix like oil and water.

5. Consider a Vice President, Consumerism.

6. Reestablish communication with the individual who has a
question, a suggestion, or a complaint; get a hearing aid for that
deaf ear. Remember, if you don't listen to the individual customer,
Government will.

7. I suggest that management philosophy, and as a consequence,
public relations programs have yet to catch up with the new mores
of our increasingly sophisticated society.

On balance, the public relations programs of our major corporations tend to be:

A. *Inward* looking rather than outward looking—the *factory*
image rather than the *consumer* image.

B. Rather naive regarding basic assumptions concerning our
modern, sophisticated society—and therefore outdated.

C. Reflections of the attitudes of the *old guard* of business rather
than reflections of the new attitudes of our public.

In this connection, "Fortune," recently remarked: "The only real
doubt about the public relations business involves the success of its
efforts to raise its standards."

The voice of a more knowledgeable, more affluent shopper will be "his master's voice" for industry. That new society compels these conclusions:

First, accelerated technological innovation will require that business provide *more* guidance to the consumer.

Second, additional consumerism legislation is made *inevitable—* and for years to come—by a more knowledgeable society.

Third, marketing in particular can avoid becoming a new type of quasi-utility *only* if it collaborates with government.

Fourth, turning a deaf ear to the highly articulate individual members of our new sophisticated society when they try to communicate with a corporation will be increasingly hazardous.

Industry's posture with respect to consumerism is a tragic reflection of corporate isolation from the mainstream of modern social dynamics! It becomes doubly tragic when it is understood that executive heads of at least 50 giant corporations have delivered brilliantly composed speeches in the last 12 months *warning industry of its social responsibilities!* Too few of those corporations are putting their policies where their mouths are!

The new challenge to industry is to be as dynamic and innovative in the ethical area as it has been in science and in production.

To date, industry has tended to fiddle in the ethical area while a more informed public has been developing a slow burn.

Industry must develop sophisticated socially responsive programs soon—or industry will face a real conflagration.

Military Conscription: Abolish the Draft

A speech by W. Allen Wallis,[4] President of the University of Rochester, delivered to the American Legion of Monroe County, New York, November 11, 1968.

To be invited to participate with you today is a pleasure which I am enjoying greatly, at least up to this point in the proceedings. To be invited to speak to you on so significant an occasion is an honor which I appreciate deeply, especially since it is an honor that you can bestow only once in every fifty years.

Today marks the fiftieth anniversary of the end of the First World War and the founding of your organization. From the looks of

[4] Reprinted from *Vital Speeches,* Vol. 35 (February 15, 1969), pp. 284–286, by permission of *Vital Speeches.*

this audience, only a minority of you can remember that historic eleventh day of November in the year nineteen hundred and eighteen.

I am among that minority. The Armistice came less than a week after my sixth birthday. It was significant to me in two ways, both purely personal. First, I was assured that the Armistice meant that my father would soon be home from the Army, in which he was a lieutenant. Second, I could sense a real change in the attitude of grownups—the lifting of doubts, worries, and uncertainties. This dramatic change of spirit was in contrast with my only other vivid recollection of the First World War, the sense of dread and gloom that infected all the grownups during Germany's Argonne offensive.

Of course I do remember some other things about the War: being admonished to eat everything on my plate because "the Belgian children were starving"—an admonition whose illogicality was transparent even to a five year old; saving tinfoil and peach seeds; and, of course, the false Armistice a few days early, which is actually more clear in my recollections than the true Armistice, for the false news reached us in daylight while my mother was in the process of buying me a new pair of shoes in a store downtown in Fresno, California.

The 1918 Armistice came more than a century after the end of the last previous war that had involved most of Europe and the United States. From the final defeat of Napoleon by the British and Prussians at Waterloo on June 18, 1815, until the declaration of war by Austria against Serbia on July 28, 1914, there was a period of 99 years and 40 days of unparalleled peace and freedom, accompanied by social progress such as had never been dreamed of earlier.

So when the Armistice came it was natural that we expected the peace after the First World War to be at least as permanent as had been the peace before the First World War. But we did not just take it for granted that peace would be permanent. We worked to make it permanent. We established the League of Nations. Many treaties were negotiated to insure peace. War was renounced as an instrument of national policy. The major naval powers, including the United States, signed and carried out disarmament agreements, scrapping enough war ships to reduce their navies substantially.

On the first day of September 1939, all the hopes, efforts, and accomplishments of twenty-one years were wiped out with the invasion of Poland by Germany.

Ironically, one of the major causes of the destruction of the peace for which so many had worked so hard and so well was an excess of passion for peace. It became apparent that for many citizens of England, France, the United States, and their friends, peace outweighed all other goals, values, and purposes together. No evil could be so great, we declared, as deliberately killing one's fellow man in war.

Even when Hitler had already imprisoned hundreds of thousands or perhaps millions of people, and even after he had begun their systematic torture and annihilation, young men in England, France, America, and other countries, took the "Oxford pledge" not under any circumstances to fight for King or Country. As a result of the pledge, and of the basic spirit of which it was only one manifestation, the leaders of these countries were deprived of credibility in international negotiations when they tried to suggest that their countries would not countenance unbridled aggression and tyranny, but would draw a line where they would stand and fight.

We know now that when Hitler's Army occupied the Rhineland they carried orders to retreat if any resistance were encountered. Hitler had issued these orders to back up the guarantees he gave his poorly armed generals that they would meet no resistance from the overwhelmingly better-armed French and the other signers of the Treaty of Versailles.

It is now more than 23 years since the end of the Second World War. This peace has already proved to be at least two years more enduring than that after the First World War. But of the Viet Nam conflict's many disastrous consequences for the United States, none seems to me so fraught with lasting peril as the fact that it has demonstrated clearly to the world that it is still true, as it has been true throughout our history, that we will not follow our leaders when they judge that the national interest requires resort to arms.

The Revolutionary War was marked by dissent no less violent than that of today. So was the War of 1812, and the Mexican War, and above all the Civil War. Only in the two World Wars, when we considered ourselves the victims of attacks initiated by aggressors, has this country shown the unity, determination, and perseverance required for the successful prosecution of a war.

Do not misunderstand me. Though I recognize that the basic pacifism of Americans is fraught with peril in the modern world, and I regret that Viet Nam has etched it in the minds of our enemies, it is one of the things that I love most about my country. I am one of those who would dearly love to see *America the Beautiful* replace our present national anthem—not only because it can be sung even if you are not an opera star, but because of the sentiments its words express so poetically: "Crown thy good with brotherhood, From sea to shining sea."

How can we preserve our national security in a world in which, unfortunately, "only the strong can be free" (as Wendell Willkie put it 28 years ago) and at the same time preserve one of the most admirable traits of our American character, our deep-seated love of peace and hatred of war and militarism?

We must not again underestimate the strength and the depth of American devotion to peace. Of all the considerations that led our forebears to come to this far-off land with its unknown risks, strange institutions, a language foreign to many, and little chance of ever again seeing home or loved-ones, probably none were more powerful than the desire for peace and freedom. These values continue to be instilled in us generation after generation by our parents, our schools, our churches, our literature, and our political leaders.

Just as we must not underestimate the strength of American devotion to peace and repugnance for war, so also must we not undervalue it. To weaken it would be to jeopardize one of the traits of character that makes America great, that makes it loved and admired throughout the world—much to the despair of the rulers of some countries who try strenuously to inculcate hate for America.

Yet we must also reckon with the danger that this peaceful spirit creates for our country in a world in which the preservation of freedom depends ultimately upon a clear and credible commitment and capacity to fight and die if necessary. It will no longer suffice to wait until after a Pearl Harbor before we firm up our resolution convincingly. It may be necessary, as the Israelis have found, to take military initiative. But such initiative clearly imposes almost impossible requirements on national leaders. How can they, much less everyone else, ever be certain that military initiative *really* was essential, or even justified? Unless such certainty is held almost unanimously, and sustained however long the conflict may require, the country is paralyzed and loses its will.

There is one measure we can take and should take immediately that would do much to resolve the dilemma that arises because, on the one horn, one of America's most fundamental—and also most admirable—characteristics is repugnance for war and, on the other horn, the ability to wage war is essential to the preservation of freedom.

The measure I propose will, I fear, shock some of you. I respectfully request that you nevertheless hear me out and think over my proposal carefully, rather than reject it out of hand. It is not a view I have come to lightly nor recently, but one I have held for over 20 years. It is not original with me nor is it without strong support from many respectable citizens of unquestionable patriotism.

A step that would do much toward resolving our dilemma is to abolish the draft: abolish it completely, lock, stock, and barrel; abolish it immediately, with no ifs, ands, or buts.

This ought to be first on the agenda when the new Congress convenes next January 20. The President-elect already is on record unambiguously as favoring abolition of the draft, though he has not, so far as I know, said unequivocally *when* it should be abolished, beyond "as soon as possible." I suggest that April 20 would be an appropriate date—90 days after the Inauguration.

At the time the draft is abolished it will be necessary to raise the pay of the military forces to obtain enough volunteers. Should a total, or near-total, mobilization become necessary, as in the two World Wars, a draft would again be appropriate.

My objections to the draft are of two kinds. First, it is immutably immoral in principle and inevitably inequitable in practice. Second, it is ineffective, inefficient, and detrimental to national security.

As to the point of principle, conscription involves taking bodily control of a person and subjecting him completely to the will of others. Nothing is more diametrically opposed to all our ethical, religious, and political principles. If this were necessary for the preservation of the nation, if it were necessary in order to assure that each person does his duty for the survival or safety of his neighbors, then the objections

in principle would be outweighed by equally cogent conflicting principles, and the draft would be justifiable. This is obviously true in total
mobilization. Equally obviously, it has been nowhere near true at any
time since 1945.

I will turn in a moment to some of the inevitable inequities in the
operation of the draft, but while we have in mind the basic immorality
of the draft, we should note that proposals to require some form of
universal national service, so that everyone will be equally mistreated,
seem to me to magnify the immorality. Under that plan, even more
people would be subjected to improper treatment. It implies that all
human beings are chattels of the government.

Inequities in the operation of the draft have been well documented in several responsible studies of Selective Service data. Thus,
one study showed that 77 percent of qualified high school graduates
serve two or more years in the military, but only 32 percent of college
graduates.

Now it is not clear how inequitable that is. It may be in some ways
a greater sacrifice for a college graduate to be drafted than for a high
school graduate. The college graduate, for example, loses more money
in civilian pay than does the high school graduate. It may not be
inequitable that an obligation be imposed mostly on those on whom
it rests most lightly.

One of the most extreme inequities is to draft a star professional
athlete, for example a heavyweight boxing champion. Such a person
has a very brief period, often only two or three years, of peak earning
power; he will probably not be able in all the rest of his life to earn
a million dollars, much less a million dollars in one or two years. The
burden on him is incomparably greater than on others. On the other
hand actual cases taper off gradually and continuously from this extreme to the man who simply has a good chance to become champion
or otherwise to earn a million dollars, or the man who is in the midst
of a period of rare artistic inspiration and achievement, or the man for
whom internal psychological factors make this the most critical year
of his life.

Local boards, of course, make some effort to allow for these special
circumstances. But every human being is special, and evaluations of
circumstances are subjective. If a boy's mother is dying, his board
would probably defer him. What if it is his aunt? Or simply a dear
friend of the family?

A lottery, which some have suggested, would not be any more fair
or equitable than the present arrangement. It is simply not fair to
subject someone who is heavyweight boxing champion, or whose
mother is dying, to exactly the same risk of being drafted as everyone
else, because the consequences for them are so much more serious than
for others. If we had one dish of diabetic ice cream, and one of regular
ice cream, and you want the diabetic serving because you have diabetes
but I want it because I have a slight preference for its flavor, would it
be fair simply to toss a coin?

One of the most serious inequities of the draft is that the draftee bears not only the personal hardship of the armed forces, but also a large part of the financial hardship. With voluntary armed forces, other taxpayers would transfer to the men in the forces enough money to make up for what they lost in civilian pay, adjusted upward or downward for the special disadvantages or advantages of the armed forces. This would come about simply by setting the pay at levels where sufficient men would volunteer.

Draftees make for ineffective armed forces. A large proportion of their whole time in the armed forces is required for processing, training, and travel. Furthermore, they may be forced into combats of which they or their relatives disapprove, thus helping to demoralize the country in pursuit of any necessary military activities.

Although there are many other arguments in favor of volunteers instead of draftees, it would not be fair to use my short remaining time on those arguments and not have time to acknowledge that there are objections to an all-volunteer force. Some of the objections seem at first glance to have merit; but on examination none that I have heard really do have merit. The case against the draft is about as lopsided a case as one ever encounters in questions of public policy.

The most common objection is that all-volunteer forces would cost too much. Actually, the true cost would probably be less than with the draft, but more of the cost would be out in the open and paid by the taxpayers. Draftees bear large hidden costs, namely the higher civilian earnings they could have made. In addition to the obvious unfairness of serving in the armed forces, a less obvious unfairness arises because draftees are usually young and impecunious in comparison with the taxpayers who avoid these hidden costs.

General Hershey and others have referred to volunteers as "mercenaries," "hired killers," and "in there just for the money." Actually, at present 90 percent of the commissioned officers and all of the highest-ranking noncommissioned officers are volunteers. As Professor Harry Gilman of the University of Rochester College of Business has asked, "Why ... are officers who are encouraged to enter and to remain in the service by reasonably high levels of pay called 'dedicated career men' but privates who would volunteer when they too received higher levels of pay called 'mercenaries'?"

In conclusion, let me reiterate that abolishing the draft promptly is important to the welfare and security of our country. That is precisely why I bring the matter before this audience. You are a group whose dedication to the welfare of our country cannot be disputed, for it is amply witnessed by your services to America and the world. My hope is that if you appreciate fully how much the draft undermines the very things for which you have risked your life, you can do our country another great service by helping to get it abolished.

It has been an interesting 50 years since 1918, in many ways a great 50 years, in some ways a terrifying 50 years. I hope you will invite me back to celebrate the completion of your next 50 years, and that all of you will be here.

Index

Acknowledgment of sources
(*see* Documentation)
Age of listeners, 15
Amplification (*see* Developmental
material)
Analogy:
argument by, 162
tests, 162
Anecdotes, 25–26 (*see also*
Illustrations)
Antonym, 93
Appeal, 41, 155
Argument (*see also* Reasoning
and Warrants):
analogy, 162
causation, 162
deduction, 163–164
definition, 162–163
essentials, 158–159
generalization. 161
layout, 159–164
testing, 159–164
Arrangement of points (*see*
Main points, patterns)
Articulation, 59, 61
defined, 61
dropping word endings, 61–62
improving, 62
slurring sounds, 61–62
Association of ideas, 73
Attention:
through eye contact, 56
in introduction, 37–38
Audience adaptation, 35–37,
82–87, 184–186

Audience adaptation (continued)
to attitudes, 184–186
characteristics, 82–87
hypothetical situation, 84–85
incorporation of audience
experience, 84
personal pronouns, 83
questions, 83
relationship of topic to
audience, 85–86
stories, 87
evaluation, 35–36
in introduction, 39–40, 86
knowing audience frame of
reference, 82
Audience analysis:
determining knowledge and
interests, 15–17
essential data, 14–15
questions, 15
samples, 16–17
Audience attitude, 184–186
in favor of proposal, 185
no opinion, 184–185
opposed to proposal, 185–186
Audience contact, 56–57
defined, 56
to hold attention, 56
maintaining, 57
to promote confidence, 56
as sign of sincerity, 56
to test audience reaction, 56–57
Audience questions as adaptation, 83
"Automobile Piston Stroke, The,"
Derek Dunn, 106–110

Baker, Sheridan, 77 *n.*
Beginning a speech (*see*
    Introductions)
Bibliography, 127–128, 133, 137
Biographical sources, 24
Bodily action:
    defined, 62
    facial expression, 62
    gesture, 62–63
    mannerisms, 63
    movement, 63
Body of the speech:
    in informative speaking, 30–37
    main points, 30–35, 148–149,
        152–154
    in outline, 42, 164–166
    in persuasive speaking, 152–154
    preparation, 30–37, 152–154
Brainstorming:
    defined, 13
    and historical exposition, 122
    samples, 13
Bronchial tubes, 58
"Buying Insurance While You Are
    Young," Elaine Horan,
    167–170
"Buy Private Label Brands,"
    Jan Scudder, 193–197

Card catalog, 23
Causation:
    argument by, 162
    tests, 162
Chalk board, as a visual aid, 104
"Changing World: Communicate,
    Learn, and Understand, A,"
    H. I. Romnes, 233–239
Cicero, 173 *n.*
Clarity, 47–50
    concreteness, 48–49
    defined, 48
    economy of words, 49–50
    specificity, 48
Classification and differentiation,
    92–93
"Classifications of Nursery Rhymes,"
    Susan Woistmann, 128–131
Common ground, 190
Communication, as dialogue, 5
Comparative advantages
    pattern, 153
Comparison, 26–27
    defined, 26
    figurative, 26
    literal, 27
    metaphor, 27
    simile, 27

Conclusions of speeches, 40–41,
    154–155
    anecdotes, 41, 155
    appeal, 41, 155
    example, 155
    goal, 40
    illustrations, 41
    narratives, 41, 155
    in outline, 44, 166
    quotations, 41
    summary, 40–41, 155
Concreteness, 48
Constant vocal pattern, 61
Contact with the audience, 56–57
Contrast, 27
Conversational quality, 58
"Corporate Deaf Ear: Consumerism,
    The," E. B. Weiss, 239–243
Creativity:
    characteristics, 126
    developing, 126
Credibility, 151
    characteristics, 152
    related to emotional appeal, 152
    related to logic, 152
    strengthening, 152
Criteria for evaluating speeches, 7
Criteria-satisfaction pattern, 154
Criticism (*see* Evaluation)

Data, 159
    refuting quality, 172–173
    refuting quantity, 172
    testing, 159, 173
Deduction:
    argument by, 163–164
    tests, 164
Definition (*see also* Speeches
    of definition):
    aid to informative speaking, 92
    antonym, 93
    argument by, 162–163
    classification and differentiation,
        92–93
    etymology, 93–94
    synonym, 93
    uses, 94
"Definition of Fossils," Frank
    Ettensohn, 97–99
Delivery, 53–65
    articulation, 54, 61–62
    bodily action, 62–63
    modes, 53–54
    practice, 53, 63–65
    standards, 54–63
    voice, 58–61
Demonstration, 104

Description (*see also* Informative speaking, descriptive speeches):
  age, 113
  color, 113
  composition, 113
  condition, 113–114
  essentials, 113–114
  location of subordinate items, 114
  weight, 113
Descriptive gestures, 62
Desire to communicate, 55–56
Determining speech purposes, 18–20
Developmental material:
  adapting, 35–37
  anecdotes, 25–26
  comparison, 26
  contrast, 27
  defined, 35
  evaluating, 35–36
  examples, 25
  illustrations, 25–26
  narrative, 25–26
  quotations, 27–28
  selecting, 35–37
  statistics, 27
Diaphragm, 58, 59
"Dining in Spain," Susan Woistmann, 79–81
Discussion:
  analysis of sample specimen, 221–224
  assignment, 221
  balance, 215–217
  content, 212–213
  defined, 205
  introduction, 220–221
  leadership, 215–216
  main points, 210–212
  objectivity, 218–219
  organization, 210–212, 213–214, 220–221
  outline, 213–214
  panel, 206
  participation, 214–221
  private, 206–207
  public, 205–206
  questions for, 208–210
  responsible contribution, 217–218
  summarizing progress in, 219–220
  symposium, 206
  t-group, 207
  topics, 207
Documentation, 28, 134
  citing in speech, 134–135
Dunn, Derek, "The Automobile Piston Stroke," 106–110

Economy of words, 49–50
Emotional appeal (*see* Motivating)
Emotional impact:
  benefits, 72–73
  in informative speaking, 72
Emphasis:
  defined, 51
  as element of style, 51
  related to clarity and vividness, 51
  transitions, 51
Encyclopedias, 23–24
Entertain, as a purpose, 18
Ethics of persuasive speaking, 150–151, 183
Ettensohn, Frank, "A Definition of Fossils," 97–99
Evaluating speeches:
  criteria for, 6
  questionnaire, 7
Evaluating speech structure, 41–44, 157–158
  annotated informative outline, 42–44
  annotated persuasive outline, 164–167
Evidence (*see* Data)
Examples:
  defined, 25
  fictitious, 25
  hypothetical, 25
  real, 25
  uses, 25
Exposition (*see also* Expository speeches):
  of critical appraisal, 124–125
  defined, 119
  of historical events and forces, 121–122
  of political, economic, and social issues, 120–121
  of theory, principle, or law, 122–124
Expository speeches, 119–131
  assignment, 126
  objectivity in, 120
  outline, 126–127
  special problems, 120, 121–122, 123, 124–125
  speech and analysis, 128–131
  topics, 121, 122, 124, 125
  types, 119–125
Extemporaneous speaking, defined, 54
External transition:
  defined, 77–78
  types, 78
Eye contact, 56–57 (*see also* Audience contact)

Facial expression, 62
Fact, questions of, 208, 210–211
Fictitious examples, 25
Forms of support (*see* Develop-
    mental material)
Frankel, Richard, "We Must Save
    Biafra," 198–201

Generalization:
    argument by, 161
    tests, 161
General purpose:
    defined, 18
    entertain, 18
    inform, 18
    persuade, 18
Gesture:
    descriptive, 62
    emphatic, 62
    use, 62–63
Group discussion (*see* Discussion)

Hendrick, James, "Interpol: History
    and Mission," 227–232
Horan, Elaine, "Buying Insurance
    While You Are Young,"
    167–170
Humor in speeches, 97, 106
Hypothetical examples, 25

Illustrations, 25–26
    defined, 25–26
    importance, 26
    related to examples, 26
    as speech conclusions, 41
    as speech introductions, 38–39
Imagination, 125
Impromptu speaking, 53–54
Indexes (*see* Source material)
"In Favor of a Voluntary Army,"
    Kathy McClure, 177–179,
    181–182
Informative speaking, 69–143
    analyzing purposes, 70–71
    association of ideas in, 73
    defined, 70
    descriptive speeches, 111–118
    development of, 70–71
    emotional impact, 72
    expository speeches, 119–131
    goals, 69–71
    requirements, 69–73
    requisites, 69
    research reports, 132–143
    speeches of definition, 92–99
    speeches illustrating audience
        adaptation, 82–91

Informative speaking (continued)
    speeches illustrating organization,
        74–81
    speeches utilizing visual aids,
        100–110
    superficiality in, 70
    tests of information in, 69
Informative speech outline,
        annotated, 42–44
Inherent speech organization, 74
Instance (*see* Examples)
Interests, for audience analysis, 15
Internal transitions:
    defined, 76–77
    types, 77
    uses, 77
"Interpol: History and Mission,"
    James Hendrick, 227–232
Introductions to speeches, 37–40,
        154–156
    anecdote, 38–39
    defined, 37
    goals, 37
    illustration, 38–39
    length, 38, 155
    narrative, 38–39
    personal reference, 39
    preparing, 37–40
    question, 38
    quotation, 38
    startling statement, 38

Jargon in expository speaking, 123

Key, 59
Knowledge:
    of audience about subject, 15–17
    for audience analysis, 15
    prior, 21–22
    verifying, 22

Language (*see* Style and Oral style)
Larynx, 58
Leadership in discussion, 215
    achieving balance, 216
    drawing conclusions, 220
    introducing discussants, 220
    summarizing, 219–220
Limiting the subject (*see* Specific
        purpose)
Listening, 3–7
    active, 5–6
    characteristics, 4–5
    defined, 4
    getting ready, 4–5
    importance, 3–4
    improving, 4–6

Listening (continued)
  ratio to speaking, 4
  related to hearing, 4
Locating material, 21–24
Logical appeal, 149–151 (see Argument and Reasoning)
Logic, testing, 157–164
Loudness (see Volume)
Lungs, 58

McClure, Kathy, "In Favor of a Voluntary Army," 177–179, 181–182
Main points:
  as complete sentences, 32
  defined, 31
  examples of, 31
  function, 148–149
  goals, 148
  idea subordination, 31
  number of, 31
  patterns:
    comparative advantages, 153
    criteria-satisfaction, 154
    negative, 154
    problem solution, 153
    space order, 33–34
    time order, 33
    topic order, 34–35
  phrasing, 31–32
  purpose of, 31
  selecting, 30–35
  stating, 30–35
  tests of, 35
Mannerisms, 63
Manuscript speaking, 54
Material (see Developmental material)
Meaning:
  changed by stresses, 61
  use of voice in conveying, 60–61
Memorization, 54
Metaphor, 27
"Military Conscription: Abolish the Draft," W. Allen Wallis, 243–248
Modes of delivery, 53–54
Monotone, 60
Motivating, 150–151
  defined, 150
  as emotional appeal, 150
  relationship to reasoning, 150
Motivation, 186–191
  common ground, 190
  conformity, 189
  defined, 183
  health, 188
  justice, 188

Motivation (continued)
  pleasure, 186–187
  responsibility, 187–188
  sex, 189
  suggestion, 190–191
Movement, 63
  problems, 63

Narratives (see Illustrations)
Negative pattern, 154
Nervousness (see Stage fright)
Newspapers, 24
Note taking, 28
  for refutation, 174–175

Observation:
  accuracy, 22
  practicing, 22
Occasion:
  adapting to, 17–18
  ceremonial, 17
  student speaking, 17
Occupation of listeners, 15
Opinions, 27–28
"Opposed to a Voluntary Army," Gerald Steltenkamp, 179–181
Oral style, 45–47
  clarity, 47–50
  emphasis, 51–52
  informal, 46
  personal, 46
  repetitive, 47
  standard, 46
  vividness, 50–51
Organization (see also Body, Conclusions, Introductions, and Main points):
  in informative speaking, 30–44
  inherent, 74
  perceptible, 75–78
  in persuasive speaking, 152–155
  placement of points, 75
  proportion of points, 76
  transitions, 51, 76–78
Originality, 125
Outline, 41–44, 164–167, 213–214
  agenda for discussion, 213
  conclusion, 44, 166
  defined, 41
  descriptive speech, 116
  expository speech, 126–127
  group, for discussion, 213
  individual, for discussion, 213
  introduction, 42, 164
  purpose sentence, 42, 164
  relation to speech, 42
  research report, 136–137
  speech illustrating audience adaptation, 88

Outline (continued)
  speech illustrating organization,
    78–79
  speech of definition, 96–97
  speech of motivation, 191–192,
    197–198
  speech of reasons, 164–167
  speech of refutation, 176
  speech utilizing visual aids,
    105–106
  symbols, 43
  wording main points, 31–32,
    42–44, 148–149

Panel discussion:
  characteristics, 206
  defined, 206
  strengths, 206
Parallelism, in phrasing main
    points, 43
Patterns of arrangement (see
    Main points, patterns)
Paul, Toni, "The Munich Hofbrau
    House," 117–118
Perceptible speech organization,
    75–78
Periodicals and magazines, 23
Personal pronouns as adaptation, 83
Personal reference introduction, 39
Persuasive speaking, 147–204
  changing belief, 148
  conclusion, 155
  credibility, 151–152
  defined, 147
  ethics, 150–151
  gaining action, 148
  goals, 148
  idea development, 141–152
  introduction, 154–155
  logical appeal, 149–151
  motivating, 150–151
  organization, 152–155
  outline for, annotated, 164–167
  purpose sentences, 147–148
  reasoning, 149–151
  reasons, 148–149
  reinforcing belief, 148
  speeches of motivation, 183–201
  speeches of reasons, 156–170
  speeches of refutation, 171–182
Pharynx, 58
Phonation, 58–59
Pitch of voice:
  defined, 59
  produced, 59
  for variety and expressiveness,
    60–61
Placement, 75

Plagiarism, 27, 29
Policy, questions of, 209–210, 211–212
Posture, 63
Practice:
  analyzing, 64
  ideas, 64
  methods, 63–64
  number of, 64
  and outline, 65
  procedure, 64
  program of, 63–65
  spontaneity in, 64–65
  value, 53, 63
  when to, 63, 64
Preparation:
  body, 30–37
  conclusion, 40–41
  introduction, 37–40
Presentation (see Delivery and
    Oral style)
Prior knowledge, 21–22
  verifying, 22
Private discussion, 206–207
Problem-solution pattern, 153
Pronunciation, 61
  defined, 61
  related to articulation, 61
Proportion, 76
  importance, 76
  related to position, 76
  showing, 76
Proposition, 147
Public discussion, 205–206 (see also
    Panel discussion and
    Symposium)
Purpose (see also General purpose
    and Specific purpose):
  speeches to inform, 18–20
  speeches to persuade, 147–148

Quality of voice, 60
Questions:
  audience, 83–84
  of fact, 208, 210–211
  general, 209
  as introduction, 38
  of policy, 209–210, 211–212
  rhetorical, 84
  specific, 209
  of value, 208–209, 211

"Race for Supersonic Aircraft, The,"
    Thomas Voss, 138–143
Rankin, Paul Tory, 4 n.
Rate of speaking, 60
Real examples, 25

Reasoning, 149–151 (*see also* Argument and Warrants)
  characteristics, 149–150
  refuting, 173–174
Reasons, 148–149 (*see also* Main points and Persuasive speaking)
  discovering, 156–157
  inventing, 157
  number of, 157
  selecting, 156–157
Recording material, 28
  note card form, 28
Refutation:
  defined, 171
  incorporating steps, 175
  outlining, 175
  steps in, 174–175
  what can be refuted, 171–174
Rehearsal (*see* Practice)
Relevancy:
  and historical exposition, 122
  as a test of informative speaking, 69–70
  of a theory, principle, or law, 123–124
Religion, of listeners, 15
Repetition:
  artless, 72
  defined, 47
  as element of style, 47
  in informative speaking, 71–72
Reports (*see* Research reports)
Research, 132–133
Research reports, 132–143
  assignment, 135
  defined, 132
  documentation in, 134
  idea development, 134–135
  outline, 136–137
  problems of, 135
  specific purpose, 133–134
  speech and analysis, 138–143
Resonance, 59
Restatement, 47, 72
  defined, 47
Rhetorical question, 84
Romnes, H. I., "A Changing World: Communicate, Learn, and Understand," 233–239

Schmit, David, "Unidentified Flying Objects," 89–91
Scudder, Jan, "Buy Private Label Brands," 193–197
Selecting a speech topic, 11–18
  audience consideration, 14–17
  for informative speeches, 12

Selecting a speech topic (continued)
  occasion, 17–18
  speaker interest, 12–13
  subdividing topics, 13
  tests, 12
Selecting reasons, 156–157
Simile, 27
Source material:
  amount needed, 29
  locating, 21–24
  note card form, 28
  what to look for, 25–28
Space order, 33
  in descriptive speeches, 114–115
Speaking, mechanics of, 58–59, 61–62
Specific instances (*see* Examples)
Specificity, 48
Specific purpose, 18–20
  contrasted with informative, 147
  defined, 18–19
  examples of evolving, 19–20
  in informative speaking, 18–20
  in outline, 42, 164
  in persuasive speaking, 147–148
  process for determining, 19
  relation to subject, area, topic, 19
  samples, 147–148
  tests, 148
Speech:
  and conversation, 58
  evaluation questionnaire, 7
  fundamental principles, 11–65
    enumerated, 11, 21, 30, 45, 53
  materials, 21–29
  and writing, 45–46
Speeches illustrating audience adaptation, 82–91
  assignment, 87
  outline, 87–88
  speech and analysis, 89–91
Speeches illustrating organization, 74–81
  assignment, 78
  outline, 78–79
  speech and analysis, 79–81
  value, 74
Speeches of definition, 92–97
  assignment, 96
  outline, 96–97
  speech and analysis, 97–99
Speeches of motivation, 183–201
  assignment, 191
  outlines, 191–192, 197–198
  speeches and analyses, 193–197, 198–201
Speeches of reasons, 156–170
  assignment, 164
  outline, 164–167

Speeches of reason (continued)
    speech and analysis, 167–170
    testing logic, 157–164
Speeches of refutation, 171–182
    assignment, 175
    explained, 171
    outline, 176
    speeches and analyses, 177–182
Speeches utilizing visual aids,
        100–110
    assignment, 105
    outline, 105–106
    speech and analysis, 106–109
Spontaneity:
    characteristics, 57–58
    defined, 57
    in practice, 64–65
    value, 57
Stage fright, 55–56
    defined, 55
    means of lessening, 55–56
Startling statement introduction, 38
Statistical sources, 24
Statistics:
    defined, 27
    uses, 27
Steltenkamp, Gerald, "Opposed to a
    Voluntary Army," 179–181
Stingley, Ronald, 78 n.
Structure (see Outline)
Style, 45–52 (see also Oral style)
    clarity, 47–50
    emphasis, 51–52
    vividness, 50–51
Subjects (see Topics)
Suggestion, 190–191
    and ethics, 191
    in persuasive speaking, 190–191
Summary, 40–41
Supporting material (see Develop-
    mental material)
Symbols, in outlining, 43
Symposium, 206
    characteristics, 206
    defined, 206
    problems, 206

Tension in speaker (see
    Stage fright)
Tests of reasoning (see Argument,
    testing)
Throat, 58
Time order, 33
Topic order, 33
Topics, for speeches:
    expository, 121, 122, 124, 125
    research reports, 132, 133
    selecting, 11–18

Toulmin, Stephen, 158 n.
Transitions, 51, 76–78
    defined, 76
    for emphasis, 51
    external, 77–78
    internal, 76–77
    types, 77

"Unidentified Flying Objects,"
    David Schmit, 89–91

Value, questions of, 208–209, 211
Variety and expressiveness, 60–61
    importance, 60
    use, 61
Verbal supporting material (see
    Developmental material)
Visual aids:
    chalk board, 104
    charts, 102
    drawings, 101–102
    films, 102
    graphs, 102
    maps, 102
    models, 101
    objects, 100–101
    passing in class, 103–104
    pictures, 101–102
    projections, 102
    sketches, 101–102
    slides, 102
    speeches utilizing, 100–110
    use, 103–105
    value, 100
Vital Speeches, 227 n., 233 n., 239 n.,
    243 n.
Vividness, 50–51
    characteristics, 50–51
    defined, 50
    of historical exposition, 122
Vocal folds, 58–59
Voice, 58–61
    key, 59
    phonation, 58–59
    pitch, 59
    production, 58–59
    quality, 60
    rate, 60
    resonance, 59
    variety and expressiveness, 60–61
    volume, 59–60
Volume, 59–60
    control, 59
Voss, Thomas, "The Race for
    Supersonic Aircraft,"
    138–143

Wallis, W. Allen, "Military Conscription: Abolish the Draft," 243–248
Warrants, 159 (*see also* Argument)
  framing, 174
  phrasing, 161
  testing, 159–161
Weiss, E. B., "The Corporate Deaf Ear: Consumerism," 239–243

"We Must Save Biafra," Richard Frankel, 198–201
Woistmann, Susan:
  "Classifications of Nursery Rhymes," 128–131
  "Dining in Spain," 79–81
Words, economy of, 49–50

Yes-response, 189–190